YO-BTB-605

THE ASEAN
SUCCESS STORY

LIB051005 R3/78

TY LIBRARY

*Based on the East–West Center's
25th Anniversary Conference on
ASEAN and the Pacific Basin,
held in Honolulu, Hawaii from
29 October to 1 November 1985.*

THE ASEAN SUCCESS STORY

Social, Economic, and Political Dimensions

Edited by
LINDA G. MARTIN

An East–West Center Book
Distributed by the University of Hawaii Press

©1987 by the East–West Center

All rights reserved

Manufactured in the United States of America

First printing 1987
Second printing 1988

Library of Congress Cataloging-in-Publication Data

The ASEAN success story.

Bibliography: p.
Includes index.
1. ASEAN—Congresses. 2. Asia, Southeastern—Economic
integration—Congresses. 3. Asia, Southeastern—Economic
conditions—Congresses. 4. Asia, Southeastern—Social
conditions—Congresses. 5. Asia, Southeastern—Politics
and government—Congresses. I. Martin, Linda G., 1947–
II. East-West Center's 25th Anniversary Conference on
ASEAN and the Pacific Basin (1958 : Honolulu, Hawaii)
HC441.A864 1987 337.1'59 86-29373
ISBN 0–8248–1107–0

Published in 1987 by the East–West Center,
1777 East–West Road, Honolulu, Hawaii 96848

Distributed by the University of Hawaii Press,
Honolulu, Hawaii 96822

CONTENTS

v

FIGURES AND TABLES

PREFACE

Since the founding of the Association of Southeast Asian Nations (ASEAN) in 1967, the social, economic, and political successes of the member countries have received increasing attention. The individual economies by and large have grown rapidly and the group as a whole has gained stature in the arena of international politics. Nevertheless, some would argue that ASEAN has not lived up to its promise in terms of economic cooperation, and others would point to the limited development of political institutions in some of the individual countries. Just what are the dimensions of ASEAN's successes and what are the challenges it will face in the future? These are the questions that this book addresses.

In 1985, the East–West Center—a public nonprofit educational institution dedicated to improving understanding in the Asia–Pacific region—celebrated its 25th anniversary. To mark the occasion it was decided to hold a major conference to examine the success of the countries of ASEAN, an association founded only seven years after the Center. In organizing the October 1985 Conference on ASEAN and the Pacific Basin, not only were we able to draw on the Center's expert staff and network of colleagues throughout the region, but also we were honored by the participation of elected officials and government leaders from ASEAN and other countries. In fact, the conference was held concurrently with the fifth in a series of parliamentarians seminars on population, resources, and development, cosponsored by the ASEAN Heads of Population Programme through funding from the United Nations Fund for Population Activities and the East–West Population Institute.

This book, based on the conference, is introduced by East–West Center President Victor Hao Li and continues in Chapter 1 with overviews of ASEAN's experience by two distinguished ASEAN leaders: His Excellency General Prem Tinsulanonda, Prime Minister of Thailand, and the

Right Honorable Dato Musa Hitam, then Deputy Prime Minister of Malaysia. The following four chapters are each composed of a major paper followed by short essays addressing related themes. Chapters 2 and 3 focus on social and economic development of the individual ASEAN countries, whereas Chapter 4 evaluates economic cooperation within the ASEAN grouping. Chapter 5 looks at the political development of the individual countries and at issues of regional order, including the Kampuchea conflict and events in the Philippines, as of October 1985. In Chapter 6, representatives of China, Japan, and the United States comment on their countries' relations with the ASEAN nations, and the final chapter presents a review of the challenges ahead for ASEAN.

A conference and publication of this scope cannot be undertaken without the efforts of many people. Victor Hao Li, Lee-Jay Cho, Seiji Naya, and Jusuf Wanandi, who serves on the East–West Center's international board of governors, all provided valuable guidance and assistance in the design and implementation of the conference, as well as contributing papers to this volume. The ASEAN Heads of Population Programme were instrumental in arranging the participation of the ASEAN parliamentarians, whose insightful and lively comments benefited all the other participants. Very special thanks must be given to Senators Prasop Ratanakorn and Tridhosyuth Devakul of Thailand for their tireless efforts on behalf of the conference and the East–West Center.

It is impossible to recognize individually all the East–West Center staff members who played important roles in the production of the conference and this book, but I want to thank Delores Gresham, Susan Palmore, Morley Gren, Betty Gordon, Marie Nomura, Norma Uejo, and Loretta Koga for their usual first-rate conference support. I also want to recognize the excellent work of Linda Loui, who took primary responsibility for preparing the manuscript. Similarly, I want to express great appreciation to David Ellis, the volume's copyeditor, for his editorial skill and painstaking effort.

Finally, there is one person, Charles Morrison, upon whom the success of all these efforts is based. An expert on ASEAN, Charles patiently educated me, provided hours of advice as I organized the conference, and critically reviewed all the papers of this volume. I am immensely grateful to him and share with him whatever credit, but certainly not any discredit, that is associated with this publication.

LINDA G. MARTIN

Honolulu, September 1986

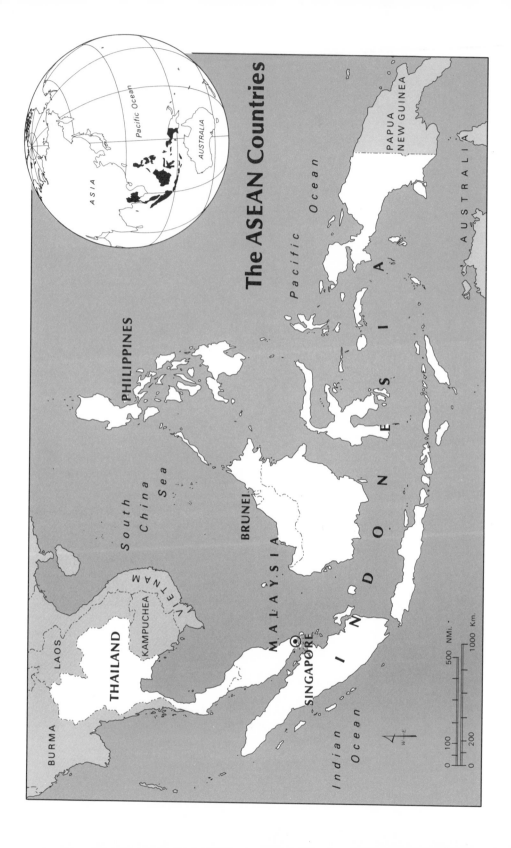

The ASEAN Countries

INTRODUCTION

Victor Hao Li

In 1960, the year the East–West Center was founded, the United States had a balance of trade surplus with Japan, South Korea was regarded as one of the world's poorest countries with little prospect for economic development, and the region's economic transformation was just beginning. Cold war tensions between the United States and the People's Republic of China cast a pall on the international politics of Asia, Bangladesh was known as East Pakistan, and none of the island nations of the Pacific was fully independent.

The concept of an Association of Southeast Asian Nations (ASEAN) had not yet come into being. Its birth was to prove, as Thai Prime Minister Prem Tinsulanonda notes in Chapter 1, "a major turning point in the history of Southeast Asia." But as Malaysian Deputy Prime Minister Musa Hitam mentions in the same chapter, in 1967 the ASEAN partners were almost strangers to each other, if not adversaries.

In 25 years, the region has undergone a true transformation. East and Southeast Asia are economically the most dynamic and the fastest-growing regions in the world today, as discussed by Seiji Naya in Chapter 3. On average, their nations have outperformed all others in real growth per capita, growth of exports, and expansion of savings and investment. In 1960, East and Southeast Asia produced 10 percent of the world's gross national product, compared to 36 percent by North America and 23 percent by Western Europe. Twenty years later, the East and Southeast Asian share had grown to 17 percent. By the end of this century, barring unforeseen developments, it will increase to 21 percent—approximately equal to North America's and Western Europe's shares of world GNP.

Large strides have also been made in social development. Population growth, birth, and death rates have all fallen. At the same time, the quality of the ASEAN populations in terms of education and skills has increased. In Chapter 2, Aline Wong and Paul Cheung document the demographic transition and educational transformation of ASEAN.

Politically, despite the turmoil in Indochina and recent problems in the Philippines, the Asia-Pacific region has been stable in comparison with the Middle East, Latin America, and Africa. Tensions do sometimes mount, but there has not been armed conflict across the 38th Parallel or the Taiwan Strait for many years. Nor are there large-scale insurgency or revolutionary movements, except perhaps in the Philippines. And the emergence of development-oriented policies in China will contribute substantially to stability and growth in the region.

A number of important issues remains to be dealt with, including the Indochina conflict, Korea, political succession in the Philippines and elsewhere, the Taiwan question, and the longer-term political and economic impact on the region of an increasingly strong China. But these issues can be managed, if not resolved, and progress is already being made in some areas. The birth and maturation of ASEAN has already contributed much to the resolution of potentially destabilizing issues. Jusuf Wanandi highlights ASEAN's political development and regional order in Chapter 5.

Technological change also has come swiftly, with several generations of technical development taking place within the span of a lifetime. The region has gone from the Green Revolution to the Gene Revolution and has mastered the mysteries of the silicon chip, robotics, and artificial intelligence. The Mercantile Age is being overtaken by the Information Age as perhaps the key component to growth in Asia and the Pacific.

In the coming Pacific Era, many of the key global developments, especially on economic matters, will shift from the Atlantic to the Pacific and from North America and Europe to Asia. But, as Wanandi argues, it may yet be premature to anticipate the formation of a "Pacific Community" that will facilitate economic, and eventually political, interaction. The Pacific Community concept is evolving slowly and hesitantly. Extensive integration for the Pacific region as a whole seems unlikely, at least in the foreseeable future. National interests and cultural backgrounds are too diverse for that level of integration to be possible or even desirable. For that reason, an eventual Pacific Community will probably differ fundamentally from the European Economic Community, where a common cultural core and geographic proximity make political and economic integration a greater possibility.

Future relations in the Pacific will be based nevertheless on the intertwining of the Pacific Basin economies. Narongchai Akrasanee critically evaluates one aspect of this—the development of ASEAN economic cooperation—in Chapter 4. Though political and cultural differences among ASEAN nations remain, economic interdependence already affects vital national issues, not just marginal matters, and there is much progress to be made in economic cooperation.

In the long run the Pacific nations—including the United States—can run, limp, or stumble together, but they cannot readily part company. On the positive side, the joining of the region's resources will yield a whole that is greater than the sum of its parts, with resulting larger shares for all.

In 1960, United States involvement with Asia was still relatively modest. Massive economic ties with Japan, and later with the newly industrialized countries (NICs) and ASEAN, were still in the future. There were no dealings of any kind with China, and the prolonged tragedy of the Vietnam War was yet unknown.

The United States at that time basically looked inward in seeking to solve its problems and meet its needs. When it did have occasion to turn outward, it looked in the direction of Europe—understandably for a society with essentially European cultural and ethnic roots. Asia and the Pacific seemed distant places both physically and, perhaps more important, psychologically. The distances were aggravated by differences in language and culture that made communication more difficult. These feelings were doubtless reciprocated.

Japan and China in 1960 were similarly preoccupied with internal economic and political questions. Japan had entered reparation agreements with the future ASEAN countries and was increasingly looking toward Southeast Asia as a supplier of the raw materials needed for its rapidly developing manufacturing industries, but the extensive economic relations that later made Japan the first or second trade and investment partner of all of the countries of the region were still in the future. China in 1960 was largely isolated from the region; it had diplomatic relations only with Indonesia and small amounts of trade moved mainly through overseas Chinese business networks.

Twenty-five years later, a great deal has changed. Southeast Asia has become very important to China, Japan, and the United States, as indicated in Chapter 6 by Bifan Cheng, Motofumi Asai, and Robert G. Torricelli. For example, in 1983 U.S. trade with the countries of ASEAN constituted 5 percent of U.S. exports and 5 percent of imports. The role of ASEAN in U.S. trade is likely to increase in coming years, partly because of the fast growth of the ASEAN economies, and partly because the American economy itself is becoming more internationalized. Twenty percent of American industrial output is now exported, double the rate of just 12 years ago.

Today in the United States, far more attention is being given to Asia and the Pacific. Senior U.S. government officials frequently visit the region. U.S. corporate activity in Asia has increased dramatically. Academic studies of the region have expanded, and media coverage of Asian news has improved. There is still a long way to go before the United States' ability to understand and to deal with Asia matches its capacities for relations with Europe. But it is making clear and significant progress.

On political matters the countries of the Pacific Basin sometimes disagree. But on the whole the degree of cooperation and mutual support is high among ASEAN, the NICs, Japan, and the United States. Similarities in values and national interests make this group of nations the bedrock of future world stability and growth.

In 1960, even though the Pacific Age was but dimly, if at all, perceived, there were men and women of vision who saw the need for a strong and enduring link between the United States and Asia. Their prescience led to the establishment of the East–West Center, located in Hawaii in the middle of the Pacific, as a meeting ground and a place for cultural and technical interchange. Efforts such as this slowly but inexorably increase mutual understanding and build national capacities for international dealings.

But there is still a long way to go. The United States' capacity to deal with Asia, while improving, is quite low. For example, Australia—with a population one-fifteenth the size of the United States—has almost as many people studying Japanese as the United States has.

Few American men and women visionaries of the Pacific Age have yet reached the higher levels of government and business, and the knowledge they possess has not yet diffused into society at large. There are excellent pockets of expertise on Asia but there is still a considerable lack of understanding in many important sectors, including policymaking sectors. This is one of the reasons why the United States has such difficulty discussing intelligently the real causes of its trade deficit. It also explains in part how anger that was initially directed at Japan can lead in a convoluted manner to protectionist legislation such as the Jenkins bill that hurts everyone except Japan and that attacks the very region whose prosperity and stability the United States wants to enhance.

I hope that understanding between our countries will be improved by the chapters in this volume, as well as by the personal interactions that accompanied their presentation as papers at the East–West Center's 25th Anniversary Conference on ASEAN and the Pacific Basin. They are the embodiment of Lyndon Johnson's vision that the East–West Center "shall bring the wise men of the West and invite the wise men of the East. From them we shall hope that many generations of young scholars will learn the wisdom of the two worlds united here and to use that wisdom for the purposes and ends of mankind's highest aspirations for peace, justice, and freedom."

CHAPTER 1

ASEAN OVERVIEW: TWO LEADERS' EVALUATIONS

ASEAN:
Meeting the Challenges of Asia and the Pacific

HIS EXCELLENCY GENERAL PREM TINSULANONDA
Prime Minister of Thailand

The countries of ASEAN share many similar values: pragmatism, adherence to principles, tolerance of the other person's viewpoint, and openness to the cultural influences of others. These values have helped Thailand to meet the challenges to its freedom and independence. Thailand, the only nation in Southeast Asia to maintain independence from colonialism, joined the United Nations in 1946 thanks to the support of our traditional friends, especially the United States, with whom we have had excellent relations since 1833. Side by side with the United States, we have fought on several battlefields to uphold freedom and preserve security in Asia and the Pacific region. As the years passed, however, it became clear that the only effective means to counter new threats to our freedom and security was, on the one hand, to increase our efforts in ensuring the well-being of our people and, on the other hand, to forge cooperation with like-minded nations who are our immediate neighbors in Southeast Asia. As a result of our diplomatic initiatives, the Association of Southeast Asian Nations, ASEAN, was founded in Bangkok in 1967.

ASEAN COOPERATION

The birth of ASEAN was a major turning point in the history of Southeast Asia. Indonesia, Malaysia, the Philippines, Singapore, and Thailand signed the Bangkok Declaration of 1967, which established ASEAN. When Brunei became independent, she was welcomed as a new member in January 1984. Over the years, ASEAN has become a strong and viable organization. It has not only minimized the differences between the

3

member countries but has also acted as a pillar of stability in the region. Without ASEAN, there might well be doubts as to the future of free societies in Southeast Asia. ASEAN has dispelled those doubts and has shown the world our vast potential for growth and prosperity.

Regional cooperation within ASEAN has progressed at a steady but measured pace. We have tried to learn from the experiences of other regions. We did not create a rigid institutional framework. We did not force a pace of cooperation beyond the absorptive capacity of individual members. ASEAN operates on the basis of consensus, equality, and mutual benefits. Our goal is to have an organization that gives more to its individual members than it demands from them. The core of trust and goodwill thus created has enabled ASEAN cooperation to expand in all directions.

Channels of communication established by ASEAN at the political level have resulted in increased economic cooperation, as well as in more technological, cultural, and other exchanges among its members. Gradually, a web of cooperative activities has been established, which has led to a growing integration of values and attitudes. We have learned to understand the needs and aspirations of one another, to be sensitive to one another's perspectives and concerns. Thus, there is now a sense of common identity among ASEAN countries, a firm commitment to work together as indicated by our common stands on several international issues as well as our concerted actions in many international forums, including the United Nations.

Economic cooperation is and will remain a basic objective of ASEAN. It encompasses both intra- as well as extra-ASEAN cooperation. Within ASEAN, the focus is on freer trade and expansion. This focus includes industrial cooperation and resource management harmonization. The lifting of trade barriers within ASEAN should encourage the expansion of regional trade and investment, thus gradually drawing the six ASEAN economies into a regional economy.

As an indication of the scope and depth of ASEAN regional cooperation, let me mention a few major examples. First, there are the ASEAN Preferential Trading Arrangements, whereby special tariff preferences are accorded to the products of fellow ASEAN countries. Then there are the ASEAN Industrial Projects, whereby each country selects an industrial project for construction in its own country and in which each ASEAN member country holds shares. The shortage of food is still a major problem in some parts of Southeast Asia. For this reason, we have created an ASEAN Food Security Reserve scheme, with rice stockpiles available when required by any member country. Other regional projects of great long-term importance include an ASEAN submarine cable system, ASEAN cultural fund, agreements on emergency sharing for crude oil and oil products, an ASEAN Finance Corporation to assist joint investment ventures, a currency swap arrangement between our central banks, an ASEAN population program, and an ASEAN development education project.

ASEAN also has a central secretariat, located in Jakarta. But this has been purposely kept small so as not to create a supranational body or a new bureaucracy. However, the central secretariat performs a valuable coordinating and supporting role for the various ASEAN committees and meetings.

In response to changes in the immediate external environment, ASEAN over the years has adopted common stands on important political issues. The best example is, of course, the Kampuchea problem. The military occupation of Kampuchea by Vietnam poses the most immediate and direct threat to the peace and security of Southeast Asia. It is in blatant contravention of international principles of self-determination and of respect for sovereignty and territorial integrity. Tremendous suffering is being imposed on the Kampuchean people by the foreign occupiers, and Thailand has had to bear an enormous humanitarian burden in caring for the tens of thousands of refugees and displaced persons forced to flee the Vietnamese occupation of Kampuchea. It has grave implications for international peace and security because it has involved major powers. That is why ASEAN and Thailand have been seeking a comprehensive political settlement for the Kampuchea problem, along the lines advocated by the United Nations General Assembly. Peace must be restored to Kampuchea and ensured for the rest of the region. We believe that we are on the right course and that we shall be able to achieve our objective in the end.

The conflict in Kampuchea is also an obstacle to the goal proclaimed by ASEAN in 1971 to transform Southeast Asia into a Zone of Peace, Freedom, and Neutrality, free of external power intervention and interference. This is the long-term political goal of ASEAN, and once the Kampuchea problem has been resolved we shall be working actively for its realization.

ECONOMIC AND SOCIAL DEVELOPMENT

In the meantime, the ASEAN countries will continue actively with economic and social development in order to raise the standards of living of our people. Already the growth rates of the ASEAN countries are among the highest in the world. We shall be cooperating closely not only among ourselves but with like-minded countries in other regions that share with us a commitment to economic growth with open economies and social development with civil liberties.

ASEAN economic cooperation has strengthened the economy of each ASEAN country and has significantly contributed to the current boom in the Pacific region as a whole. Although the prospect for Pacific cooperation has been on the agenda of businessmen and academics for the past several years, ASEAN actually convened a meeting for this purpose in 1984 with the five Pacific Dialogue Partners; namely, Australia, Canada, Japan, New Zealand, and the United States. The discussion resulted in a pragmatic proposal in line with the ASEAN spirit. In July 1985, the 11 foreign ministers of ASEAN and its Pacific Dialogue Partners further agreed to initiate a program on human resources development. The program is open for participation by other countries in the Pacific region, particularly the developing countries of the South Pacific. With the success of this first program, cooperation in other fields leading toward a better utilization of the potentials within the Pacific region can be envisaged.

With a combined population of almost 300 million people, ASEAN is destined to become a major market and important trading bloc. But we cannot rely on quantity alone. We must also emphasize quality. Thailand has pursued a population program with satisfactory results. The population growth rate in Thailand has been reduced from 3.2 percent in 1972 to about 1.5 percent at present. In the future though, one challenge will be to effectively utilize the talents and resources of the aging, whose number is on the increase. As in the past, the East–West Center can contribute to the development of successful population policy for Thailand.

CONCLUSION

ASEAN has come a long way in a short span of time. However, we are keenly aware that new challenges continue to confront us. With the present international economic slowdown, coupled with the realization that there is much more that can be done to improve economic cooperation among the member countries, ASEAN governments are now looking at the prospect of holding another summit of heads of government, possibly in 1987 to coincide with the twentieth anniversary of the founding of ASEAN, where among many important matters it is hoped the following will also be discussed:

- review of ASEAN progress in the first 20 years;
- adaptation of ASEAN machinery to meet new needs; and
- ways and means of achieving closer economic cooperation and responding to the challenges of the international economic environment.

In summary, in its 18-year history, ASEAN has been able to shape an environment of stable interstate relations among member countries. It has established clear political directions to foster wide-ranging economic, social, and cultural cooperation. ASEAN is a going concern with a sense of community, a commitment to shared ideals and values, and a willingness to respond to the needs and interests of one another. We are united on many issues relating to international peace and progress in our region. We are now looking toward possible cooperation between ourselves and other groupings. We are convinced that such cooperation will be a positive contribution to the cause of peace, progress, and prosperity, not only for Asia and the Pacific region, but for the world community as a whole.

We must all play a part to create better understanding among peoples. The East–West Center has been exemplary in this regard. Its concept—to bring together highly qualified people from the whole region of Asia and the Pacific in a joint effort to seek solutions to the region's most pressing problems—is noble and, at the same time, refreshingly innovative. This is because the opportunity to share a diversity of knowledge and cultural experience leads to new perspectives and valuable insights into problems. More often than not, this opportunity will produce imaginative and effective solutions. Such experiences create permanent goodwill and a better understanding among peoples.

Since the Center's inception in 1960, some 2,000 Thai scholars have directly benefited from training at the East–West Center. These same scholars are now active in key sectors of Thai society. They join me in expressing our sincere appreciation to the Center for its support and contribution to the socioeconomic development of the region.

For our part, we in ASEAN have not been afraid to reach out and to meet new challenges. We are dedicated to bringing about a peaceful, prosperous, and secure region. With a lot of hard work and a little luck, we will succeed.

ASEAN and the Pacific Basin

THE RIGHT HONORABLE DATO MUSA HITAM
Deputy Prime Minister of Malaysia

WHY ASEAN IS VITAL

The vitality of ASEAN the community, ASEAN the concert of nations, ASEAN the organization, ASEAN the process, and ASEAN the spirit is essential to us in the ASEAN subregion in three arenas—the diplomatic, the political, and the economic.

Most obviously, ASEAN has given member states diplomatic strength. One U.S. ambassador to the United Nations has stated that while the ASEAN concert is the smallest "bloc" in the United Nations, on many occasions it has been the second most influential political grouping in the U.N. General Assembly. There is no doubt that the whole has been much more than the sum of its parts. Because of our wealth of relations with the First, Second, and Third Worlds, and because of the richness of our international affiliations, our membership in so many international "clubs"—the nonaligned movement, the Organization of Islamic Conference, the Commonwealth, the Organization of Petroleum Exporting Countries, etc.—the ASEAN states have been able to acquire and influence a whole array of natural allies and some unlikely friends. Our success, arising from concerted action on a range of issues, is sufficient testimony to the value of ASEAN to its member states.

While the diplomatic contribution and value of ASEAN—what ASEAN has been able to do with regard to the outside world—has been the most dramatic and, therefore, the most noted even in the ASEAN countries, in my view the internal political contribution has been far more profound.

First, ASEAN has prevented the rise of a sense of isolation that might have led to the sort of patron–client relationship with the Big Powers that is an invitation to Big Power competition. If ASEAN had not been there to provide psychological solace and support when the Vietnam War ended and when Kampuchea was conquered, the spillover effect on Thailand and other states would certainly have widened the conflict and risked dragging the Big Powers into the situation.

Second, ASEAN has given each of its members the self-confidence to assert that they are not the objects of international politics—not pawns on a chessboard—but the subjects of international relations, fully fit to participate in the affairs of our region and the wider world. We are neither queen, nor rook, nor even bishop. But we are at least a small knight, able to jump out of harm's way and, on occasion, to check the maneuvers of the bigger players. Pawns are virtually powerless, and powerlessness can corrupt as surely as power. ASEAN has helped member states to avoid the corruption of powerlessness.

Third, because much of our foreign policy is made within the multilateral framework of ASEAN, with all its checks and balances, we have been able to arrive at mature positions, take mature actions, and establish mature policies. To be sure, some good policies may have been checked and balanced out of the picture, and that is a loss to the ASEAN community. But the ASEAN process has tended to ensure that the policies of each member state are not made strictly on a unilateral basis, in splendid isolation, outside a multilateral framework, and oblivious to the concerns and interests of our neighbors. I am constantly amazed how smart people can be when they sit down together to talk openly and candidly, and how much better even the most brilliant idea can become when it has gone through the crucible of honest debate by intelligent men and women of goodwill. ASEAN has been fortunate in having a fund of intelligence and goodwill.

Fourth, the ASEAN process has resulted in the creation of an ASEAN sense of community, of family feeling; not a negative attitude of "we versus others" but a positive sense of our own interests and our own togetherness. It is not as wide or as deep as I would like it to be, but it is there. Because of the ASEAN sense of community, which we must all seek to strengthen, we are more sensitive to each other's interests, more inclined to think of community. Malaysian Prime Minister Datuk Seri Mahathir Mohamad has spoken of "an almost telepathic belief in partnership for progress, interdependence, and mutuality of interests" arising out of ASEAN.

Fifth, the ASEAN process has played a major role in the creation of a sturdy structure of mutual predictability, understanding, confidence, trust, and goodwill among the ASEAN six, without which Southeast Asia would be a different place today. When ASEAN was formed in 1967, we were almost strangers to one another. Some of us were almost adversaries and did not even want to know each other. Many of us were deeply suspicious of each other. Some of us frankly distrusted each other.

There was goodwill, but there was ill will too. Today, all is certainly not sweetness and light, but it is better than before.

Sixth, the ASEAN spirit has helped to resolve several conflicts between us and, much more important, has helped to prevent the rise of misunderstanding and conflict in the first place.

Seventh, because of ASEAN we have been able to establish four fundamental ground rules for peace and amity between us all: first, the principle of strict noninterference in each other's internal affairs; second, the principle of pacific settlement of disputes; third, respect for each other's independence; and fourth, strict respect for the territorial integrity of each of the ASEAN states. The ASEAN position on Kampuchea makes sense only in the context of ASEAN insistence on adherence to these fundamental ground rules by all of Southeast Asia—and by all the external players in the regional game.

The ASEAN states have declared these ground rules and, as demonstrated by our stance on Vietnam, have acted and lived by them. This is why Malaysia has consistently supported the territorial integrity of the Philippines and Thailand in discussions of Muslim minorities within the Organization of Islamic Conference. This is why every ASEAN state judiciously and meticulously has acted towards the Philippines in a way that cannot be construed by anyone as intervention, despite our desire to be of assistance to that country. The successful establishment of these basic rules of the game in the ASEAN community has without doubt made a major contribution to the peace, security, and prosperity of the area and will continue to do so.

Eighth, and perhaps most important of all, ASEAN has enabled the building of a zone of peace, an area of amity, a community of friendship encompassing six of the ten states of Southeast Asia, about 70 percent of Southeast Asian territory, and nearly four out of every five Southeast Asians. ASEAN today is already a zone of peace, freedom, and (save only for the Philippines, which has American bases for reasons that we do not oppose) of neutrality also.

The creation of an area of amity, to my mind, has been the supreme achievement of ASEAN. It is an achievement that we must be prepared to fight to maintain. It is an achievement that dwarfs whatever has been achieved on the diplomatic front and in the economic arena.

ECONOMIC COOPERATION

Nevertheless, ASEAN has contributed economically in at least four ways. *First,* through concerted diplomatic action (for example, *vis-à-vis* its dialogue partners) economic gains have been and are being extracted from time to time.

Second, because of the respect ASEAN has earned, the confidence it has built, and the stability it has helped to ensure, the ASEAN area has become a magnet for foreign investment, without which the national resilience of each ASEAN member would have been negatively affected, with consequences that range from substantial to dramatic.

Third, although there are grounds for dissatisfaction with regard to intra-ASEAN economic cooperation—trade among the ASEAN states, for example, amounts to only about 20 percent of our trade with the outside world—there is no doubt in my mind that without ASEAN, economic cooperation and economic relations among the present ASEAN member states would have been much narrower and much shallower.

Fourth, while they fall far short of our hopes and sometimes our expectations, the achievements of economic cooperation are not to be casually dismissed. Examples are:

- the Agreement of Mutual Assistance on Rice;
- an emergency sharing scheme on crude oil and oil products;
- an ASEAN Preferential Trading Arrangements system under which more than 18,000 items have been granted tariff preferences (although there are exclusion lists). Intra-ASEAN trade has increased 300 percent between 1976 and 1983—from U.S.$7.4 billion to U.S.$28.8 billion;
- cooperation on tourism;
- an ASEAN Minerals Cooperation Plan;
- an ASEAN Food Handling Bureau;
- a Plant Quarantine Training Center;
- an Agricultural Development Planning Center;
- an ASEAN Forest Tree Seed Center;

and finally three ambitious programs whose progress leaves much to be desired:

- an ASEAN Industrial Projects program;
- an ASEAN Industrial Complementation program; and
- an ASEAN Industrial Joint Ventures program.

The list is quite substantial but more needs to be done. Fortunately, the ASEAN states are fast approaching a time when they will be pushing for greater progress in cooperation.

I have emphasized the importance of ASEAN to the ASEAN community because I believe that we have managed to contribute something to the world as well as to our own small corner of it. ASEAN, indeed, has made a historic difference to the way Southeast Asia has evolved, particularly in the last ten years. ASEAN will continue to develop, as it must.

PACIFIC BASIN COOPERATION

Today, there is much talk of the Pacific Basin and of ASEAN's place in that wider community. An American President, Theodore Roosevelt, stated 82 years ago that, "The Atlantic is now at the height of its development and must soon exhaust the resources at its command. The Pacific Era, destined to be the greatest of all, is just at its dawn." Theodore Roosevelt was somewhat premature. But there can be no doubt that the dawn of the Pacific Era has come and gone, even as many of us slept through it. The thickening of the web of affiliations, increased economic and other interactions, and greater pan-Pacific cooperation, are inevitable, unless war intervenes. The imperatives that should guide these developments are:

First, it is absolutely premature to be thinking of a single overarching organization or institution for the Pacific. The problems of membership, purpose, and value are overwhelming. As the ASEAN experience has shown, there is virtue in structural ambiguity. The Pacific Era will be built not by architects with grand designs. The steps to be taken will not be the type of which great mythology is spun and heroic stories told.

Second, we must take not the political road but the functionalist road. Participation should be based on interest and on the ability to contribute to a particular functional collaborative effort.

Third, in pushing the process along we must not only be pragmatic and flexible but also patient. Patient bricklayers, not impatient men behind the steering wheels of giant bulldozers, will be needed.

Fourth, no one should try to create a strategic design, still less a Brezhnev Doctrine in reverse.

Fifth, it is essential to create in the Pacific not a rich man's club, not a hierarchical system, but a series of arrangements and collaborative efforts that are egalitarian in character and in content.

Sixth, and above all, from the point of view of the ASEAN community, it is absolutely essential that nothing be done that would retard or jeopardize the development of the ASEAN spirit, process, concert, sense of community, and organization. Too much has been invested in ASEAN. The viability of ASEAN is essential to its participation in the Pacific process and to the enrichment of the web of interdependence in the Pacific. ASEAN is too important an enterprise to be sacrificed for anything that does not promise much more.

For ASEAN, the future is pregnant with possibilities richer and more profound than the already considerable successes it has achieved. As Pacific Basin developments intensify in the coming years, they too promise possibilities that can alter the economic landscape not only of the region but of the wider world beyond. These possibilities—for the ASEAN states as well as for the Pacific states—spell opportunity in the coming years. The challenge lies in whether we possess the political sensitivities, the diplomatic skills, and the will, energy, and commitment to turn these possibilities into reality.

CHAPTER 2
DEMOGRAPHIC AND SOCIAL CHANGE

Demographic and Social Development: Taking Stock for the Morrow

ALINE K. WONG AND PAUL P. L. CHEUNG

INTRODUCTION

Since its formation in 1967, ASEAN[1] has developed into one of the world's fastest-growing regions. In the first fifteen years, the then five ASEAN countries experienced unprecedented high economic growth, with annual growth rates at 6 to 10 percent. The same period has also seen rapid infrastructural developments in the provision of health, education, communication, and other essential services. The economic and infrastructural changes are closely associated with sociostructural transformations in each society. Some of these changes have been instrumental in quickening economic growth, while others may have incurred social and economic costs. On balance, there seems to have been significant social progress in the region, marked by a steady rise in the standard of living and a surging sense of optimism.

As ASEAN entered the 1980s, the economic growth of the member countries slowed considerably, due to the world market situation and, to a certain degree, internal structural and institutional problems. With the prospect of a sustained economic slowdown looming large on the horizon, it is perhaps timely to take stock of the gains made in the past two decades. This paper examines the social implications of ASEAN's past economic growth and some emerging problems that could have significant bearing on the countries' efforts to sustain social development. It reviews some of the critical dimensions of ASEAN's social and demographic changes, including demographic development, urbanization and migration, educational transformation, changing roles of women, changes in family structure and relations, and, finally, the rise of the middle class and income inequality.

---

1. This paper does not cover Brunei, which joined ASEAN in 1984 as the sixth member, because of the focus on *past* development trends in ASEAN.

17

DEMOGRAPHIC DEVELOPMENT

Demographic development in the ASEAN region in the past two decades
is notable for two features: accelerated progress in mortality reduction,
which commenced after World War II, and remarkable success in lowering fertility and curbing population growth. As a result, the region as a
whole is making rapid strides towards the completion of the so-called
"demographic transition," the movement from high fertility and mortality to low fertility and mortality conditions. It is notable that Singapore,
the demographic forerunner, completed the transition in barely 20 years
and lowered its fertility by 1975 to the replacement level—2.1 children
per woman, the number necessary if she and her husband are to be just
replaced in the next generation, allowing for mortality.

The reduction in mortality has been rapid in all ASEAN countries,
which is not surprising given the spread of modern public health and
medical technologies throughout the world since World War II. Table 2.1
documents the upward trends in life expectancy at birth and the decline
in infant mortality from 1960 to 1985. Note that although the absolute
gains are similar, between-country differentials remain large, reflecting
divergent stages of socioeconomic development within the region. Indonesia had a fairly low life expectancy of 42.5 years in the 1960s. Steady
gains were made in the early 1970s when life expectancy was raised by
five years to 47.5, and, by the early 1980s, another five years were
added. In the 1960s, Malaysia, the Philippines, and Thailand already
had life expectancies of around 55. By the early 1980s, the life expectancies in these countries had risen to 66.9, 64.5, and 62.7 years respectively. Among the three, Malaysia has shown the largest gain and enjoys
the second highest life expectancy in the region. Singapore's mortality
level is fast approaching the level of the developed countries, with a life
expectancy of 72.2 years and an infant mortality rate of only 11 infant
deaths per 1,000 live births.

The rapid decline from high to moderate or low mortality is associated
with three factors: the effective implementation of public health and disease control measures, better access to and utilization of medical services, and the general improvement in the standard of living as reflected
in the increase in average daily protein and caloric intake.[2] Future mortality reduction on a national basis, of course, will depend on the contin-

---

2. The increase in average daily caloric intake is largest in Indonesia and the Philippines,
where daily intake increased from below 2,000 to around 2,400 between 1965 and 1981.
For the same period, the increases for Singapore, Malaysia, and Thailand were also substantial. See Asian Development Bank (1984).

Table 2.1   Selected mortality indicators, 1960–85

	Life expectancy at birth (years)			Infant mortality rate (deaths per 1000 live births)		
	1960–65	1970–75	1980–85	1960–65	1970–75	1980–85
Indonesia						
Both sexes	42.5	47.5	52.5	145	112	87
Males	41.7	46.4	51.2			
Females	43.4	48.7	53.9			
Malaysia						
Both sexes	55.7	63.0	66.9	63	40	29
Males	54.2	61.4	65.0			
Females	57.4	64.7	68.8			
Philippines						
Both sexes	54.5	60.4	64.5	97	68	50
Males	52.9	58.8	62.8			
Females	56.2	62.1	66.3			
Singapore						
Both sexes	65.8	69.5	72.2	30	19	11
Males	64.1	67.4	69.1			
Females	67.6	71.8	75.5			
Thailand						
Both sexes	53.9	59.6	62.7	95	65	51
Males	51.9	57.7	60.8			
Females	56.1	61.6	64.8			

Source: United Nations, *World Population Prospects: Estimates and Projections as Assessed in 1982* (New York: United Nations, 1985).

uation of these efforts. Furthermore, research has shown the persistence of significant mortality differentials by localities and socioeconomic characteristics (Herrin et al. 1981). The extension of cheap, easily available health services to the rural areas and to the lower class is as much a prerequisite for future mortality reduction as the adoption of advanced medical technology. However, as experiences in other countries have shown, the size and the tempo of future reductions are likely to be smaller and slower unless there is significant improvement in the standard of living among the majority of the population (Palloni 1981).

The region's pattern of fertility decline, especially its magnitude and tempo, has received considerable research attention. For example, Singapore's total fertility rate (TFR) stood at 6.5 children per woman of reproductive age in 1957. As Table 2.2 shows, it declined to 4.9 in the early

Table 2.2   Selected fertility and population growth indicators, 1960–95

	1960–65		1970–75		1980–85		1990–95	
	TFR[a]	Annual growth rate (percent)	TFR	Annual growth rate (percent)	TFR	Annual growth rate (percent)	TFR	Annual growth rate (percent)
Indonesia	5.4	2.1	5.5	2.4	3.9	1.8	2.9	1.5
Malaysia	6.7	3.0	4.9	2.5	3.7	2.3	2.9	1.9
Philippines	6.6	3.0	5.0	2.5	4.2	2.5	3.3	2.1
Singapore	4.9	2.8	2.6	1.7	1.7	1.3	1.7	1.0
Thailand	6.4	3.0	5.0	2.6	3.6	2.1	2.6	1.7

Source: United Nations, *World Population Prospects: Estimates and Projections as Assessed in 1982* (New York: United Nations, 1985).
[a] TFR stands for the total fertility rate, which is measured in terms of children per woman.

1960s, and by the early 1980s it was 1.7—below-replacement fertility, as defined above. Singapore's fertility is now among the lowest in the world. Thailand and Malaysia have shown equally remarkable drops in their total fertility rates, from a high of around 6.5 children per woman in the early 1960s to less than 4.0 in the 1980s. The decline has been less swift in the cases of Indonesia and the Philippines. Nonetheless, significant fertility reductions were made in these two countries. By 1995, if current trends continue, the ASEAN countries (with the exception of the Philippines) are expected to have TFRs of below 3.0.

Three additional features characterize the fertility decline in the ASEAN region. First, the impressive decline is due largely to a drop in marital fertility, with the increase in age at marriage playing a secondary role (Herrin et al. 1981). This change in marital fertility signifies the increasingly widespread adoption of modern contraceptives for the explicit purpose of birth control. Second, the decline in marital fertility is thought to have begun among older women in the prevention of unwanted births and to have been followed by the lowering of the number of wanted births through a downward shift in fertility preference. Third, the diffusion of modern contraceptive technology has been rapid and pervasive across geographical and socioeconomic boundaries. The rapid decline in marital fertility among rural populations and the less educated has been noted especially in the cases of Thailand and Indonesia (Knodel et al. 1984; Hull et al. 1977).

The decline is the outcome of interplay between social and economic changes on the one hand and governments' intense efforts on the other

(Bulatao 1984). Demographers in the region have generally acknowl-edged the effectiveness of governmental involvement in organizing and promoting fertility control measures. The concern over rapid population growth led Singapore in 1965, Malaysia in 1966, Indonesia in 1968, and Thailand and the Philippines in 1970 to adopt official anti-natalist poli-cies. Subsequently, all ASEAN countries instituted country-wide family planning programs, with well-developed organizational infrastructure. The programs in Indonesia, Thailand, and Malaysia have been particu-larly commendable in their effective delivery of services to rural residents through health stations or outreach networks. In Indonesia, the involve-ment of community leaders in the program has resulted in strong com-munity-wide participation. In Singapore, the program is reinforced by a wide-ranging set of social policies with anti-natalist intentions.

The systematic introduction of modern contraceptives, though legiti-mized by the government, could not have wholly accounted for the fertil-ity decline. Latent demand for birth control is clearly met by the pro-gram, and the prevention of one or two unwanted births per woman could amount to a noticeable aggregate fertility reduction. However, unless fertility preferences are substantially lowered, rational birth con-trol could do little to effect a significant fertility decline. In the ASEAN region, research has shown that fertility decline is probably precipitated by a downward shift in fertility preference (Knodel et al. 1984).

Changes in fertility preferences are indicative of the changing balance in the familial calculus of the value and cost of children. Reduction of the economic contribution of children to the family, partly because of a grad-ual shift to a wage economy and the constraints on land utilization imposed by the size of landholdings, places a limit on the economic value of children. At the same time, parents, with higher education than past generations and having still higher aspirations for their children, are increasingly aware of the rising cost of educating their children up to expectation. The net result of these changes is that large family size is increasingly viewed as an avoidable economic burden. This realization, coupled with the growing emphasis on the psychological value of chil-dren, may have tipped the balance in trading quantity for quality of chil-dren.[3]

Changes in fertility preference over time have not been documented in a comparative framework,[4] but the decline for each country is nonethe-

---

3. For a detailed discussion on the value and cost of children and their effect on fertility decisions, see publications in the seven-volume series *The Value of Children: A Cross-National Study,* published by the East–West Population Institute on various dates between 1975 and 1979.

4. Some estimates are presented in a World Fertility Survey report on family size prefer-ences. See Lightbourne and MacDonald (1982).

less noticeable. Among Chinese in Singapore, the desired number of children dropped from an average of 3.6 in 1973 to 2.6 in 1982. The evidence from Thailand also indicates a significant drop in the past two decades, but the number has leveled off at about two to three. The leveling off of fertility preference will no doubt pose a constraint to some countries' efforts to control the size of their populations.

The issue is, therefore, whether the governments concerned will be able to devise additional measures or policies to encourage further declines in fertility preference. The case of Malaysia constitutes an interesting and exceptional reversal of the ASEAN countries' population control policies. The recent pro-natalist shift in Malaysia's population policy, if implemented rigorously, may reverse that country's fertility trend. For successful implementation, it would require some strong inducements at the family level in order to counter the past trend of fertility decline. Pending further developments, it is unclear how such a pro-natalist shift would alter the relationship between Malaysia's population, resources, and economic development.

As for Thailand, Indonesia, and the Philippines, further fertility declines would require not just continuing government efforts to promote family planning programs, but also accelerated growth in standards of living and social infrastructural development, which facilitate the decline in fertility preference. In any case, the data suggest that it would be unlikely for these countries to reach replacement levels of fertility in the immediate future.

The case of Singapore illustrates the population concerns the other countries may face in the long run. With its below-replacement fertility, Singapore has been sensitized to the quality of its future cohorts. Its recent attempts to adjust the "lopsided" procreation pattern as related to educational levels, i.e., the tendency of more-educated women to have fewer babies, and attempts to search for talent through overseas recruitment exercises, provide some indication of the future direction of Singapore's population policy. At the same time, the sustained declines in fertility and mortality have led to concern about an aging population, with far-reaching implications for the welfare burden of the aged, the shortage of labor, adjustments in infrastructural provisions, as well as the sociocultural ethos of the society (Martin 1985).

URBANIZATION AND MIGRATION

It is often observed that the rapid growth of urban agglomerations in developing countries constitutes a problem second only to the high rate of population growth, in that both are proceeding faster than the pace of

Table 2.3   Urbanization trends, 1960–2000

	Urban population (in millions)			Urban population as percent of total			Percent of urban population in largest city	
	1960	1980	Percent increase	1960	1980	2000	1960	1980
Indonesia	14.0	33.5	139.3	15	22	37	20	23
Malaysia	2.1	4.1	95.2	25	29	42	19	27
Philippines	8.5	18.1	112.9	30	37	49	27	30
Singapore	1.3	1.8	38.5	78	74	79	100	100
Thailand	3.4	6.7	97.1	13	14	23	65	69

Sources: United Nations, *World Population Prospects: Estimates and Projections as Assessed in 1982* (New York: United Nations, 1985); World Bank, *World Development Report* (Washington D.C.: World Bank, 1983).

economic development. If a degree of success can be said to have been achieved in curbing population growth in the ASEAN region in the past two decades, the same is not true for moderating urban growth. Although ASEAN is still one of the least-urbanized regions of the world, rapid growth in the absolute size of its urban populations seems to continue unabated.

In 1960, with the exception of Singapore, urban populations in the ASEAN countries constituted not more than 30 percent of the respective total populations. The Philippines and Malaysia were on the high side with 30 and 25 percent urban respectively and Thailand and Indonesia were only 13 and 15 percent respectively (Table 2.3). By 1980, the percentages had increased moderately by one to seven percentage points, but none of the four countries exceeded 50 percent urban. United Nations projections indicate that the 50 percent mark is not likely to be reached by 2000 (United Nations 1985). This slow rate of urbanization is largely explained by the facts that the natural increase (births minus deaths) in rural populations has kept pace with growth in urban areas and the labor absorptive capacity of the rural sector has been relatively stable (Herrin et al. 1981).

In contrast, the absolute growth of the urban populations in these four ASEAN countries has been remarkable. In a twenty-year span, from 1960 to 1980, all of them doubled the size of their urban populations. Furthermore, the high concentration of the urban populations in the largest cities further increased. In 1980, Bangkok had some 69 percent of Thailand's urban population. The corresponding figures for Manila, Kuala Lumpur, and Jakarta were 30, 27, and 23 percent respectively.

Growth in the urban population is attributable to three sources: urban natural increase, net migration, and net gains in reclassification of urban boundaries. Research has shown that across the region the contribution of natural increase has gained prominence over time, although migration continues to be a major source (Pryor 1979). Rural–urban migration has remained the dominant type of migration stream in the ASEAN region in recent periods. Although other forms of migration, such as seasonal circulation and return migration, are present, they are not likely to offset the urban growth through rural–urban migration.

Despite the many difficulties they encounter in the city and despite the efforts of some governments to discourage migration to the cities (such as Indonesia's declaration of Jakarta as a "closed city"), the rural migrants are by no means deterred. For many, the city offers hope for a better life, particularly for their children, no matter how harsh the present conditions are, no matter how low a wage they can fetch in either the formal or the informal sector of the city economy. Arguments revolving around the "push versus pull" hypothesis of this cityward migration are well known. An additional feature is seen in the case of Malaysia, where the government's policy of attracting Malays to the urban areas for social and political reasons plays as much a role in the country's cityward migration as the familiar push and pull factors.

In ASEAN, as in other developing regions, the urban-biased pattern of development has raised doubts over the viability of this type of growth strategy because of the apparent urban diseconomies (Yeung 1984). In the main, there are three major areas of concern. The first is employment —or rather, unemployment and underemployment. The labor-absorptive capacity of the urban centers is often limited and its growth consistently outstripped by the growth of the urban workforce. As a result, a large proportion of the migrants and the urban poor are either unemployed or are struggling for subsistence in the informal sector. (For example, it has been estimated that 46 percent of Jakarta's workforce is employed in the informal sector.) The relentless pressure for employment opportunities from the ever-expanding urban workforce has important implications for the social and political stability of these countries.

The second major area of concern is the deterioration in the quality of life in the cities. The conditions and adequacy of the urban infrastructure and essential services are found wanting in many respects. Housing shortages, snarled traffic, pollution, and sprawling squatter settlements are common problems in the cities of the region. To ameliorate these problems would mean huge capital expenditures in infrastructural improvements, further straining already tight national budgets and diverting resources away from essential rural development.

The third concern is the plight of the migrants, especially the females who flock to the city in large numbers. While many of them succeed in securing a livelihood in the informal sector, a sizable number are drawn into the illicit trades. Their poverty and their exploitation for immoral purposes are issues that require the urgent attention of governments.[5]

A newly emerging issue relating to the migrants is the notable increase in international labor migration among the ASEAN countries. The Philippines has by far the largest number of workers overseas. In 1975, the number totaled about 12,500, mostly professional and service workers. By 1983, the number had increased to 380,263, mostly production workers. Thailand and Indonesia have fewer workers overseas, but a significant increase was also observed in those countries between 1980 and 1983 (Stahl 1983). It is undoubtedly true that labor export has certain economic advantages at both the macro- and the micro-levels. But social costs have also emerged. Abuse and exploitation of the workers in the receiving countries are not uncommon. The separation of the workers from their families further gives rise to family and emotional problems. Moreover, large-scale external migration may create shortages in some skilled occupations in the labor-exporting country, as Thailand and Malaysia have experienced in the construction industry. It would also seem that the demand for labor export is unlikely to be a sustained one. The current world economic recession has begun to cause the repatriation of foreign workers in large numbers. The reintegration of returned migrants into their native societies, together with the question of their employment absorption, poses additional problems to the ASEAN countries, themselves suffering from the effects of the world recession.

LITERACY AND EDUCATION

Another major aspect of ASEAN's social development is its educational transformation. In the postwar era, both the process of education and the distribution of schooling opportunities have undergone significant changes. The trend toward broad-based and longer formal education is clearly evident in all ASEAN countries. Table 2.4 shows that younger age groups in each country are more likely to have received primary and secondary education. With the exception of Indonesia, the ASEAN countries moved rapidly in the 1960s to universal primary education. Thus, young people just entering the labor force in the late 1970s and early 1980s were equipped with at least a primary education. For countries

---

5. For more details on this topic, see Fawcett et al. (1984).

Table 2.4 Proportion attained primary and secondary schooling, by age and sex

	Ages 15–19		Ages 20–24		Ages 25–34	
	Primary	Secondary	Primary	Secondary	Primary	Secondary
Indonesia (1980)						
Total	.60	N.A.	.57	.24	.54	.22
Male	.63	N.A.	.62	.30	.60	.26
Female	.57	N.A.	.52	.19	.51	.17
Malaysia[a] (1980)						
Total	.93	N.A.	.90	.30	.85	.19
Male	.95	N.A.	.93	.33	.91	.23
Female	.92	N.A.	.87	.27	.79	.15
Philippines (1985)						
Total	.96	N.A.	.96	.48	.94	.37
Male	.96	N.A.	.96	.48	.94	.40
Female	.96	N.A.	.96	.48	.93	.35
Singapore (1980)						
Total	.92	N.A.	.89	.32	.85	.29
Male	.93	N.A.	.91	.30	.89	.31
Female	.92	N.A.	.88	.33	.81	.27
Thailand (1980)						
Total	.97	N.A.	.96	.23	.94	.15
Male	.97	N.A.	.97	.27	.96	.19
Female	.96	N.A.	.95	.20	.93	.12

Source: United Nations, *Demographic Yearbook, 1982* (New York: United Nations, 1983).
N.A.: Not applicable.
[a] Malaysia figures from Khoo Teik Huat, *General Report of the Population Census* (Kuala Lumpur: Department of Statistics, 1983).

that already had a high level of primary education, significant progress in the attainment of secondary education can be observed in the same period. Even in the case of Indonesia, the proportion of primary-school-age children who were actually in school in 1980 stood close to 100 per-cent,[6] suggesting that the steady gain in primary education had quickened in the decade.

A notable region-wide phenomenon in the educational transformation is the diminishing sex differential in educational attainment. Table 2.4 shows that for most countries the gap between the sexes has narrowed.

---

6. This is a net enrollment ratio, adjusted for age-grade retardation.

Table 2.5   Enrollment ratios at primary and secondary level by sex, 1970–80

	Primary			Secondary		
	Total	Male	Female	Total	Male	Female
Indonesia						
1970	77	83	71	15	20	10
1975	83	90	76	19	24	15
1980	112	119	104	28	33	22
Malaysia						
1970	87	91	84	34	40	28
1975	91	93	89	43	48	39
1980	92	93	91	51	52	49
Philippines						
1970	108	N.A.	N.A.	46	N.A.	N.A.
1975	108	N.A.	N.A.	54	N.A.	N.A.
1980	110	111	108	63	58	68
Singapore						
1970	106	110	102	46	47	45
1975	111	114	107	53	52	53
1980	107	108	105	59	58	61
Thailand						
1970	83	86	79	17	20	15
1975	84	87	81	26	28	23
1980	96	98	94	29	30	28

Sources: 1970 and 1975 data—United Nations, *Demographic Yearbook, 1982* (New York: United Nations, 1983). 1980 data—United Nations Educational, Scientific and Cultural Organization, *UNESCO Statistical Yearbook, 1984* (Paris: UNESCO, 1984).

Note: The enrollment ratio is the number of students enrolled divided by the appropriate school-age population. It is possible for the ratio to exceed 100 because of age-grade retardation; i.e., the number of students at a given level could exceed the population of the expected schooling age for that level.

N.A.: Figures not available.

In the case of the Philippines, studies have shown that a crossover may have occurred in favor of females (Smith and Cheung 1981), and the data in Table 2.5 substantiate it. Similarly, signs of a crossover are already apparent for Singapore, but enrollment figures shown in Table 2.5 suggest that crossover is not likely to occur in the other ASEAN countries in the immediate future in spite of some recent rapid gains made toward a balanced sex ratio at the tertiary levels in Malaysia and Thailand. In general, sex inequality in educational attainment is not yet totally removed, especially at the family level where educational investment decisions have to be made for the children. In Indonesia, Malaysia, and the Philippines, research has revealed a tendency for poorer families to favor boys in the allocation of scarce family resources for education (Mani 1983; Smith and Cheung 1981; Wang 1980).

Underlying this transformation is a subtle shift in the premise of social stratification by education in the region. Clearly, the distribution of primary education has become more equitable across socioeconomic strata. A child from a poor family now stands as much chance of beginning and completing primary education as his well-off counterparts. This equality in access provides a definite avenue of upward mobility for the more able from the lower socioeconomic groups. However, the relevance of inherited social advantages has persisted. Research has shown that family background characteristics remain important determinants in the attainment of post-primary education, especially at the tertiary level (Smith and Cheung 1986). School performance and educational aspiration are also positively associated with family background, giving the well-off an added advantage. In the case of the Philippines, where progression to tertiary level is common, socioeconomic status determines to a large extent the quality of college education received, which in turn is reflected in the ability to be admitted to quality schools. It is therefore not surprising to find that, within a given level of educational attainment, the perceived quality of the school becomes an important determinant of the ease in job search and labor market entry.

A critical problem that has surfaced in the midst of the educational transformation is the dearth of opportunities for the effective utilization of the educated. For example, in Indonesia and the Philippines economic development has not proceeded at a pace that allows adequate absorption of the college-educated. The limited absorptive capacity of the labor market in general will undoubtedly have a dampening effect on the future growth of average educational attainment. On the other hand, as in the case of Singapore, rapid economic growth has resulted in a shortage of highly qualified personnel, thus necessitating programs of expansion of educational opportunities and emphasis on science and technology, as well as intensive efforts in foreign recruitment.

CHANGING ROLE AND STATUS OF WOMEN

Women in the ASEAN region have traditionally had high status. With the exception of Indian and Chinese women in Singapore and Malaysia, equality of the sexes has been a common characteristic of the traditional cultures in the region. Women's status is founded on the basis of interdependent and complementary roles in social, economic, cultural, and even political affairs, and is reinforced by a favorable disposition of the folk religions toward women. The complementarity of the sexes is nowhere more evident than in the village subsistence economy, where farming and trading activities are shared.

With modernization and the disruption of the village economy, the traditional fabric of communal life began to change. However, observers have noted the striking continuities, rather than the discontinuities, with the past with respect to many of the women's roles (Wong 1979). Indeed, many of the so-called modern roles of women are extensions of their traditional roles. The concentration of the economically active women in trade, commerce, and personal services can thus be perceived as a carryover from their past activities in these areas, albeit in a more monetized, modern setting.

In the village, the fact that women's economic activities can be easily combined with their daily family responsibilities means that the performance of familial roles does not prevent women's economic participation. In the cities, the position of women is more relegated to the home, resulting in a more rigid differentiation of sex roles. Thus, in spite of better educational and employment opportunities for women in the cities, the division of labor within the household is such that housework remains the priority responsibility of the wife. It is perhaps among the small proportion of urban middle-class women that, with Western influence, the husband–wife relationship becomes more egalitarian and a more equitable division of housework prevails. Among these couples, the working wives have a greater role in family decision making and have greater control over their own social and work activities.

Between 1970 and 1980, the female industrial labor force in developing countries in general increased by 50 to 60 percent (International Labour Office 1985). In ASEAN, as elsewhere in the developing world, whether the industrial establishments are national enterprises or the offshore branches of multinational corporations, whether the industries are of the import-substitution or the export-oriented type, women workers are employed mainly in labor-intensive operations such as garment and footwear manufacturing, food processing, and electronics. The majority of the female workers are young, single girls who are employed for their manual dexterity, tolerance for repetitive and monotonous tasks, keen eyesight, patience, and concentration. Their work is low-skilled and low-paid. Employment can fluctuate widely with world market conditions, and unionization is sometimes disallowed. Another feature of women's work in multinational offshore manufacturing in the ASEAN region is the commonly found "export-processing" or "free-trade" zones, which are often fenced-off compounds where the girls, many of whom come from rural areas, work and live. The female workers' wages, employment conditions, and adjustment to factory work and urban life have been the subject of a number of recent studies (Lim 1978; Grossman 1979; Jamilah 1980; Heyzer 1982; Chapkis and Enloe 1983; Blake 1984; Fawcett et al. 1984).

Despite the increase in average educational attainment, women in the ASEAN region in general do not enjoy so great a return from their level of education as do men, because they tend to concentrate in a limited number of academic specializations that do not match the demand of a modern technology-based economy. Furthermore, such sex-role segregation usually starts early in the educational process, inculcating a domesticated and non-achieving image. Thus, in spite of the rising level of education, women still occupy only a small percentage of the higher paid professional, administrative, executive, and managerial jobs (Wong 1979).[7] Institutional rigidity in hiring women for top positions further explains the slow gain. Given the fact that the middle-class populations in the ASEAN countries are still very small, both in absolute and proportionate terms, the few highly educated women who succeed in making inroads into the male world of occupational elites may symbolize the persistence of social inequalities rather than the advent of social equality to women in the lower and working classes. Thus, the impact of industrialization and economic development on changing sex roles and raising women's status in society remains a questionable one.

CHANGES IN FAMILY STRUCTURE AND RELATIONS

Changes in family structure and relations in the ASEAN countries reflect in many ways the structural transformation that has occurred in each society. The increase in educational and economic opportunities, the persistent search for a better life through social and geographical mobility, the demographic changes, and the changes in the roles of women, all have affected the family in one way or another.

Three major structural changes in the family in the ASEAN countries are evident. First, average family size has experienced a gradual decline

---

7. Singapore seems to have done less well in terms of the proportion of women among the professional, technical, administrative, executive, and managerial occupations. Singapore's 31 percent (1984) compares favorably with Indonesia's 37 percent (1980) and Thailand's and West Malaysia's 35 percent (1980), but it pales when compared to the Philippines' 60 percent (1981).

in recent decades. A positive result of this is the expected redistribution of parental resources with an increase in the share per child. Moreover, the parents, especially the mother, are freed from the tending of young children at an earlier stage of marriage, thus giving them more time for career pursuits. Yet the decline in family size may also reduce the caring capacity of the average family at later stages of the family's life course. The caring function of the family will be taxed as more parents survive to the vulnerable years of old age. The availability of persons to perform this function at the family level is positively related to family size. Whether the one- or two-child family will be able to cope with the caring function is an important question to address.

Second, improvement in life expectancy has inevitably lengthened the duration of the life course of a family (Mason and Martin 1985). As a result, there is increased opportunity for multigenerational living, the transition of headship of the family from the older to the younger generation has been delayed, and the passage of inheritance from one generation to the next is similarly delayed. These changes may, however, be offset by a rising preference for nuclear households. The effect of these changes on family relations is unclear and a topic for further research.

Third, with the increase in migration, there appears to be a troubling trend in the fragmentation of the family and kin groups. At the place of origin, the sending families, in exchange for possible remittances, face a depletion of human resources. At the destination, however, the family is often reconfigured in some form to provide mutual assistance by the congregation of family members or kin. The predominance of non-nuclear households in some migrant settlements reflects this adaptive strategy.

However, it is important to realize that changes in the family, especially the relational aspects, tend to come about slowly and gradually. In this respect, the family serves as an invaluable stabilizer in a society undergoing rapid social and economic changes. Signs of the tenacity of family relations are many. The sending of remittances by migrant workers back to their homes is indicative of the strong and continuing link between the migrants and their families. The care of the aged has remained primarily the responsibility of the family and children's obligations toward parents persist at the core of parent–child relations. Within the family economy the children—male or female, married or unmarried —continue to play a major role. In many respects the family remains the locus of decision making for the individual.

Nevertheless, changes are emerging in the realm of family relations. The rise of women's status has resulted in a greater tendency toward an egalitarian basis of family decision making. The adoption of modern contraceptives for the purpose of family planning introduces a degree of rationality to both the childbearing and childrearing processes. The parents are more aware of the costs of children, apart from the possible contributions the children may bring. Thus, investment in children, educationally or otherwise, becomes a more conscious choice.

In Singapore, the perceived changes in family relations have caused swift government intervention in the form of social policies to counteract what the government considers to be the undesirable consequences of these changes. Various public housing schemes have been implemented to encourage extended-family living, and income tax incentives and medical expense schemes have been adopted to enable children to contribute toward care and maintenance of their aging parents and grandparents. Furthermore, there is now a concerted effort to revitalize traditional family values through emphasizing Confucianism. Traditional Asian values in general are heralded as the cultural ballast for a society going through rapid changes under the influence of Westernization. The current signs of a return to more fundamental religious faiths among certain sections of the Singapore and Malaysian populations can also be seen as indigenous responses to the similar trends of changes in family and social relations across the region. The issue, for Singapore and other countries, is thus whether such government and nongovernment efforts can effectively contain the tide of social change so as to remain open to external, global trends while maintaining cultural traditions.

THE RISE OF THE MIDDLE CLASS AND INCOME INEQUALITY

Rapid economic growth is inevitably associated with a diversification and further differentiation of the occupational structure. New occupational roles arise because of emerging societal needs, while traditional roles may become obsolete. Associated with these changes is the broadening of the social mobility process, and perhaps the movement towards equality in the distribution of monetary rewards among the population.

Observers have noted that the pace of diversification and differentiation of the occupational structure in the ASEAN region has quickened only in the past two decades. Prior to that the process had been slow, with the proportion of nonagricultural workers remaining at about the 20 percent level in the agriculture-based countries (Evers 1973). The substantial shift of workers from agricultural to nonagricultural occupations is a product of both industrialization and urbanization. Among the non-agricultural occupations there has been an increase, in proportion as well as in absolute numbers, of administrative, managerial, and professional workers. All the ASEAN countries witnessed a doubling in the number of this group of workers in the decade 1970–80. If these workers can be considered constituents of the middle class then the social stratification in ASEAN countries has indeed witnessed a thickening of the middle layers.

The broadening of the middle class over time has profound social implications. First, the attainment of administrative, managerial, and professional occupations is usually indicative of an open system of social mobility based on educational level and individual merits. The new professionals are therefore markedly different from their older counterparts, who tend to be indigenous aristocrats transferred to modern occupational roles (Evers 1973). The opening-up of the social mobility process to the lower classes is an important structural transformation. While rapid social mobility represents the fulfillment of popular aspirations and raises the sense of well-being in society, it is important to note that social unrest could easily result from the frustration of these aspirations brought about by a slowdown in the rate of economic growth. Second, members of the middle class, partly because of their education and partly because of their access to scarce resources, are prone to external influences on their values and life styles. In a sense, they become social trend-setters and cultural innovators. Their impact on traditional orientations to life should not be underestimated.

The emergence of the middle class does not mean that an equitable distribution of societal rewards and benefits is in effect. Observers have often noted the coexistence of an emerging middle class and a greater inequality in income distribution in some of the ASEAN countries. With the exception of Singapore, the equity performance in ASEAN countries has not kept pace with economic development (Wong and Wong 1984). In the Philippines, income inequality, as measured by the Gini ratio, has shown only a small decline from the early 1960s to the mid-1970s; the Gini ratio dropped from around .50 in the 1960s to .45 in 1975. This slight decline occurred while the Philippine economy was undergoing rapid expansion and growth. In Indonesia and Thailand, the trends show an increase in inequality, with the ratios deteriorating from .35 in 1965 to .41 in 1976 for Indonesia, and from .56 in 1963 to .60 in 1972 for Thailand, although recent evidence in Thailand seems to show that the situation has improved since 1972. In Malaysia, the Gini ratio increased between 1957 and 1970, after which it started on a downward trend (from .50 in 1970 to .44 in 1973) in part because of the redistribution-oriented New Economic Policy. In Singapore the trend has shown rapid progress toward greater equality; the ratio decreased from .50 in 1966 to .38 in 1977. This is attributable to an industrial economy with nearly full employment over a long period of time.

It should be emphasized that summary measures such as the Gini ratio should be interpreted with great care, because any change in the pattern and trends of income inequality of a country has to be analyzed in the context of its particular structural and institutional characteristics, which in turn provide the source of such inequality. Suffice it to say that for four of the five ASEAN countries considered here the disturbing feature is that income inequality has been reduced slowly or has even increased during the period in which all of these countries have experienced impressive economic growth. The serious implications for their social and political stability, should economic growth slow down for sustained periods in the future, are obvious. It is, however, heartening to note that since the 1970s there has been a growing awareness among the ASEAN governments of the equity issue, and that they have explicitly incorporated the reduction of inequality and poverty as important objectives in their various development plans.

CONCLUSION

As reviewed in this chapter, economic growth in ASEAN has been accompanied by remarkable social transformations signifying considerable social progress in the region. Demographic changes over the past two decades have lengthened life expectancy, reduced average family size, and brought down population growth. Expansion of educational opportunities has raised the average level of educational attainment and improved the life chances of the poor. The social structure has become more open, and there has been a broadening of the middle class. Women in general have more educational and employment opportunities and are enjoying some changes in traditional roles.

On the other hand, rampant urban growth has incurred considerable economic and social costs, with the familiar problems of "over-urbanization" highlighted by the conditions of migrants and deteriorating quality of life in cities. In the area of education, an emerging issue is that of unemployment among the educated. Even though women's education has increased, their employment patterns do not necessarily indicate a substantial rise in social status or equality with men. Changes in family structure may have adversely affected the caring capacity of the family unit, while changes in family and social relations raise concern about a possible decline in traditional values. But by far the most serious implications for ASEAN's future development and stability lie in the problem of income inequality. In spite of rapid economic growth in the past, the income gap has not significantly closed and in some cases is actually widening. Income inequality may be tolerated by the population during times of economic expansion (i.e., so long as the cake is getting bigger); this may not be the case if the economy stagnates. Furthermore, income inequality in ASEAN is closely linked with ethnic differentials. Given the ethnic diversity in the region and the past history of ethnic conflicts that have periodically erupted into violence, the specter of economic slow-down is indeed a very dark cloud on ASEAN's horizon. The immediate challenge to ASEAN is thus to sustain some minimal rate of growth in order that past gains in social development will not be obliterated.

REFERENCES

Asian Development Bank
  1984 *Key Indicators of Member Developing Countries of ADB* (April) XV.

Blake, Myrna
  1984 Constraints on the Organization of Women Industrial Workers. In Gavin W. Jones (ed.), *Women in the Urban and Industrial Workforce: Southeast and East Asia.* Canberra: Development Studies Center, Australian National University.

Bulatao, Rodolfo
  1984 Reducing Fertility in Developing Countries: A Review of Determinants and Policy Levers. *World Bank Staff Working Papers* 680. Washington, D.C.: World Bank.

Chapkis, Wendy, and Cynthia Enloe (eds.)
  1983 *Of Common Cloth, Women in the Global Textile Industry.* Amsterdam/Washington, D.C.: Transnational Institute.

Evers, Hans-Dieter
  1973 Group Conflict and Class Formation in Southeast Asia. In H. D. Evers (ed.), *Modernization in South-East Asia.* Singapore: Oxford University Press.

Fawcett, James T., Siew-Ean Khoo, and Peter C. Smith (eds.)
  1984 *Women in the Cities of Asia: Migration and Urban Adaptation.* Boulder, Colorado: Westview Press.

Grossman, Rachael
  1979 Women's Place in the Integrated Circuit. *Southeast Asia Chronicle* 66:2–17.

Herrin, Alejandro, H. Pardoko, L. Lim, and C. Hongladarom
  1981 Demographic Development in ASEAN: A Comparative Overview. *Philippine Review of Economics and Business* 18.

Heyzer, Noeleen
  1982 From Rural Subsistence to an Industrial Peripheral Work Force: An Examination of Female Malaysian Migrants and Capital Accumulation in Singapore. In Lourdes Beneria (ed.), *Women and Development: Sexual Division of Labour in Rural Societies.* New York: Praeger Special Studies for the World Employment Programme of the International Labour Office.

Hull, Terrence, V. Hull, and M. Singarimbun
  1977 Indonesia's Family Planning Story: Success and Challenge. *Population Bulletin* 32 (6). Washington, D.C.: Population Reference Bureau.

International Labour Office
  1985 *Women Workers in Multinational Enterprises in Developing Countries.* Geneva: ILO.

Jamilah, Ariffin
   1980   Industrial Development in Peninsular Malaysia and Rural–Urban Migration of Women Workers: Impact and Implications. *Journal Ekonomi Malaysia* 1:41–60.
Knodel, John, N. Havanon, and A. Pramualratana
   1984   Fertility Transition in Thailand: A Qualitative Analysis. *Population and Development Review* 10:297–328.
Lightbourne, Robert, and A. MacDonald
   1982   *Family Size Preferences.* London: World Fertility Survey.
Lim, Linda
   1978   Women Workers in Multinational Corporations: The Case of the Electronics Industry in Malaysia and Singapore. *Michigan Occasional Papers* 9. Ann Arbor: Women's Studies Program, University of Michigan.
Mani, A.
   1983   *Determinants of Educational Aspirations among Indonesian Youth.* Singapore: Maruzen Asia.
Martin, Linda G.
   1985   The Aging of Asia. Unpublished paper, East–West Population Institute, Honolulu, Hawaii.
Mason, Andrew, and Linda G. Martin
   1985   Recent Trends in Household Structure in Asia. Paper presented at the annual meeting of Population Association of America, 28–30 March 1985.
Palloni, Alberto
   1981   Mortality in Latin America: Emerging Patterns. *Population and Development Review* 7:623–649.
Pryor, Richard (ed.)
   1979   *Migration and Development in South-East Asia.* Kuala Lumpur: Oxford University Press.
Smith, Peter, and Paul P. L. Cheung
   1981   Social Origins and Sex-Differential Schooling in the Philippines. *Comparative Education Review* 25:28–44.
Smith, Herbert, and Paul P. L. Cheung
   1986   Trends in the Effects of Family Background on Educational Attainment in the Philippines. *American Journal of Sociology* 91:1387–1408.
Stahl, Charles
   1983   International Labor Migration and the ASEAN Economies. Unpublished paper, Department of Economics, University of Newcastle.
United Nations
   1985   *World Population Prospects: Estimates and Projections as Assessed in 1982.* New York: United Nations.
Wang, Bee-Lan
   1980   Sex and Ethnic Differences in Educational Investment in Malaysia: The Effect of Reward Structures. *Comparative Education Review* 24:5140–59.
Wong, Aline
   1979   The Changing Roles and Status of Women in ASEAN. *Contemporary Southeast Asia* 1:179–193.
Wong, John, and A. Wong
   1984   Equity Performance: Some Social Implications of Development in ASEAN. In M. Suh (ed.), *Aspects of ASEAN.* Munich: Weltforum Verlag.
Yeung, Yue Man
   1984   The Great Cities of Eastern Asia: Growing Pains and Policy Options. Unpublished paper, Geography Department, Chinese University of Hong Kong.

Micro-Level Aspects of Demographic Change

PETER C. SMITH

I would like to supplement Wong and Cheung's paper by stressing the micro-level—the status of families and persons—and the ambiguities inherent in recent demographic and social trends in ASEAN.

Three specific trends should be considered. First is the historic decline in mortality and the resulting extension of life. While the decline in mortality is unambiguously a positive development, the speed of the decline has placed some stress on traditional social arrangements and cultural values in the region. To cite one example among many, the ASEAN societies are aging rapidly—that is, there is a growing share of population in the older ages and, increasingly, at the very old ages. Family-based arrangements for the care of older family members worked well when families contained proportionally few older people, but these traditional arrangements will have to be strengthened and perhaps supplemented from outside the family if the elderly are to be cared for properly in the future.

Second, later marriage and earlier achievement of sexual maturity (both trends universal in the region) have produced prolonged periods of adolescence, defined as the period between the two events. In the past, in many ASEAN societies adolescence was either very brief or did not occur at all. Parental control during this formative stage of life is weakened by the long duration involved and is further weakened by other changes, notably the extension of schooling into adolescence (Figure 2.1) and the rise of youth migration to cities.

Third is the urbanization of youth resulting from cityward migration. The fact that this migration is, in most ASEAN countries, so disproportionately female in composition and so heavily made up of young single females raises questions regarding the immediate costs and benefits to the young women involved, not to mention the implications for their life

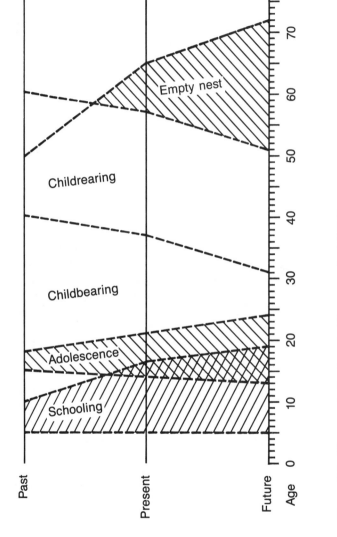

Figure 2.1. Changes in the female life course in ASEAN

chances in the longer term. Thus, it is not clear whether the urban jobs available to young women represent dead-end positions in terms of incomes and occupational advancement, or footholds in the urban economy that can be exploited to the women's advantage.

Where Wong and Cheung emphasize mainly positive implications of demographic and social trends for macrosocietal and macroeconomic issues, I would argue that the implications indicated here are in fact less sanguine and should be considered in this light by ASEAN planners.

Ethnicity and Religion in Social Development

GUNGWU WANG

In presenting my views on the roles of religion and ethnicity in the social development of the ASEAN region, I do not discuss the main themes addressed by Wong and Cheung; rather, I begin with their three direct references to religion and ethnicity.

The one reference to religion in the section on *Changes in Family Structure and Relations* mentions the return to more fundamental religious faiths in Singapore and Malaysia as an example of response to rapid social change. In the discussion of migration, the Malaysian government's "policy of attracting Malays to the urban areas for social and political reasons" is referred to, and in the paper's conclusion, income inequalities are cited as a most serious problem, in part because they may be closely linked with ethnic differentials. This last important point, however, is not elaborated.

Although the references are brief, their implications are worth noting. Religion and the traditional cultural values represented in religion may ameliorate the consequences of rapid economic change and may even protect newly evolving societies from various kinds of alienation. One wonders whether traditional values do not also play a role in determining the kind of change favored by any state or society.

As for ethnicity, there is the implication that ethnic tension could increase if an economic slowdown in ASEAN led to greater income inequalities, implying in turn that ethnic relations would be more harmonious if there were economic expansion and successful development, that is, if the pie grew steadily larger. There is truth in this, but I would ask if certain kinds of rapid development would not actually exacerbate income inequalities and thus also damage ethnic harmony.

However, the paper "takes stock for the morrow" very well. In particular, by focusing on variables and indicators that are clearly secular and by placing no emphasis on ethnic factors, it is refreshingly different in approach from previous writings on ASEAN.

Islam is ASEAN's largest religion, though it is not predominant in all six countries. Next are Christianity, Buddhism, and the Chinese religions based on varying mixes of Buddhism, philosophy, and folklore, most notable in Malaysia and Singapore. The noteworthy point is that ASEAN subscribes to religious tolerance, and religion has never been allowed to affect the good relations between its members, in which secular considerations are paramount.

Problems of ethnicity in the ASEAN countries (except for Singapore, where migrant peoples form the majority) derive mainly from two sources: firstly, from migrant minorities (mainly urban-based Chinese and Indian), whose problems have nothing directly to do with religion; and secondly, from territorially based minorities, whose religious differences with the majority peoples have led some of them to challenge the authority and legitimacy of the nation-state, as in the case of the Moslem populations of southern Thailand and the southern Philippines.

With this background in mind, and before considering the political implications of religion and ethnicity in ASEAN, some historical observations are in order.

HISTORICAL PHASES

Recent history in the ASEAN region breaks down broadly into three phases: an external first phase, an internal second phase, and an external third phase, summarized as follows:

1ST PHASE: 1950–65, characterized by reaction against external influence, whether in the form of colonial ideas and institutions or neocolonial interference, and by fear of external subversion, especially communism.

2ND PHASE: 1965 to the late 1970s, which saw a shift of emphasis to issues of internal control, of order, of balancing democracy, and of economic development. During this period, ASEAN countries confidently opened themselves to the world economy.

3RD PHASE: The late 1970s to the mid-1980s, in which there has been renewed concern not only about external factors, especially vulnerability to foreign economic power, but also about threats to indigenous cultural values.

Examining the role of religion through the three phases, it can be observed that:

1. Buddhism in Thailand does not seem to have been affected by the shifts of emphasis through the phases.

2. Minority Chinese and Indian religions were affected in the second phase by the weakening of direct ties with China and India.

3. Christianity was favored through the first phase but weakened as controls and restrictions were imposed upon its external links.

4. Islam was purposefully controlled if not suppressed by colonial powers until well into the first phase, but was widely revived in the second phase, and the revival was largely generated from within each country. There is some current interest in whether the resurgence of Islam in ASEAN since the late 1970s was externally stimulated by West Asian influences. I believe it was generated initially by political factors within each country; for example, by feelings of neglect and discrimination in Thailand and the Philippines and by the perceived threat from migrant communities in Malaysia. But today it is also a cultural and spiritual response to rapid economic change perceived as threatening traditional values. I also believe that the ASEAN grouping has been a moderating check on the excesses of radical and revolutionary Islam.

Issues of ethnicity can also be analyzed using the same three phases. If local and territorial ethnic minorities still constitute problems today, they can be managed internally. Migrant minorities, however, and notably the Chinese, certainly went through the first phase as threats to the new nation–states (when there was fear of communist subversion) to the second phase in which they became internally manageable problems for each country. This transition was the case even in Malaysia, whose Chinese minority was the largest in the region. The question is: has the third phase (of renewed concern about their external links) been reached now that China has adopted an open-door policy? Are there fresh external pressures on the ASEAN minorities of Chinese descent? And the minority question apart, is China an economic threat? Is there cause for alarm?

I would suggest that if there is an economic slowdown—or simply the fear of economic stagnation—then China offers growth opportunities that may provide mutual benefits for both the ASEAN states and China. Moreover, while individual ASEAN countries may be justified in feeling concern, ASEAN as a group need have no fears, partly because ASEAN's economic development is more advanced than China's and partly because ASEAN's ethnic Chinese businessmen seem to prefer to advance their fortunes in their ASEAN homes and with ASEAN's established partners.

All the same, it is worth noting the interesting juxtaposition between ASEAN's containment of Islam in its radical form and as a political force, and ASEAN's resistance to the pull of China (for ethnic Chinese) by acting in concert and gaining diplomatic leverage with China.

POLITICAL IMPLICATIONS

My second main comment is with regard to the political implications of religion and ethnicity. The relationship between religious faith and the power of the modern state seems to vary among countries in ASEAN. For example, in countries that have one clearly dominant faith (as in Thailand, the Philippines, and Indonesia) there has been a trend toward a secular state that acknowledges the diversity of religious groups whether large or small. Such states play down the political role of religion and encourage religions to provide educational services and to support the spiritual life of citizens. The dominant religion is strong, but it is neither dependent on nor does it seek to control the state.

The political implications of ethnicity are bound up in three kinds of rights that apply to the ASEAN states. First, there are traditional rights, which were often taken away by the colonial powers. For different ethnic minorities, they included tributary rights, feudal rights, and special trading-port rights for alien or migrant communities, sometimes accompanied by some kind of extraterritoriality allowing these communities to be governed by their own laws and customs. Such traditional rights evolved over centuries and lasted until the onset of World War II.

The second kind of rights are the new citizenship rights of republican or nationalist states. These are largely legal and political rights and, in theory, are equal and nondiscriminatory. But they are often difficult to implement fairly for minorities, especially in the early stages of nation-building. In the period of modernization, most ASEAN states experienced these difficulties.

The third kind of rights are minority rights, derived more recently from the abstract philosophical idea of "human rights" as a universal phenomenon. Exponents of such rights have sometimes claimed the necessity of international intervention on their behalf, and the resulting debate has had an effect on the question of ethnicity in multicultural societies in many parts of the world.

ASEAN has thus far been successful in projecting an image of growth, security, and confidence. Its existence provides a comparative perspective on ethnic and other rights. Its experience with its members' social, cultural, and political issues has heightened its sensitivity as a group to wider common issues. This sensitivity has had a beneficial influence on each state's attitude toward ethnic minority rights and is yet another reason why I share the sentiments expressed by Dato Musa Hitam in the previous chapter about having faith in and being optimistic about the future of ASEAN.

CHAPTER 3
ECONOMIC GROWTH

Economic Performance and Growth Factors of the ASEAN Countries

Seiji Naya

The economic dynamism and the growing importance to world trade and industry of the developing countries in the Asia–Pacific region, particularly those that comprise the Association of Southeast Asian Nations (ASEAN), have stimulated a new interest in the Pacific. The major countries involved are the United States and Japan, but the emergence of a "Pacific Century" or increased Pacific cooperation would be virtually impossible without the participation of the ASEAN countries. Although the ASEAN countries were initially lukewarm to the concept of increased Pacific cooperation, there is growing awareness of its potential benefits.

Through rapid economic growth and falling population growth rates, Indonesia, Malaysia, the Philippines, Singapore, and Thailand have graduated from the ranks of low-income countries as classified by the World Bank to the ranks of middle- and in some cases upper middle-income countries.[1] Despite external shocks—notably oil price hikes, recession, high interest rates, and protectionism—in the past decade the ASEAN countries, along with the East Asian newly industrialized countries (NICs), have attained higher rates of real output growth and export expansion with lower rates of inflation than any other group of developing nations. Real growth rates for 1984 were in the 5–9 percent range (except for the Philippines), and despite a fall in 1985, long-term growth prospects remain excellent.

The author acknowledges the assistance of Pearl Imada and Eric Ramstetter in preparing the manuscript.

1. Brunei, a small oil-rich country with a little more than 200,000 people and per capita income of approximately U.S. $20,000, became a member of ASEAN in 1984. However, its oil- and natural gas-based economy resembles those of Persian Gulf states. Throughout this paper, references to ASEAN do not take Brunei into account.

The ASEAN countries have set aside some major differences to launch a wide range of cooperative activities, including the ASEAN Preferential Trading Arrangement, several large-scale industrial projects, and industrial complementation schemes. Admittedly, some of these projects have had little economic impact and others have not moved beyond the talking stage, but regional cooperation among developing countries was never easy and ASEAN has had more success than any other regional organization, in large part because its leaders have set a realistic pace for cooperative efforts.

Politically, the formation of ASEAN is one of the most significant events to have occurred in the postwar history of the region. The display of ASEAN solidarity and the resulting regional stability enhance the group's dealings with other countries. This sometimes gives an illusion that the organization wields more economic power than is actually the case.

The growth in the economies, trade, and investment potential of member countries has been due not to the combined market or any cooperative efforts, but rather to the good economic performance of individual countries. It is important, therefore, to look at the five countries as separate entities.

The first five members of ASEAN, which are focused on in this paper, are a diverse group of countries in size, resource endowment, economic development, and culture. Per capita income for 1984 ranged from U.S.$540 for Indonesia to $7,260 for Singapore (Table 3.1). Indonesia is the largest of the five countries in land area and population. With 162 million people, it is the fifth most populous country in the world. Indonesia, with the lowest per capita income of the five countries, has over half

Table 3.1   Basic economic indicators of ASEAN
             countries, 1984

	Population (millions)	GDP (U.S. $ millions)	GDP per capita[a] (U.S.$)
Indonesia	161.6	80,590	540
Malaysia	15.3	29,280	1,980
Philippines	53.3	32,840	660
Singapore	2.5	18,220	7,260
Thailand	50.7	41,960	860

Source: World Bank, *World Development Report* (1986).
[a] World Bank Atlas Methodology, 1982–84 base period, rounded to the nearest ten dollars.

of the ASEAN group's population, making development efforts there especially important.

The Philippines and Thailand are next in size of population, with approximately 50 million people each. Although in the 1960s per capita income in the Philippines was higher than in Thailand, in 1984 per capita income in Thailand was U.S.$860 as compared to U.S.$660 for the Philippines. Political tension and uncertainty about economic policies have held back growth in the Philippines. Thailand has had rapid economic growth and has entered into a new era of middle-income status.

Malaysia is a smaller but richer country, with a population of approximately 15 million. It has an efficient primary-product sector and a fairly diversified industrial sector, making it an upper middle-income country with a per capita income of $1,980 in 1984, similar to that of South

Table 3.2   Average annual rates of growth of real GDP and GNP per capita of selected ASEAN countries and other areas of the world (percent), 1960–85

	Real GDP		GNP per capita
	1960–85[a]	1985[a]	1965–84
ASEAN	6.5	0.8	4.8
Indonesia	5.4	2.9	4.9
Malaysia	6.9	2.8	4.5
Philippines	4.4	−3.7	2.6
Singapore	8.7	−1.8	7.8
Thailand	7.1	4.0	4.2
World	4.0[b]	2.9	
Industrialized countries	3.7	2.8	
United States	3.3	2.2	
Japan	7.5	4.6	
Developing countries	5.0[b]	3.2	
Africa	3.4	1.6	
Latin America[c]	4.1	3.8	
Middle East	6.2[b]	−1.6	

Sources: International Monetary Fund, *International Financial Statistics, Yearbook 1985* (June 1986); World Bank, *World Development Report* (1986); Asian Development Bank, *ADB Annual Report* (1985); International Monetary Fund, *World Economic Outlook* (April 1986).

Note: Classification of countries according to IMF.

[a] 1985 preliminary estimates.

[b] 1961–85.

[c] Excluding countries in the Western hemisphere with populations of less than one million.

Korea. Singapore, a city–state with a population of 2.5 million, has the highest per capita income of the five ASEAN countries and can be considered, in fact, to have graduated from the ranks of developing countries to become an industrialized country. Growth, however, slowed in 1985 because of a combination of long-term and cyclical factors (such as the slowdown in world trade and the government's high wage policies), which damaged Singapore's competitiveness in the world market.

Despite these different characteristics, rapid economic growth is common to all (Table 3.2). Over the past quarter century, real gross domestic product (GDP) growth rates of more than 8 percent for Singapore, about 7 percent for Malaysia and Thailand, and 5 percent for Indonesia were higher than those of other developing countries as a whole. The Philip-

Table 3.3   Growth of merchandise exports[a] (percent), 1960–85

	1960–70	1970–80	1980–85[b]	1985 (FOB; U.S $ billions)
ASEAN	4.1	25.9	0.2	68.4[b]
Indonesia	2.8	34.8	–3.4	18.5[b]
Malaysia	3.6	22.6	3.6	15.4
Philippines	5.3	18.6	–4.3	4.6
Singapore	3.2	28.7	3.3	22.8
Thailand	5.6	24.8	1.8	7.1
World	9.3	20.7	–1.0	1,783.8
Industrialized countries	10.1	18.9	0.3	1,258.3
U.S.	7.7	17.7	–0.7	213.1
Japan	16.9	21.0	3.1	177.2
Developing countries	6.7	25.2	–4.3	494.8
East Asia	25.5	29.4	9.7	90.5[b]
South Asia	–0.5	14.2	4.7	14.4[b]
Africa	6.5	22.1	–7.9[c]	68.4[d]
Middle East	11.5	33.3	–14.5	105.1
Latin America	5.6	20.6	–0.9	99.3

Sources: IMF, *International Financial Statistics, Yearbook 1985* (June 1986); IMF, *International Financial Statistics,* monthly (June 1986); ADB, *ADB Annual Report* (1985); Republic of China Council for Economic Planning and Development, *Taiwan Statistical Data Book* (1985).
[a] Compound annual rates of growth based on current prices.
[b] Estimate for 1985.
[c] 1980–84.
[d] 1984.

Table 3.4   Ratio of exports and imports of goods and services to GNP of selected countries, 1970–71 and 1983–84

	Exports		Imports	
	1970–71	1983–84	1970–71	1983–84
ASEAN				
Indonesia	13.9	29.0	16.5	27.6
Malaysia	44.3	58.4	42.5	60.5
Philippines	19.0	21.0	19.6	24.2
Singapore	80.3[a]	135.4[a]	127.8[a]	164.2[a]
Thailand	17.0	24.1	21.0	27.9
Other Asian developing countries				
Hong Kong	68.9[b]	83.5[b]	80.5[b]	87.2[b]
India	4.3	6.9[c]	4.8	9.8[c]
Korea, Rep. of	14.7	37.9	24.7	38.1
Pakistan	7.9	10.9	14.7	21.0
Sri Lanka	27.2	28.6	29.9	38.9
United States	5.3	7.5	5.6	9.9
Japan	11.8	16.5	10.0	14.0

Sources: ADB, *Key Indicators of Developing Member Countries of ADB* (1984 and Supplement October 1985); IMF, *International Financial Statistics, Yearbook 1985* (June 1986); IMF, *International Financial Statistics,* monthly (May 1986); World Bank, *World Tables* (1983).

[a] Value of merchandise goods only.
[b] Value of merchandise goods as percent of GDP.
[c] 1981–82.

pines is the lone exception, with a lower average growth rate of real GDP and per capita gross national product (GNP). Differences in resource endowment and policy orientation, among other things, make it difficult to generalize about why the ASEAN countries have generally been successful. Some similarities, however, can be seen. With the exception of Singapore, the ASEAN countries are comparatively rich in resource potential and primary products have been the mainstays of their economies and export earnings. More importantly, the ASEAN countries have market-oriented, open economies and trade has contributed significantly to their growth. The rapid rate of growth of exports has made their export-to-income ratios very high (Tables 3.3 and 3.4). The ratio of exports to GNP in 1983–84 in ASEAN countries ranged from 21 percent for the Philippines to 135 percent for Singapore. In general, they have also welcomed foreign investment and have become increasingly integrated into the world financial market. External factors therefore play a major role in these countries.

There have been major changes in the development strategies of ASEAN countries. In the 1960s, industrial policy was generally based on import substitution; export-promotion policies were not instituted until the 1970s for most of the countries. The changeover has not been easy— some major structural adjustments are still being made. The process has been slower for the ASEAN countries than it was for the Asian NICs. Ironically, the abundance of natural resources has impeded the process. Exploitation of natural resources has allowed the four larger ASEAN countries to postpone difficult economic policy adjustments. Abundant natural wealth has had the undesirable side effect of encouraging rent-seeking behavior.

This paper examines some of the complex issues and challenges facing the ASEAN countries in their attempts to continue high rates of economic growth. The sections that follow look at factors contributing to the rapid growth and prospects for the future in these areas. The factors are: (1) the availability of resources, including energy; (2) the changing structure of the region's economy with the increasing importance of the industrial and trade sectors; (3) the rapid growth of exports and the changing composition and direction of trade; (4) the large inflows of direct foreign investment; and (5) the high rates of domestic saving and the subsequent decrease in dependence on external debt-creating flows. Although similarities are present among the countries in all of these areas, the differences are responsible for variations in the development paths of the five countries.

RESOURCES

The ASEAN countries' abundant endowment of natural resources has been a major source of growth. Together, they have most of the important minerals required by industry. ASEAN is a major supplier of key raw materials—petroleum, rubber, palm oil, tin, sawn wood, and a variety of other tropical agricultural and marine products.

Indonesia is particularly rich in natural resources, including oil and gas, timber, rubber, tin, and copper, and is a member of the Organization of Petroleum Exporting Countries (OPEC). Indonesia currently enjoys an oil production capacity of 1.6 million barrels per day (BD), which is projected to rise to 1.8 million BD by 1990 (Fesharaki forthcoming).

Malaysia's oil production outlook has improved significantly as well. Only three years ago, people predicted Malaysia would become an oil importer by 1985. Today, Malaysia's output is 440,000 BD, which could rise to 600,000 BD in 1990. Unlike Indonesia, however, Malaysia has not been successful in arresting the growth of domestic oil demand. The jump in oil prices in the 1970s accelerated growth in these countries, although the recent softening of the oil market necessitated reappraisal of development strategies. Thailand and the Philippines, being almost entirely dependent on imports for their petroleum needs, are less fortunate than Indonesia and Malaysia, but they too have rich endowments of natural resources that have formed the basis of their development.

In spite of the great reliance of ASEAN countries on resource-based exports, to date there has not been a comprehensive assessment of the resource potential of any country in the region. For example, one study estimates that, based on geologic analogy with the United States, Indonesia in relation to its size may be as well endowed in nonfuel minerals as the United States; the major difference being that in the United States the majority of nonfuel minerals have already been mined and developed, whereas in Indonesia relatively little production of nonfuel minerals has taken place (Dorian and Clark 1984). With such huge potential in terms of nonfuel mineral resources, Indonesia can and should diversify away from oil and natural gas, on which it is overly dependent, into major nonfuel minerals, including metals. Clearly, given the need to expand the export base, thorough assessments could be profitable.

There is some fear, however, that an abundance of resources can be a constraint to growth. A high degree of dependence on resource-based development has caused some serious problems. Adverse impacts on other sectors—particularly on traditional agriculture and nontraditional manufacturing through changes in exchange rates, inflation, and competition for scarce managerial and technical human resources—are not usually foreseen. "Dutch disease" (the decline in competitiveness of export-oriented industries in the nonresource sector) has been acute in some energy-exporting developed and developing nations.[2] With limited employment generation in the energy or minerals sector, this could have devastating results unless effective countermeasures are taken. Indonesia

---

2. "Dutch disease" refers to the adverse impact on nonresource exports resulting from a boom in the resource sector. The increase in investment inflows accompanying a resource boom causes a real appreciation of the exchange rate, thus depressing the revenue from nonresource exports and increasing expenditure on imports. The term "Dutch disease" was originally used to describe the decline in industrial exports of the Netherlands that resulted from the increase in petroleum exports (Corden 1981).

and Malaysia increased investment in sectors such as agriculture to offset the effects of the petroleum boom and to lessen their dependence on oil.

The high rates of real output growth in agriculture, averaging close to 4 percent per annum, have provided a strong impetus to overall economic growth (Vyas 1983). In Thailand and Malaysia, labor productivity grew at close to 4 percent per year between 1970 and 1980, while in the Philippines and Indonesia it rose by 1.5 percent and 2.4 percent, respectively. Substantial progress has been made toward full self-sufficiency in major cereal crops. Indonesia and the Philippines have both emphasized rice production. With new high-yield hybrids, the Philippines achieved a modest rice surplus in the late 1970s. Although Indonesia was forced to continue imports of rice because of droughts in 1982–83, by 1984 it had reached self-sufficiency. In spite of subsidies, Malaysia continues to be a large importer of rice, but given its strong balance-of-payments position and its factor endowment, self-sufficiency in rice may not be a desirable economic goal. Thailand, on the other hand, is one of the largest rice exporters in the world.

The export-crop sector also did well in Thailand and Malaysia. Thailand has diversified its agricultural activity from rice and rubber into tapioca, maize, pineapples, natural fibers, canned fruit, sugar, and marine products. Malaysia developed oil palm into a new and thriving export sector, as a substitute for rubber. It also expanded exports of wood, marine products, and a variety of other crops. Yields of traditional export crops such as sugar and copra stagnated in the Philippines under the control of quasi-government marketing monopolies while other crops, such as banana, cassava, cacao, corn, pineapple, and coffee, did better under private initiative. Indonesia's agricultural exports fared poorly until the second half of the 1970s. Indonesia neglected agricultural exports in its pursuit of rice self-sufficiency until the 1980s, when petroleum prices weakened.

Continued high agricultural growth will be required to meet rural employment needs and balance-of-payments objectives. However, external demand for commodities is likely to grow slowly, and supply is prone to fluctuations caused by weather. Furthermore, recession in the Organization for Economic Cooperation and Development (OECD) countries can cause demand to fall sharply. Recent experience has shown that the mobilization of a variety of stabilization instruments, including export quotas, buffer stocks, and even production cutbacks, has been unsuccessful in reversing price declines or improving export volumes.

ASEAN countries will, therefore, have to continue to diversify exports and expand production of manufactured goods. The next section looks at industrial and trade policies established for this purpose.

INDUSTRIAL AND TRADE POLICIES

Early growth in the industrial sector in most ASEAN countries was related to processing of primary products. Agro-based industries such as vegetable oils and wood products were predominant, especially in Thailand and Malaysia. The Philippines, with its wealth in human resources and its preferential relationship with the United States, began to develop its manufacturing sector in the 1950s, and by 1960 20 percent of its GDP was in manufacturing. Indonesia was the slowest to begin its industrialization process.

Singapore became virtually a free-trade economy after a brief period of import substitution in the first half of the 1960s. The other ASEAN countries, like most developing countries, adopted import-substituting strategies to stimulate industrialization. They have relied primarily on policies that provide selective protection for domestic producers against foreign competition by raising domestic output prices over world market prices. Tariffs and import quantity ceilings and surcharges have been frequently used to achieve this protection.

Because protection allows domestic industries to produce goods with a higher added value and higher profits than under free trade, productive resources are induced to move into the protected industries. These policies, therefore, often discourage both export-oriented industrial production and non-industrial activities via reduced availability of productive factors, i.e., higher factor costs and higher prices of inputs. Simultaneously, an overvalued domestic currency sustained by import protection has the effect of further discouraging exports.

Indonesia has the most inward-looking industrial orientation, with a history of large-scale government intervention, ownership, and regulation of the economy. The present government partially dismantled the import licensing and exchange controls erected under the Sukarno regime, but continued in the 1970s to make extensive use of non-tariff trade barriers and price controls.

Malaysia also followed the usual pattern of import substitution in the 1960s and early 1970s but did not discriminate seriously against other traded goods nor overvalue the domestic currency. It had few non-tariff trade restrictions, and though tariff rates diverged widely, tariffs on manufactures were quite low in general. Thailand, like Malaysia, did not favor widespread import substitution, although its tariffs were higher than Malaysia's. The Philippines, on the other hand, began its import-substitution process early (in the 1950s) and provided substantial protection to domestic producers of consumer goods.

In addition to import protection, these countries strongly favored and subsidized the use of physical capital while disfavoring the use of labor—an obviously distorted set of incentives and disincentives in labor-abundant economies.

In the second half of the 1970s, in an effort to adjust to the increases in the oil import bill, the governments of Thailand and the Philippines attempted to increase manufactured exports. Export controls were relaxed and export taxes abolished. Governments granted duty-free importation allowances for necessary inputs to exporters, introduced special rebates on income and turnover taxes, and opened new (mostly short-term) export-credit facilities.

Malaysia's trade policy also changed drastically during the 1970s (Akrasanee 1984; Ariff and Hill 1985). The labor-intensive manufacturing sector was developed by the government to alleviate poverty and racial inequality. With increased income in the mid-1970s, resulting from the discovery and development of petroleum, the government expanded its efforts to develop new manufactures for export.

The Philippines and Indonesia even made cautious attempts to reduce the overvaluation of their currencies, but because their domestic inflation rates remained above those of their major trading partners, real exchange rates soon returned to their former levels (Bautista et al. 1979:29–30 and 79ff).[3] Indonesia's 1978 rupiah devaluation was designed to prevent the erosion of incomes in the non-oil sectors of the economy, particularly for smallholders in agriculture. It had a surprisingly strong positive effect on manufacturing exports, which surged until the inflation differential and a boom in the domestic economy took a toll on manufactured export growth. The second oil price bonanza of 1979 and 1980 put any worries regarding foreign exchange earnings on the back burner until oil prices fell and current account deficits mounted between 1981 and 1983. It then became apparent that Indonesia would have to make a major effort to expand non-oil exports if it were to attain acceptable economic growth without unacceptable foreign debt into the 1990s. As a result, a second major devaluation occurred in March 1984. The devaluation was part of a major policy reform toward liberalization and privatization of the economy that included a tighter government budget, a decrease in subsidies, and a rescheduling of a number of large developmental projects.

Thailand, a country that studiously avoided devaluation in the 1970s, took a bold step in devaluating the baht substantially in 1984. In con-

---

3. Rana (1983) also found that real effective exchange rates appreciated in the Philippines, Thailand, and Indonesia between 1967 and 1979, including a loss of competitiveness in export markets.

Table 3.5   Average tariff rate of
selected Asian countries

	Simple average tariff rate (percent)
Pakistan	71
India	66
Sri Lanka	44
Indonesia	33
Thailand	31
Philippines	28
Malaysia	25
Korea, Rep. of	24
Singapore	6

Sources: Data computed by Philippine Tariff Commission from: Indonesia's Customs Tariff 1980; Malaysian Practical Guide to Customs Duties Order 1982; Philippine Tariff and Customs Code 1982; Singapore Trade Classification and Customs Duties 1983; Customs Tariff of Thailand, 1983; Pakistan Douanes 1979–80; Korea Douanes 1982–83; India Douanes 1979–80; Sri Lanka Douanes 1983–84.

junction with World Bank "structural adjustment loan" programs, Thailand and the Philippines have sought to provide more balance to the incentive systems in order to promote a more efficient and resilient industrial growth pattern. Indonesia and Malaysia have undertaken similar reviews of their trade and industrial policies in the mid-1980s with a view toward promoting more vigorous manufacturing export growth.

The anti-export bias of import substitution has been a major obstacle to the continued rapid growth of ASEAN exports, especially for manufactured goods. This bias against exports had been offset to some extent by countervailing subsidies and exemptions. In addition, protection has declined over time and is much lower than in the South Asian countries listed in Table 3.5. But other than Singapore, which has average tariff rates of 6 percent, the rates are still high (between 20 and 30 percent for the other four countries) and highly variable.[4]

As a result, the average effective rate of protection seems to have risen and then declined for some industrial sectors, the export incentives thus

---

4. The rate for the Philippines is especially low due to recent effort to rationalize the tariff system (De Rosa 1986).

having little impact on the sectoral pattern of incentives. These measures have generally been inadequate, however, and also represent a second- or third-best solution. Discrimination against exports has been only partly mitigated by the new measures. The incentive structure favoring capital- and energy-using industrial activities remains basically unchallenged in the four larger ASEAN countries.

The Singapore government opted to intervene in the labor market. It was thought that because administered wages were too low, productivity was suffering (Tan 1985). Thus, the Tripartite National Wages Council, which had controlled wage increases since 1972, implemented a wage correction policy. Administered wages were raised in several successive increments by a total of about 80 percent over the 1979–81 period, and at the same time measures were taken to upgrade the skills of the labor force. The wage increases were meant to induce a shift from unskilled to skilled labor-intensive activities, in which higher labor productivity would allow higher wages without granting specific advantages to physical capital-intensive industries. Although this policy was to be implemented for only three years, the council continued to increase wages through 1984. Singapore's growth slowdown in the mid-1980s is causing the government to take a hard look at its strategies and policies in the science-based, skill-intensive sectors.

Significant structural transformation has occurred in these countries, with industry's share of GDP rising and agriculture's falling (Table 3.6). The share of industry in GDP increased rapidly in Indonesia, from a low base of 14 percent in 1960 to 40 percent in 1984, but much of this gain was due to the petroleum sector. The Philippines started at the highest base, 28 percent in 1960, with slower rates of growth through the 1970s. Industry accounted for less than 20 percent of GDP in 1960 for Malaysia, Singapore, and Thailand, later increasing to 35, 39, and 28 percent respectively. Industrial employment, however, has not grown as rapidly. In 1984 it comprised approximately 10 percent of the total labor force in Indonesia, the Philippines, and Thailand, 17 percent in Malaysia, and 28 percent in Singapore. The growth of the industrial sector was not very successful in absorbing labor during the 1970s because of severe distortion in factor prices and other incentives for capital-intensive development.

Despite remaining biases against exports, as well as the slower growth of world trade and external disturbances such as the first oil shock, ASEAN exports grew at an average of more than 25 percent annually in the 1970s (Table 3.3). In addition, the share of manufactures in total exports in 1981 rose to about 20 percent in Malaysia, the Philippines, and Thailand (Table 3.7). The least industrialized Southeast Asian country, Indonesia, achieved a similarly high rate of growth in manufactured

Table 3.6 Structure of production and employment (percentage of GDP and employment)[a], 1960, 1970, and 1984

	Agriculture			Industry			Services		
	1960[b]	1970	1984	1960[b]	1970	1984	1960[b]	1970	1984
ASEAN									
Indonesia	54 (75)	47 (71)[c]	26 (55)[d]	14 (8)	18 (9)[c]	40 (11)[d]	32 (17)	35 (20)[c]	34 (34)[d]
Malaysia	37 (63)	29[e] (53)	21 (36)	18 (12)	27[e] (12)	35 (17)	46 (25)	44[e] (36)	44 (47)
Philippines	26 (61)	28 (54)	25 (50)	28 (15)	30 (12)	34 (10)	46 (24)	42 (34)	41 (40)
Singapore	4 (8)	2 (3)	1 (1)	18 (23)	30 (22)	39 (28)	78 (69)	68 (75)	60 (71)
Thailand	40 (84)	32 (72)[f]	20 (69)	19 (4)	24 (8)[f]	28 (8)	41 (12)	44 (20)[f]	52 (23)
Other Asian developing countries									
Hong Kong	4 (8)	2 (2)[g]	1 (1)	39 (52)	37 (35)[g]	22 (37)	57 (40)	61 (63)[g]	78 (62)
India	50 (74)	47 (73)[g]	35 (53)[h]	20 (11)	22 (13)[g]	27 (20)[h]	30 (15)	31 (14)[g]	38 (27)[h]
Korea, Rep. of	37 (66)	31 (50)	14 (27)	20 (9)	26 (13)	40 (24)	43 (25)	43 (36)	47 (49)
Pakistan	46 (61)	39 (57)	24 (53)	16 (18)	23 (15)	29 (14)	38 (21)	38 (28)	47 (34)
Sri Lanka	32 (56)	35 (50)[g]	28 (46)[h]	20 (14)	18 (10)[g]	26 (11)[h]	48 (30)	47 (40)[g]	46 (43)[h]

Sources: ADB, *Key Indicators of Developing Member Countries of ADB* (April 1983, 1984, 1985, Supplement October 1985); World Bank, *World Development Report* (1980, 1984, 1986); The Economist Intelligence Unit, *Quarterly Economic Review of India and Nepal* (Annual Supplement 1985).

[a] Numbers in parentheses represent percentage of employed, except as indicated in following notes.
[b] Percentage of labor force.
[c] 1965, percentage of labor force.
[d] 1982.
[e] 1973.
[f] 1972.
[g] 1971.
[h] 1981.

Table 3.7 Exports of ASEAN by principal commodity groups (as a percentage of exports), 1970 and 1981

	Indonesia 1970	Indonesia 1981	Malaysia 1970	Malaysia 1981	Philippines 1970	Philippines 1981	Singapore 1970	Singapore 1981	Thailand 1970	Thailand 1981
Primary commodities	98.6	96.8	92.8	80.0	89.5	55.4	69.0	51.5	89.5	71.6
Raw materials	79.0	91.7	80.2	63.1	49.5	21.2	52.8	44.5	39.0	17.6
Ag. & food products	19.6	5.1	12.6	16.9	40.0	34.2	16.2	7.0	50.5	54.0
Manufactured exports[a]	1.2	2.9	6.3	19.5	6.4	22.8	28.0	41.1	5.2	24.8
Resource-based manuf.	—	1.1	2.6	2.3	4.4	4.3	3.5	2.7	2.1	5.1
Misc. manufactures	—	0.1	0.3	0.5	0.6	2.9	2.1	2.0	0.4	1.7
Textiles	0.2	0.2	0.4	1.2	0.5	1.2	3.6	1.4	1.2	4.9
Clothing	—	0.4	0.3	1.4	—	6.1	1.9	2.1	0.1	4.9
Transport equip.	—	0.3	0.6	0.3	—	0.7	3.4	4.2	0.3	0.2
Chemicals	0.5	0.3	0.7	0.7	0.5	1.8	2.8	3.6	0.4	0.8
Electrical machinery	—	0.3	0.3	10.9	—	1.9	4.0	14.6	0.1	4.5
Non-electrical machinery	0.3	0.1	0.7	1.0	0.1	0.2	4.4	7.0	0.2	0.4
Precision instruments	—	—	0.1	0.3	—	0.5	0.7	1.6	0.2	0.5
Total commodities	100.0	100.0	100.0	100.0	100.0	100.0	100.0	100.0	100.0	100.0
(U.S.$ million)	(1,055.1)	(22,260.3)	(1,686.6)	(11,737.7)	(1,059.7)	(5,722.2)	(1,598.2)	(22,098.4)	(710.3)	(7,035.7)

Source: United Nations, *Commodity Trade Statistics* (1970 and 1981).

Note: Dash indicates <0.1%.

[a] The categories of manufactured exports do not add up to total manufactured exports since not all of the categories are listed. Does not include SITC Section 9 (commodities and transactions not classified elsewhere).

exports. However, because of the rise in oil export earnings following the oil price hikes, the share of manufactures in the total exports of OPEC member Indonesia was still low (3 percent) at the end of the decade. The next section will look at the composition and destination of exports of the ASEAN countries.

TRADE PATTERNS AND EXPORT PERFORMANCE

In the 1980s, exports of primary commodities continue to account for the bulk of total exports of the four resource-rich ASEAN countries, ranging from 97 percent of total exports in Indonesia to 55 percent in the Philippines (Table 3.7). Over the years, the ASEAN countries have diversified their primary commodity exports to include natural rubber, wood, tin, sugar, maize, palm oil, fruit, and (for Malaysia and Indonesia) oil and liquified natural gas. The share of raw material exports is especially high in Indonesia, reflecting the large volume and relatively high unit price of petroleum exports in the 1970s. This effect is less evident in Malaysia, which did not become a net oil exporter until 1975.

But the overwhelming importance of primary commodities in the trade of the four resource-rich countries has decreased somewhat. Based on combined figures for the four countries, manufactured exports rose from less than 5 percent of total exports in 1970 to nearly 13 percent in 1981. In 1970, when the industrial base was still very small, almost one-half of manufactured exports consisted of resource-based manufactures. The four ASEAN countries, in general, remained competitive in the production of resource-based manufactures throughout the 1970s, but the share of these products in total manufactured exports declined from 47 percent to 19 percent between 1970 and 1981. New manufactured products— electronic components (particularly in Malaysia), followed by clothing and petrochemicals—have become important in the export composition of these countries.

Singapore shows less reliance on primary exports than other ASEAN countries. Though the share of primary products declined by almost 20 percentage points since 1970, primary products still accounted for over 50 percent of total exports in 1981. These were predominantly exports of petroleum, petroleum products, and natural rubber, reflecting Singapore's traditional role in entrepôt trade, with a large share of primary products being exported through Singapore from surrounding countries. Singapore has recently diversified its manufactured exports away from export of traditional labor-intensive products to exports of transport equipment and electrical and non-electrical machinery.

↗TRADE WITH JAPAN AND THE UNITED STATES

Japan and the United States are ASEAN's most important trading partners (Table 3.8). In 1985, Japan alone accounted for 24 and 21 percent of ASEAN exports and imports, respectively. U.S. trade is slightly lower, comprising more than 20 percent of ASEAN's exports and 15 percent of its imports. The ASEAN countries, Japan, and the United States form a triangular relationship that in no small measure has contributed to the prosperity of the Asia–Pacific region in recent years.

Trade relations between the ASEAN countries and Japan, however, have maintained the typical "North–South" pattern, with Japan importing energy and raw materials and exporting manufactures. This pattern is also apparent in Japan's trade relationships with Korea and Taiwan. Japan's large trade surpluses reflect the difficulty that manufactured exports, from both developed and developing countries, have in penetrating the Japanese markets. For example, in 1981 the United States purchased 28 percent of ASEAN's manufactured exports, while Japan took slightly less than 7 percent—only one-fourth as much (Naya forthcoming).

In addition to the structural differences in its trade pattern with Japan and the United States, ASEAN's export growth to Japan has lagged behind. From 1973 to 1985, exports to Japan fell from 27 to 24 percent of total ASEAN exports, whereas exports to the United States rose from 17 to 20 percent. But in both the U.S. and Japanese markets, ASEAN countries have done comparatively well. From 1973 to 1983, ASEAN's share of the Japanese import market rose from 12 to 14 percent, and in the same 20-year period ASEAN increased its share of U.S. imports from 3 to 5 percent.

ASEAN exports to the United States are affected by three factors:[5]

---

5. The analytical device used here is known as the constant market-share model. For a good theoretical evaluation of this model, see Richardson (1971). The algebraic formula used is:

$$dx \equiv s^0 dM + (\Sigma s_k^0 dM_k - s^0 dM) + (\Sigma ds_k M_k^0 + ds_k dM_k)$$

where x, M, and s refer to ASEAN exports to the United States, total U.S. imports, and x/M, respectively. The superscript 0 refers to the base period (1972–73) and the subscript k refers to commodity classifications. Although the constant market-share model is usually discussed in terms of the share, it is useful to express it in terms of the growth rate, as follows:

$$dx \equiv gx^0 + (\Sigma g_k x_k^0 - gx^0) + [(dx - \Sigma r_k x_k') + (\Sigma r_k x_k') - \Sigma g_k x_k^0)]$$

where g and r are the growth rate of imports with M^0 and M^1 (total imports in the end year) as the base, respectively. The three right-hand terms in each equation correspond to W, C, and S, as discussed in the text, though all of these terms in the text are expressed as a proportion of x^0 or the growth rate of exports.

Table 3.8 Direction of trade of ASEAN countries, 1985

	Indonesia		Malaysia		Philippines		Singapore		Thailand		ASEAN	
	Amount[a]	(Percent)	Amount	(Percent)	Amount	(Percent)	Amount	(Percent)	Amount	(Percent)	Amount	(Percent)
Total exports	18,330	(100.0)	15,408	(100.0)	4,614	(100.0)	23,234	(100.0)	7,170	(100.0)	68,756	(100.0)
Japan	9,007	(49.1)	3,784	(24.6)	875	(19.0)	2,184	(9.4)	951	(13.3)	16,801	(24.4)
United States	4,168	(22.7)	1,970	(12.8)	1,658	(35.9)	4,830	(20.8)	1,402	(19.6)	14,029	(20.4)
EEC	1,207	(6.6)	2,221	(14.4)	647	(14.1)	2,416	(10.4)	1,357	(18.9)	7,848	(11.4)
Asian developing[b]	2,708	(14.8)	6,045	(39.2)	902	(19.5)	8,394	(36.1)	1,642	(22.9)	19,691	(28.6)
Total imports	9,321	(100.0)	12,301	(100.0)	5,351	(100.0)	27,513	(100.0)	9,409	(100.0)	63,895	(100.0)
Japan	2,619	(28.1)	2,833	(23.0)	750	(14.0)	4,486	(16.3)	2,448	(26.0)	13,135	(20.6)
United States	1,341	(14.4)	1,881	(15.3)	1,344	(25.1)	3,988	(14.5)	1,053	(11.2)	9,606	(15.0)
EEC	2,020	(21.7)	1,775	(14.4)	455	(8.5)	2,977	(10.8)	1,545	(16.4)	8,772	(13.7)
Asian developing[b]	1,277	(13.7)	3,717	(30.2)	1,385	(25.9)	7,931	(28.8)	1,756	(18.7)	16,065	(25.1)

Sources: IMF, *Direction of Trade Statistics* (Yearbook 1986); Ministry of Finance, *Monthly Statistics of Exports and Imports of Republic of China* (October 1984); Republic of China Council for Economic Planning and Development, *Taiwan Statistical Data Book* (1985).

[a] Amounts are in U.S. $ millions.

[b] Includes ASEAN trade with East Asian NICs, ASEAN countries, Bangladesh, Burma, India, Nepal, Pakistan, and Sri Lanka.

1. The rate of growth of the total U.S. market;
2. The degree of concentration of ASEAN exports in those products that are growing rapidly or slowly in U.S. imports; and
3. The ability of ASEAN countries to expand their exports of individual commodities more rapidly than competing exporters to the United States.

The first factor is defined as the average growth effect *(W)* measured by the growth rate of total imports. The second factor is defined as the (commodity) compositional effect *(C)*, while the third, which measures the commodity share of ASEAN exports in the U.S. market, is defined as the share effect *(S)*.

The difference between the export growth of ASEAN countries to the United States *(A)* and the average growth of U.S. imports *(W)* indicates how the export growth of these countries has deviated from the average

Table 3.9   Export performance of ASEAN and selected other developing

	Exports to the United States						
	Export growth rate (A)[a]	Aver- age growth (W)	Commodity compo- sition effect (C)	Share effect (S)	Export perfor- mance (A−W)	Average total exports (U.S.$ millions)	
						1972–73	1982–83
ASEAN							
Indonesia	119.9	32.0	6.9	81.0	87.9	391.4	5,082.7
Malaysia	46.2	32.0	8.5	5.8	14.2	370.4	2,082.0
Philippines	25.4	32.0	−12.4	5.8	−6.6	580.6	2,057.5
Singapore	61.7	32.0	9.3	20.4	29.7	365.6	2,621.3
Thailand	67.7	32.0	3.2	32.6	35.7	128.1	995.8
World developing	53.3	32.0	2.4	18.9	19.1	17,189.8	105,117.3
Asia and Pacific developing	54.5	32.0	13.2	9.3	22.5	6,151.8	39,678.6
Hong Kong	37.1	32.0	0.3	4.8	5.1	1,349.6	6,359.9
India	34.7	32.0	−19.1	21.7	2.7	431.8	1,928.0
Korea, Rep. of	71.3	32.0	0.1	39.2	39.3	840.7	6,832.6
Pakistan	35.6	32.0	−15.5	19.1	3.6	39.8	181.7
Latin America developing	40.1	32.0	−0.1	8.3	8.1	8,293.8	41,559.1

Source: United Nations, *Commodity Trade Statistics* (various years).
[a] See text for explanation of notation.

trend. This difference is referred to as export performance *(A − W)*. This same procedure is also applied to ASEAN exports to Japan.

In explaining export performance, it is reasonable to suppose that the commodity compositional effect is affected more by external (U.S. and Japan) than by internal (ASEAN) conditions, and *vice versa* for the share effect. That is, external factors (e.g., import demand and policies of developed countries) favoring (or not favoring) the particular export structure of ASEAN are regarded in sum as a major determinant of the compositional effect. On the other hand, the share effect reflects the competitive position and whether—and to what extent—ASEAN countries have kept up with external demand. The share effect also indicates the scope for policymaking by the exporting countries to encourage or discourage, directly or indirectly, their exports.

To compute export performance, U.S. and Japan import data are used

countries, 1972–73 to 1982–83 (simple averages)

					Exports to Japan	
Export growth rate (A)	Average growth (W)	Commodity composition effect (C)	Share effect (S)	Export performance (A−W)	Average total exports (U.S.$ millions) 1972–73	1982–83
55.7	31.8	6.4	17.5	23.9	1,707.0	11,218.7
124.2	31.8	4.4	88.0	92.4	228.8	3,070.1
12.4	31.8	5.6	−25.1	−19.4	644.6	1,441.4
85.7	31.8	5.0	48.9	53.9	172.1	1,646.8
21.9	31.8	17.7	−27.6	−9.9	323.1	1,029.7
47.0	31.8	3.0	12.2	15.2	12,769.0	72,809.7
39.6	31.8	1.5	6.3	7.8	5,848.4	28,986.5
22.6	31.8	5.7	−14.9	−9.2	197.7	646.2
12.9	31.8	−0.1	−18.8	−18.9	492.2	1,126.5
30.6	31.8	−4.6	3.4	1.2	815.3	3,309.4
9.2	31.8	−8.7	−13.9	−22.6	130.1	249.6
27.5	31.8	0.2	−4.5	−4.3	1,679.8	6,294.4

to represent a given country's exports to those countries. The growth rates were obtained by simple averaging of the growth rate of trade from 1972–73 to 1982–83. The numerical results of one (simple) application of this methodology are presented in Table 3.9. Results for selected other Asian countries are also included for comparison.

Several noteworthy points emerge. First, as mentioned previously, ASEAN countries have done considerably better in the American than in the Japanese market, but with substantial variation in export performance between individual ASEAN countries. The Philippines, however, was the only ASEAN member to lose market shares in both Japan and the United States.

Second, export expansion of the Philippines and Thailand has been limited by their poor commodity composition in the United States. The external demand factor has not been very favorable for these countries. In the United States, imports of raw materials, particularly petroleum and petroleum products, grew fast relative to agricultural and food products and manufactured imports. Thus, Indonesia, Malaysia, and Singapore have the strongest commodity composition components.

Finally, there is a close association between export performance and the share effect. The countries that do well in their exports are generally those that have a large positive share effect. In fact, in many instances, countries have been able to more than offset their unfavorable commodity makeup with favorable share or competitive effects to yield rapid export expansion and favorable export performance.

Of the factors affecting ASEAN export performance, a positive share effect is clearly very influential. I interpret a positive (negative) share effect as an indication of an improved (worsened) competitive export position, but it is very difficult to pinpoint exactly what "competitiveness" is comprised of or what it means. Obviously, price is an important variable. But other factors such as product quality and uniqueness, distance (transport cost), speed of delivery, after-sales service, and commercial and financial ties and arrangements may also be important determinants of competitiveness.

Although this analysis shows that ASEAN has improved its competitive position *vis à vis* the rest of the world in the Japanese and particularly the U.S. markets, the increasing trend toward protectionism could hurt it through worsening the average growth and compositional effects. With exports looming so large in the economic performance of ASEAN countries it is important to ascertain whether exports can be expected to rise substantially, given the somewhat restrictive trade-policy environment in many developed countries. ASEAN must promote greater trade within the region. Cultivating markets in developing countries is difficult, but will be important for trade.

⌐⌐ INTRA-ASEAN TRADE

The South–South trade of ASEAN countries is largely intra-ASEAN. Intraregional trade among the ASEAN countries has always been higher than among any other regional grouping of less developed countries. Intra-ASEAN trade not only is substantial but also has been rising for the last ten years, reversing the declining trend of the period before the mid-1970s. As shown in Table 3.10, trade among ASEAN countries rose from 14.1 percent of their total trade in 1974 to nearly 23 percent in 1983. The large increase in trade with the United States in 1984, however, contributed to the decline of intra-ASEAN trade as a percentage of total trade. In addition, the development of refineries in Indonesia and Malaysia and the oil glut in the 1980s have reduced Singapore's trade in petroleum and petroleum products.

Despite ASEAN's trade cooperation efforts, intra-ASEAN trade has not increased as much as hoped. The ASEAN Preferential Trading Arrangement (PTA), approved in February 1977, was the first major commitment toward joint efforts to liberalize and expand intra-ASEAN trade. The number of tariff concessions exchanged among ASEAN countries increased from 71 items when the PTA was begun to around 20,000 items in 1985. Intra-ASEAN trade cooperation has also been shifting to improve preferential arrangements. For example, after 1980 the cumbersome product-by-product approach to PTA was replaced by across-the-board tariff reductions, and a 20-percent margin of preference was given to items with import values of under U.S. $50,000. Further, in 1982 the margin of preference was raised to 20–25 percent on items with import value up to U.S. $10 million.

There are, however, several problems inherent in the tariff-cutting exercise of the PTA, namely:

1. Tariff cuts are too limited to induce trade promotion and trade creation in the ASEAN countries;

2. The prevalence of non-tariff measures make the tariff concessions ineffective;

3. The magnitude of the exclusion lists virtually eliminates all potentially tradable items in the region;

4. Bilateral negotiations under the matrix approach are tedious and cumbersome; and

5. The different industrial and tariff policies of the member countries tend to compete with each other.

In fact, what seems to be rapidly expanding intra-ASEAN trade is more apparent than real. If Singapore is excluded, intra-ASEAN trade (among the four resource-rich countries) amounts to no more than 4 to 5 percent of the total. This is due to Singapore's role in entrepôt trade and

Table 3.10 Trend of intra-ASEAN trade as a percentage of total trade for ASEAN as a whole and for individual countries[a], 1974–85

	ASEAN			Indonesia		Malaysia		Philippines		Singapore		Thailand	
	Total Trade	Exports	Imports	Exports	Imports	Exports	Imports	Exports	Imports	Exports	Imports	Exports	Imports
1974	14.1	15.3	13.0	8.7	9.4	23.9	14.4	1.3	2.3	22.8	21.8	17.8	2.1
1975	14.7	16.9	12.8	10.3	8.7	24.2	15.2	2.7	4.8	26.0	20.9	17.2	2.7
1976	14.9	15.5	14.2	8.7	13.7	21.2	14.0	3.1	6.3	23.1	21.2	16.7	3.3
1977	15.6	15.7	15.6	10.6	14.3	18.9	14.6	3.9	6.4	22.9	24.6	18.0	4.3
1978	15.6	16.3	14.9	12.7	9.6	18.5	14.3	6.2	4.6	22.3	24.1	15.4	5.9
1979	17.0	17.4	16.5	14.2	11.6	20.1	14.5	4.1	5.7	23.0	26.0	16.7	7.5
1980	17.3	17.7	16.9	12.6	12.4	22.4	16.4	6.5	6.2	24.0	24.8	16.2	9.6
1981	17.3	18.4	16.1	11.9	12.8	26.5	17.9	7.2	6.6	25.3	21.5	14.6	10.1
1982	21.3	23.1	19.6	15.7	19.6	30.0	19.9	7.2	6.5	32.2	24.9	15.5	12.0
1983	22.9	23.7	22.0	16.4	23.9	28.2	18.9	7.1	8.6	33.0	29.7	15.6	12.0
1984	19.4	19.7	19.1	11.4	14.0	26.0	,9.4	9.7	11.6	26.6	24.4	14.1	13.7
1985	17.6	17.6	17.6	7.9	6.6	25.6	22.4	11.4	14.2	22.1	20.9	14.3	14.3

Sources: IMF, *Direction of Trade Statistics* (Yearbooks 1977, 1984, 1985, 1986); IMF, *International Financial Statistics* (Yearbook 1985).

Note: Singapore trade with Indonesia derived from Indonesian trade data using Singapore conversion factor CIF/FOB for each year. Therefore, Singapore total trade shown here includes trade with Indonesia, although original source does not.

[a] Intra-ASEAN trade as a percentage of total trade is 100 times intra-ASEAN trade (exports plus imports) divided by total ASEAN trade to the world (exports plus imports). Intra-ASEAN exports (or imports) as a percentage of exports (or imports) to (from) the world is defined accordingly for ASEAN as a whole and for the individual countries.

also to the complementarity between Singapore and other ASEAN countries. While ASEAN has gone a long way in increasing the number of tariff concessions exchanged in the PTA, the impact of the ASEAN PTA on intra-ASEAN trade has been limited, and its potential remains to be fully explored. Other schemes to increase intra-ASEAN trade will not have much impact unless there is more significant liberalization.

But intra-ASEAN trade is likely to become even more important. As mentioned above, the increasing trend toward protectionism in the more developed countries may to some extent close markets to ASEAN countries' exports. Also, the more developed countries are not growing as rapidly, thus limiting the expansion of the market. But trade flows depend on complementarities; the four research-rich ASEAN countries have complementary economic structures with the East Asian NICs and Singapore. As the Asian developing countries proceed with economic development, industrial complementarity will strengthen. This has already been occurring with changes in the comparative advantage of the NICs toward the production of skill- and technology-intensive goods, while ASEAN countries concentrate on resource- and labor-intensive goods, replacing exports of NICs in some of these products. The scope for increase of intra-Asian trade is large.

⌐7 INVESTMENT AND TECHNOLOGY

The trade-oriented policies and rapid growth of the ASEAN countries have attracted foreign direct investment (FDI). During the last two decades, the inflow of FDI into the ASEAN countries has increased rapidly. However, FDI from the Development Assistance Committee countries has not steadily increased as a share of total net resource flows. Average combined total resource inflows amounted to U.S. $8.1 billion a year for the ASEAN countries in 1981–84, with FDI accounting for as much as 28 percent of total resource inflows for Indonesia and 65 percent for Singapore (Table 3.11).

On the other hand, FDI has accounted for far smaller portions of gross domestic capital formation. International Monetary Fund (IMF) figures (Table 3.12) show that FDI accounted for more than 10 percent of gross domestic capital formation only in Malaysia and Singapore, but usually well under 5 percent in the other countries.

Due to the lack of a standardized data base, these (and all other) FDI figures must be viewed with some skepticism. Differences in data processing methodology, the nature of the data base itself (i.e., approvals vs. arrivals, flows vs. stocks), the sectoral coverage involved, and the number of investing countries covered lead to great differences between data

Table 3.11   Total net resource flows to ASEAN countries (average annual,
U.S.$ millions) and official, private, and direct investment
percentages, 1969–84

	1969–71	1972–76	1977–80	1981–84
Indonesia	521.4	1,647.6	1,136.0	3,452.1
Percentage of total:[a]				
Official[a]	90.6	47.1	88.2	44.7
Private[b]	9.4	52.9	11.8	55.3
(direct investment)	(13.7)	(32.2)	(5.5)	(27.9)
Malaysia	80.4	245.5	446.5	1,214.1
Percentage of total:				
Official	71.3	49.7	44.0	27.6
Private	28.7	50.3	56.0	72.4
(direct investment)	(31.3)	(36.7)	(21.4)	(3.0)
Philippines	225.8	469.8	974.7	1,159.2
Percentage of total:				
Official	64.1	57.6	48.9	76.4
Private	35.9	42.4	51.1	23.6
(direct investment)	(12.4)	(20.5)	(18.3)	(4.3)
Singapore	81.3	165.5	444.7	893.5
Percentage of total:				
Official	55.3	34.4	14.0	2.5
Private	44.7	65.6	86.0	97.5
(direct investment)	(19.4)	(42.8)	(65.1)	(64.7)
Thailand	208.7	142.3	746.6	1,380.6
Percentage of total:				
Official	53.4	74.9	68.0	63.4
Private	46.6	25.1	32.0	36.6
(direct investment)	(6.1)	(16.8)	(11.3)	(15.7)

Sources: Hal Hill and Brian Johns, "The Role of Direct Foreign Investment in Developing
East Asian Countries," in *Weltwirtschaftliches Archiv,* table 1 (forthcoming); OECD,
Geographical Distribution of Financial Flows to Developing Countries (1981–84).

Note: Due to the possible incomplete recording of all the investment inflows, data from different sources may differ.

[a] Total and official refer to net disbursements from DAC (Development Assistance Committee) and OPEC countries as well as most multilateral sources.

[b] Private (including direct investment) refers to net disbursements from DAC countries
only.

Table 3.12   Total net inflows of foreign direct investment (FDI) in the host
country (in U.S.$ millions and as a percentage of gross domestic
capital formation (GDCF)), 1965–84

	Annual Average				Total
	1965–71	1972–76	1977–80	1981–84	1965–84
Indonesia FDI	48.5[a]	198.7	230.9	218.7	3,034.2[b]
(Percentage of GDCF)	(5.10)[a]	(4.28)	(2.02)	(1.04)	(1.92)[b]
Malaysia FDI	69.5[a]	317.5	603.5	1,240.7	9,311.8[b]
(Percentage of GDCF)	(10.58)[a]	(15.19)	(12.54)	(13.15)	(13.17)[b]
Philippines FDI	−8.3	55.3	52.9	71.6	716.1
(Pecentage of GDCF)	(−0.53)	(1.50)	(0.64)	(0.74)	(0.71)
Singapore FDI	61.5[a]	487.6	920.7	1,655.5	13,050.2[b]
(Percentage of GDCF)	(11.27)[a]	(25.74)	(27.16)	(25.44)[c]	(25.17)[d]
Thailand FDI	43.6	87.2	101.7	297.5	2,338.1
(Percentage of GDCF)	(3.17)	(2.91)	(1.44)	(3.35)	(2.65)

Sources: IMF, *Balance of Payments Yearbook* (various issues); IMF, *International Financial Statistics* (various issues).
[a] 1967–71.
[b] 1967–84.
[c] 1981–83.
[d] 1967–83.

sets. Nevertheless, some conclusions about FDI in ASEAN can be reached. First, Japan and the United States are the largest investors in ASEAN, according to host-country data.[6] Second, when all sectors are accounted for the United States is the largest investor in ASEAN countries, with Japan following. Although investing-country sources (Table 3.13) imply that Japan is the larger investor in Indonesia and therefore in ASEAN, host-country sources covering all sectors (not shown here) indi-

---

6. Host-country data covering economy-wide actual FDI by country of origin can be found in the following sources: Indonesia—Thee Kian Wie (1984), Hill (1984), Pangetsu (1985:tables 2, A.1.1, and Appendix 1, p.1); Philippines—Central Bank of the Philippines as cited in Japan External Trade Organization (JETRO) (1986:364); Singapore—Singapore Economic Planning Board as cited in JETRO (1986:359); Thailand—Bank of Thailand data as cited in Tambunlertchai (1977:7).

Table 3.13 United States and Japanese foreign direct investments in Asia (U.S.$ millions), 1976 and 1984

	Japan[a]						United States[b]					
	All industries		Manufacturing		Mining		All industries		Manufacturing		Petroleum	
	1976	1984	1976	1984	1976	1984	1976	1984	1976	1984	1976	1984
ASEAN	3,946	12,534	1,372	5,199	2,059	5,767	3,051	9,946	609	1,978+D	1,786	5,148+D
Indonesia	2,703	8,015	682	2,270	1,755	5,261	1,298	4,409	103	152	1,029	3,892
Malaysia	356	1,046	205	759	102	120	419	1,153	76	370	278	720
Philippines	354	832	92	311	197	378	698	1,185	274	443	215	D
Singapore	305	1,930	221	1,352	0	3	402	2,232	109	1,013	148	536
Thailand	228	711	172	507	5	5	234	967	47	D	116	D
East Asia	1,365	4,994	796	1,713	3	10	1,770	5,450	518	1,304	276+D	454+D
Hong Kong	448	2,799	100	233	0	5	1,166	3,799	195	629	260	348
Korea, Rep. of	690	1,548	485	908	2	3	359	823	149	211	D	D
Taiwan	227	647	211	572	1	2	245	828	174	464	16	106
World	14,661	71,431	6,035	22,048	4,859	11,158	133,335	233,412	57,651	93,012	26,636	63,319

Sources: Japanese Ministry of Finance, Monthly Statistical Review of Public Finance and Money (September 1977 and December 1985); U.S. Department of Commerce, U.S. Direct Investment Abroad, 1977 (Washington, D.C.: Dept. of Commerce, 1981); U.S. Department of Commerce, Survey of Current Business 65(8) (August 1985).

D: Not disclosed.

[a] Fiscal years end March 31 of the following calendar year. Petroleum is not listed as a separate category. Total actual FDI for 1965–84 as reported in balance of payments statistics was U.S.$37,974 million while total approved FDI for the same period was U.S.$70,100 million; thus, approval figures apparently overstate the true amount of Japanese FDI.

[b] Mining figures are very small or not disclosed.

cate that the United States is the largest investor in Indonesia, Singapore, and Thailand.[7] The Japanese figures based on government approvals rather than actual FDI substantially overstate outflows from Japan. Third, most sources show that investment in ASEAN countries from other Asian countries, especially the East Asian NICs, Singapore, and India, has become significant in recent years.

Turning to sectoral distributions, a large proportion of FDI takes place in the mining and petroleum sectors of the four resource-rich ASEAN countries, especially Indonesia. Host-country figures reveal shares of about 65 to 90 percent for Indonesia and about 10 to 20 percent in the other three countries (Table 3.14). Investing-country figures for available years (Table 3.13) indicate that U.S. petroleum shares of FDI were about 30 to 65 percent in these three countries and that the Japanese mining share was about 45 to 55 percent in the Philippines. Thus, the mining and petroleum shares may be somewhat underestimated in Table 3.14. Nevertheless, manufacturing FDI has also been a key element of FDI in ASEAN countries other than Indonesia. A variety of manufacturing subsectors have been able to attract substantial FDI. These include metals (all ASEAN), electrical products (Malaysia, Singapore, Thailand), and textiles (all ASEAN). Foreign investment in the service sector is also quite significant, with its share growing rapidly in Malaysia and Singapore.

Some of the manufacturing, petroleum, and mining subsectors are very capital-intensive. The capital-intensity of resource-based industries is often underestimated, and inadequate attention is paid to the sensitivity of capital requirements to different technologies that are available at different stages of resource development, from extraction and refinement to processing, fabrication, and final consumption. The costs of resource extraction projects and the development of related industries as well as physical and social infrastructure are often unfeasible in Southeast Asian countries. The Asahan project, a massive package consisting of power stations using North Sumatra's water resources and an aluminum smelter, will have cost more than U.S. $1.6 billion when completed. Thailand's planned development of its natural gas resources will also be an enormous project. Such projects rely heavily not only on foreign financial help but also on services and technology; indeed, one of their purposes is

---

7. It should be noted that host-country data based on approvals rather than on actual FDI show that the Japanese share is larger in Indonesia, Malaysia, and Thailand. Yet these data often exclude several key sectors of U.S. FDI, such as oil. See: Indonesia—BKPM (Investment Board) as cited in JETRO (1986:363); Malaysia—MIDA (Malaysia Industrial Development Authority) as cited in JETRO (1986:362); Philippines—Central Bank of the Philippines as cited in JETRO (1986:364); Thailand—Board of Investment of Thailand (1984:table C, p.5).

Table 3.14   ASEAN: Estimates of foreign direct investment flows by sectoral

Sector and Subsector	Indonesia[b]			Malaysia[c]		
	1967–70	1971–76	1977–83	1966–70	1971–76	1977–80
Agriculture, forestry, and fishery	14.1	4.7	1.3	34.6	27.3	18.6
Mining and petroleum	64.8	64.8	88.3	12.4	12.3	11.9
Manufacturing	17.4	25.8	9.5	21.3	25.1	29.6
Food, beverages, and tobacco	4.8	1.8	0.4	4.8	2.1	3.1
Chemical products	4.1	3.4	2.8	2.8	2.0	1.2
Metal products	4.0	5.3	2.9	2.7	0.8	2.0
Machinery and transport equip.	N.A.	N.A.	N.A.	0.4	0.3	0.3
Electrical products	N.A.	N.A.	N.A.	1.0	5.6	4.9
Textiles	2.9	11.0	2.0	1.3	5.4	2.2
Wood and pulp	0.1	0.6	0.4	0.4	0.8	0.1
Petroleum and coal	N.A.	N.A.	N.A.	5.7	2.7	6.9
Others	1.6	3.4	1.0	2.1	5.4	8.9
Services	3.4	4.2	0.7	17.0	26.8	34.3
Construction	0.3	0.5	0.1	0.8	1.0	1.3
Others	—	—	0.1	13.9	7.5	4.5
Total	100.0	100.0	100.0	100.0	100.0	100.0

Source: Mari Pangestu, "The Pattern of Direct Foreign Investment in ASEAN: The U.S. vs. Japan," a paper presented at the ASEAN–U.S. Economic Relations Workshop, Institute of Southeast Asian Studies, Singapore (22–24 April 1985), table 4 .
[a] From all investor companies.
[b] Net approvals (except banking and oil) from Bank Indonesia, *Indonesian Financial Statistics* (various issues) combined with oil exploration and development totals from U.S. Embassy, *Industry Outlook Report: Indonesia's Petroleum Sector* (various years).
[c] Estimated from Malaysia, Dept. of Statistics, *Report of the Financial Survey of Limited Companies* (various years).
[d] From Central Bank approval data.

to stimulate the transfer of technology. With the assistance of foreign capital and technology, ASEAN countries have been able to develop their natural resource and manufacturing sectors and increase their exports to the rest of the world.

Technology transferred through direct investment carries the characteristics of its country of origin, such as that country's factor endowment and level of economic development (Kojima 1985: Ch.5–11). For example, Japanese FDI in manufacturing industries is relatively large in traditional industries such as textiles, clothing, processing, and fabrication (e.g., motor vehicle assembly), and in the production of parts and components for electronic machinery. Firms in such industries are suited to

breakdown (percent),[a] 1967–83

	Philippines[d]			Singapore[e]			Thailand[f]		
	1970	1970–76	1977–83	1970	1971–76	1977–82	1972	1973–76	1977–83
	—	1.3	0.9	—	—	—	0.3	0.3	0.3
	14.5	11.2	22.3	—	—	—	12.0	15.6	17.3
	57.7	48.7	35.7	75.6	68.5	64.4	21.6	30.5	34.2
	14.8	4.5	8.2	2.3	2.5	2.1	0.4	3.3	1.2
	7.2	7.4	11.6	4.6	3.5	2.5	4.8	4.6	3.7
	4.0	14.8	3.9	4.0	2.2	2.8	0.2	4.1	5.3
	2.3	1.6	2.9	3.9	13.3	7.7	1.9	0.8	4.2
	2.5	N.A.	N.A.	6.2	8.2	10.4	3.2	4.4	10.5
	1.9	3.3	1.6	3.4	4.6	3.7	12.5	13.2	3.4
	5.9	N.A.	N.A.	2.6	4.0	3.0	N.A.	N.A.	N.A.
	N.A.	5.5	0.4	42.2	24.1	27.0	N.A.	N.A.	N.A.
	19.0	11.6	7.1	4.9	6.5	5.2	3.4	0.1	1.6
	27.4	38.3	15.0	24.4[g]	31.5[h]	36.5[i]	44.0	47.4	31.5
	0.3	0.1	1.0	N.A.	N.A.	N.A.	22.1	6.3	15.9
	0.1	0.1	—	N.A.	N.A.	N.A.	—	—	—
	100.0	100.0	100.0	100.0	100.0	100.0	100.0	100.0	100.0

[e] Manufacturing sector data from Singapore Economic Development Board, *Annual Report* (various years). Service sector data estimated from Singapore, Dept. of Statistics, *Census of Services* and *Report on the Survey of Wholesale and Retail Trade, Restaurants and Hotels* (1974–note 5 & 1980–note 7) and from G. F. H. Seow, *The Service Sector in Singapore's Economy: Performance and Structure,* Economic Research Center, Univ. of Singapore, 12/79) (1975/76–note 6).

[f] From Bank of Thailand net inflow data.

[g] 1974.

[h] 1976.

[i] 1980.

joint ventures and local ownership in areas afforded some kind of "most-favored" status (with investment incentives such as tax holidays and favorable profit repatriation) by host governments. U.S. FDI, on the other hand, tends to be in the industries using new and highly sophisticated technology often unique to the firm. This type of arrangement requires a high level of management skills and thus generally takes the form of wholly-owned subsidiaries. Partly because of these differences in the ownership pattern, Japanese investment tends to concentrate more in promoted sectors than does U.S. investment.

FDI is not the only means by which technology is transferred to developing countries, but it is an important factor in ASEAN. Another princi-

Table 3.15   Major sources of technology, selected ASEAN countries (percent)

	Recipient Country		
	Malaysia 1960–81	Philippines 1978–79	Thailand 1980–81
Japan	30.5	20.6	36.3
United States	14.7	46.0	18.8
United Kingdom	13.5	6.7	7.7
Other developed countries	25.8	22.7	25.6
Developing countries	15.5	4.0	11.6
Total	100.0	100.0	100.0
(No. of agreements)	(348)	(150)	(388)

Source: United Nations, *Costs and Conditions of Technology Transfer through Transnational Corporations,* ESCAP/UNCTC Publication Series B No. 3 (Bangkok, 1984).

pal form of technology transfer is through arms-length licensing arrangements.[8] Table 3.15 shows major sources of technology, measured in terms of the number of licensing agreements, for selected ASEAN countries. For Malaysia, the Philippines, and Thailand, the two major suppliers of technology in recent years have been Japan and the United States. Together, they account for approximately one-half of the licensing agreements made by the three ASEAN countries. Surprisingly, however, less developed countries were also a significant source of technology for Malaysia and Thailand. Although the identity of these countries is not disclosed, the Asian NICs are believed to be replacing Japan as a source of standardized, labor-intensive technology.

The foregoing trends suggest that the supply of technology to ASEAN is strong because of substantial growth in Japanese FDI in technology in the region, increased competition between Japan and the United States in sectors demanding more sophisticated technology, and growth of the NICs as suppliers of more standardized technology (Hill and Johns forthcoming). Thus, the ASEAN countries seem to be relatively well placed to obtain the technology they need from abroad. How effectively that technology is actually transferred, however, depends on their policies in areas such as personnel development and training, which need to be strengthened to expand their ability to absorb foreign technology.

All the ASEAN countries consider FDI desirable for its overall contri-

---

8. The measurement of technology and its transfer is extremely difficult, as there is no natural unit of measurement. The number of licensing agreements has been used here as a proxy for technology transferred.

bution to their economic development efforts. They promote FDI as a source of new technologies and of employment opportunities for their abundant labor, as well as for its contribution to trade and payments. Although the priorities differ somewhat, they especially encourage FDI in manufacturing activities where they lack the technical know-how, management expertise, and export market outlets.

In order to attract FDI, every ASEAN country has an elaborate incentive and guarantee scheme. All guarantee that earnings can be repatriated and assets will not be appropriated. Exemptions from taxes on imported capital goods and raw materials are also a common feature. Different countries, however, allow different rates of deduction from taxable corporate income with respect to depreciation allowance, carryover of capital allowance during the relief period, and company expenses. Malaysia and the Philippines offer the largest number of guarantees and incentives, followed by Thailand, Singapore, and Indonesia (Table 3.16).

The ASEAN countries should review the incentives they give to foreign investors. Tax holidays, accelerated depreciation, provision of infrastructure, and other incentives have been built up piecemeal, and apparently no government has attempted to systematically assess their overall effects. The proliferation of incentives may not have a significant effect on bringing in new investment, and if done competitively by several countries may have the effect of subsidizing private FDI at high cost to the host countries. It is more important to make resources attractive and to provide a stable, profitable business environment and consistent regulation of business over time.

Now is a critical time because recession, the debt crisis, and the fall in oil earnings have forced countries to reexamine FDI policies. Until recently, ASEAN countries were moving in the direction of increased regulation. Now, however, FDI policies are less rigid and incentives to firms have increased for several reasons. First, external financial flows, particularly official development assistance (ODA) or aid to developing countries, have slowed. At the same time, concern about the large external debt of developing countries has limited private inflows from financial institutions. The slowdown in other sources of external capital and the desire of ASEAN countries to control external debt make FDI more attractive. Second, in the past, direct foreign investment was often viewed by developing countries as being exploitative. More recently, it has become less politically controversial. Singapore provides a good example of the economic benefits that can accrue from FDI. Third, with China's entry into the international market, there is an increase in competition for financial flows, which may result in more incentives being

Table 3.16   Summary of investment incentives of ASEAN countries, 1984

	I	M	P	S	T
Basic rights and guarantees to investors					
Guarantee against appropriation	X	X	X	X	X
Guarantee against loss due to					
–Nationalization	X	X		X	X
–Damage caused by war		X			
–Inconvertibility of currency	X				
Remittance of foreign exchange					
earnings and payments	X	X	X	X	X
Repatriation of capital	X		X	X	X
Protection scheme and priorities given to investors and aliens					
Employment of aliens	X	X	X	X	X
Patent protection	X	X	X	X	X
Preference in the granting of					
government loans		X	X	X	X
Protection against competition					
–Import competition	X	X	X^a		X
–Government competition			X^a		X
–Local competition		X	X^a		X
Real estate ownership by alien					
investors	X	X		X	X
Exemptions from taxes and tariffs					
Capital gain tax		X	X		
Corporate income tax		X		X	X
Taxes on imported capital goods	X	X	X	X	X
Taxes on imported raw materials	X	X	X	X	X
Taxes on royalties		X		X	X
Withholding tax on interest on					
foreign loan (tax credit)		X	X^a	X	X
Other taxes and fees	X	X	X	X	X
Deductions from taxable corporate income					
Accelerated depreciation allowance		X	X	X	X
Carry-over of capital allowance					
during the relief period		X		X	
Carry-over of loss	X	X	X	X	X
Export allowance/deduction		X	X	X	X
Deduction of organization and					
preoperating expenses					
–Organizational expenses	X	X	X		X
–Preoperating expenses	X		X		X
Reinvested profits			X		
Investment allowance		X	X	X	

Table 3.16 *(continued)*

	I	M	P	S	T
Tax credits (direct deduction from corporate income tax)					
Investment tax credit		X			
Tax credit on domestic capital equipment			X		
Other tax credit		X	X		X
Extension of incentive availment period		X	X	X	
Special incentives					
To multinational companies			X		
To exporters	X	X	X	X	X
To offshore banking units		X	X	X	
Other laws granting benefits to foreign investors		X	X	X	
Assistance to investors					
Joint venture brokerage	X	X	X[a]	X	X
Technical assistance		X	X[a]	X	X
Processing of application and other requirements	X	X	X	X	X

Source: The SGV Group, *Comparative Investment Incentives 1984* (Manila: SVG and Co., 1984).

I: Indonesia; M: Malaysia; P: Philippines; S: Singapore; T: Thailand.

[a] Not applicable to all firms or enterprises.

offered by ASEAN countries. Finally, ASEAN countries hope to encourage more U.S. investment (as well as investment from other more developed countries) to enable them to lessen the large share of Japanese investment in their countries.

FINANCIAL FLOWS AND DOMESTIC RESOURCE MOBILIZATION

The ASEAN countries have been very successful in mobilizing both foreign and domestic financial flows. They have become increasingly linked to world financial markets. Despite the slowdown in external financial flows in the mid-1980s, flows into these countries have increased more than fourfold since the early 1970s. More important, private capital flows (banks and investors) increased in the 1970s as a percentage of total flows in all countries (except Indonesia where the share of private flows declined during 1977–80). Although much of this increase of private flows was in the form of non-debt-creating flows, such as direct investment, the increase in private flows corresponds to the increase in external debt of these countries.

Debt-service ratios indicate that the debt-servicing capacity of the Southeast Asian countries, like those of other developing countries, has diminished since the second oil shock. However, except for the Philippines, the debt-servicing burden in less developed Asia is still significantly lower than that of major debtors in Africa and Latin America and, more important, the long-term capacity for repayment of external debt in Asia is quite strong. Only in the Philippines has the situation reached a point where rescheduling was mandatory. The Philippine short-term debt became excessive, and all available foreign exchange has had to be used to make stopgap payments.[9]

The absence of debt repayment crises in the rest of ASEAN is primarily due to effective domestic economic policies. Borrowing supplements efforts to generate internal resources, thus financing the excess of imports over exports so that the rate of investment and growth can be raised. External funds have been used mainly to finance investments in agriculture, industry, and energy production. In addition, saving rates have risen to high levels over the past two decades (Table 3.17), increasing the amount of internal funds available for investment. This large mobilization of domestic resources has been a major factor in the development success of these countries and in their attempts to avoid serious external debt problems. If the less developed countries in Asia are to continue to have high and sustained rates of economic development, they will need to mobilize more domestic resources to finance the requisite high levels of investment without increasing their dependence on external capital.

National saving rates have either increased remarkably or maintained high levels since 1960 for the ASEAN countries, ranging from 18 percent for the Philippines to 43 percent for Singapore in 1984. Except for the Philippines, they all had average growth rates above 6 percent during the 1970s, and their saving ratios in 1984 were above 20 percent. But Indonesia and Malaysia achieved high saving ratios with the aid of high earnings from oil exports that may not continue in the future. The Philippines had to curtail domestic investment in order to avoid a larger resource gap, since saving was not sufficient.

---

9. The roots of the crisis lie in long-term problems associated with macroeconomic, industrialization, and trade policies that weakened foreign exchange earning capacity, leading to heavy reliance on imports as inputs and encouraging excessively capital-intensive activities. See Naya and James (1986).

Table 3.17   Domestic saving, investment, and resource balance (as a percentage of GDP), 1960 and 1984

	Gross domestic saving		Gross domestic investment		Resource balance	
	1960	1984	1960	1984	1960	1984
ASEAN						
Indonesia	8	20	8	21	0	−1
Malaysia	27	32	14	31	13	1
Philippines	16	18	16	18	0	−1
Singapore	−3	43	11	47	−14	−4
Thailand	14	21	16	23	−2	−2
Other Asian developing countries						
Hong Kong	6	29	18	24	−12	5
India	14	22	17	24	−3	−3
Korea, Rep. of	1	30	11	29	−10	0
Pakistan	5	6	12	17	−7	−12
Sri Lanka	9	20	14	26	−5	−6
United States	19	16	18	19	1	−3
Japan	34	31	34	28	0	3

Sources: World Bank, *World Development Report* (1982, 1986); ADB, *ADB Annual Report* (1985).

A useful rough measure of the degree of financial development and of the potential for raising the household saving rate through increased bank intermediation is the ratio of broad money M_2 (currency plus demand, time, and savings deposits) to GDP. Increases in the ratio (M_2/GDP) represent greater use of financial assets.[10] Excluding Singapore, the average M_2/GDP ratio during the 1970s was 27 percent for the ASEAN countries, a low figure compared to that of the NICs (62 percent) and Japan's in 1955 (55 percent). These figures indicate *prima facie* that the role of money used as transferable savings and the role of deposit banks in the economies of the ASEAN and South Asian countries can be expanded.

---

10. McKinnon (1980:98–99) points out two reasons why this ratio can be used as a measure of the flow of loanable funds in the economy. First, it gives an indication of the absolute size of the banking system and measures the stock of liquidity available for self-financed investments. Second, increases in the ratio provide an indication of real additions to the ongoing loanable funds capacity of the banking system, because the flow of private savings shows up in part as changes in the assets and liabilities of the banking system.

Financial development in Thailand has been a significant factor in the increase in the domestic saving rate (Asian Development Bank 1984). Liberalization of the Thai financial system encouraged rapid increases between 1960 and 1982 in the number of rural branches of commercial banks, which dominate the Thai financial system. Indonesia also significantly liberalized its financial system in 1983, including eliminating credit ceilings and freeing interest rates. These policy changes stimulated competition within the banking system and encouraged both state-owned and private banks to become more aggressive in providing business loans and longer-term credits. Despite the rapid growth of the private sector in recent years, however, it is still not well developed because of limitations placed on foreign and non-indigenous bankers. State-owned banks continue to dominate the financial sector in Indonesia.

It is important for the low-saving and moderate-saving countries of ASEAN to continue to enhance their financial systems and to broaden their role in mobilization and allocation of funds. Potential saving of the household sector is not fully mobilized, primarily because of inadequate financial development. A financial sector that provides consumers of financial services with the greatest choice in terms of accessibility and variety of instruments with respect to size and maturity, while guaranteeing depositors a positive real rate of return, is more likely to call forth additional savings than one that denies them. This response is not only because of direct positive effects, but also through longer-term reinforcing effects of improved investment efficiency and higher real economic growth rates.

Increasing the rate of domestic saving and investment is a necessary but perhaps not sufficient condition for sustained high growth. Resource mobilization efforts of ASEAN countries have been impressive, but if capacity utilization is low and inefficient, overall growth rates will be retarded, again underscoring the point that the allocation of investable funds must also be efficient if accelerated economic growth is to be attained.

The uses to which savings from all sources are put are extremely important in this context. The incremental capital–output ratio (ICOR) is an approximate measure of the efficiency of investment. It is defined as the ratio of the change in capital stock to the change in GDP. The lower the ICOR, the faster the increase in real income for a given level of investment. Estimates of the size and direction of change of the ICORs and marginal savings rates (MSRs) for Asian less developed countries over the last two decades are presented in Table 3.18. MSRs remained high (but with decreases for the Philippines and Thailand) while ICORs

Table 3.18   Incremental capital–output ratio and marginal saving rate, 1966–82

	Incremental capital–output ratio		Marginal saving rate (percent)	
	1966–75	1976–82	1966–75	1976–82
ASEAN				
Indonesia[a]	2.2	3.3	18.0	22.6
Malaysia	3.2	3.7	24.6	26.0
Philippines	3.3	4.7	26.5	21.8
Singapore	3.2	4.3	33.8	48.2
Thailand	3.3	3.7	24.2	21.8
Other Asian developing countries				
Hong Kong	2.8	2.5	24.3	24.6
India[a]	4.4	4.7	20.2	21.8
Korea, Rep. of	2.7	4.3	24.6	31.2
Pakistan	2.6	2.2	9.0	5.5
Sri Lanka	2.5	3.4	8.5	10.7

Source: Seiji Naya and William James, "External Shocks, Policy Responses, and External Debt of Asian Developing Countries," in Augustine H. H. Tan and Basant Kapur (eds.), *Pacific Growth and Financial Interdependence* (Sydney: Allen and Unwin, 1986).
[a] The data cover only up to 1981.

increased (worsened) reflecting not only declining efficiency of investment but also the deep recession that characterized the end of the period (1982). The rise of the ICOR was most pronounced in the Philippines.

CONCLUDING REMARKS

During the past few decades ASEAN countries have become known for the attainment of high rates of growth. Industrialization has proceeded rapidly during the past two decades and export growth rates have been outstanding. Despite the slowdown in the 1980s, ASEAN countries have done very well in terms of long-term economic growth. With their rich resources and abundant labor, they have tremendous potential for growth and development.

Continued economic growth, however, assumes the continuation of export-oriented policies and high rates of resource mobilization. The

ASEAN countries have been able to mobilize domestic savings to maintain high rates of investment, while at the same time reducing their reliance on foreign capital. However, with the emergence of "aid fatigue" and the slowdown of external flows from developed countries, less foreign savings will be available to finance investment, making greater domestic resource mobilization even more vital, along with increased efficiency of investment. The declines in the marginal saving rates in the Philippines and Thailand must be reversed.

Their adherence to relatively market-oriented, outward-looking development strategies has also been a major factor in their success, having contributed to the high rates of export growth and the expansion of new export-oriented industries through increases in the efficiency, competitiveness, and overall growth prospects of the entire economy. In turn, these dynamic gains are reinforced by domestic economic policies that allow market forces both to work and to improve the infrastructural and institutional framework of the economy.

Although I advocate the use of outward-looking development stategies for ASEAN countries, I do not recommend they follow the development path of Korea or Taiwan. The smallest of the five ASEAN countries, Malaysia and Singapore, like the East Asian countries have large trade dependency ratios. Due to the larger domestic markets and natural resource wealth of the other three ASEAN countries, however, trade–GNP ratios are about 20–25 percent, much lower than those of the two smaller ASEAN countries. Industrialization of these resource-rich ASEAN countries should emphasize processing of primary products along with labor-intensive manufactured products.

The ASEAN countries are endowed with rich natural resources. Natural resource-based exports have financed necessary imports and provided impetus to growth. But to some degree, wealth in natural resources in these labor-abundant countries makes it more difficult to adopt policies that promote growth with equity through labor absorption in an outward-looking manufacturing sector. Resource wealth tends to encourage rent-seeking behavior. It often has concentrated ownership and requires capital-intensive technologies for development. In addition, the effect of natural resource booms on non-resource sectors capable of producing exports is often negative because of "Dutch disease" effects. The sectors that are most often adversely affected are labor-intensive.

A major shortcoming of development patterns of the resource-rich ASEAN countries has been weak labor absorption in manufacturing. The growth in manufacturing exports and GDP shares has not been matched by growth in manufacturing employment. Despite measures to promote manufactures, exports, and efficiency, government industrial planning continues to favor import substitution and investment in capital-intensive heavy industries that have not been able to provide sufficient employment opportunities. This failure is due to the fact that export-promotion policies have been implemented on top of import-substitution policies and have not necessarily been a correction of the distortions created by the latter. Although the Philippines attempted to replace import-substituting policies in the early 1980s, they were swamped by political events and not able to improve labor absorption. Unless the pattern is changed in the other resource-rich countries, serious social problems—including high rates of unemployment and poverty—will result, as labor force growth is extremely high.

Finally, the importance of world trade expansion and the trade policies of industrial nations has been discussed in this chapter but requires elaboration. The openness of the ASEAN countries makes external conditions very important, and the international trading environment is a crucial aspect of any development strategy. Commercial policies of advanced industrial countries have substantial effect on the ability of less developed nations to expand exports. The general trend toward protectionism in more developed countries is a cause for concern. Even more dangerous for ASEAN countries than direct legislation in industrial countries to restrict imports from ASEAN could be the indirect fallout from trade frictions between industrial nations. The handling of the U.S.–Japan trade conflict has serious implications for ASEAN. Failure to achieve market opening by Japan could lead to wide-ranging U.S. restrictions. More than 300 protectionist bills are presently in Congress, including the Jenkins bill, which would limit textile, footwear, and clothing imports. The cost of a protectionist approach to settling trade imbalances between the United States and Japan would be very high for ASEAN. Not only would their exports to the United States be restricted, but their exports to Japan would also probably decrease as the pressure on Japan to open its market disappears. ASEAN countries must use their political unity to oppose protectionism and get a better deal from Japan. In turn, ASEAN trade policies should be responsive to consumers' and firms' needs to purchase competitive products from the industrial countries. Increases in South–South trade will also be important, providing rapidly growing markets for ASEAN exports, while further measures to remove distortions will encourage export growth.

The worsening of the external environment, however, does not mean that export-oriented policies are no longer appropriate. The analysis in this chapter indicates that supply conditions and competitiveness have been important factors in export growth. More important, the dynamic gains of outward-looking policies, including increased efficiency and competitiveness of domestic production, have significant long-run effects on economic growth and development. Outward-looking development strategies encourage efficient resource allocation and the development of industries using abundant factors of production. For the labor-abundant ASEAN countries, such a strategy will have a significant effect on equity and employment. It can be a powerful implement for pulling people out of poverty.

REFERENCES

Akrasanee, Narongchai
    1984 Export Promotion Policies in ASEAN. In Pitou van Dijck and Harmen Verbrug-
          gen (eds.), *Export-Oriented Industrialization and Employment: Policies and
          Responses*. Amsterdam: Council for Asian Manpower Studies.
Ariff, Mohamed, and Hal Hill
    1985 *Export-Oriented Industrialization: The ASEAN Experience*. Sydney: Allen and
          Unwin (Publishers) Ltd.
Asian Development Bank
    1984 *Domestic Resource Mobilization Through Financial Development* 1. Manila:
          ADB.
Bautista, Romeo M., and John H. Power and Associates
    1979 *Industrial Promotion Policies in the Philippines*. Manila: Philippine Institute for
          Developing Studies.
Board of Investment of Thailand
    1984 *Activity Report for the Month of June 1984*.
Corden, W. M.
    1981 The Exchange Rate, Monetary Policy and the North Sea Oil: The Economic The-
          ory of the Squeeze on Tradables. *Oxford Economic Papers* (supplement, July)
          33:23–46.
De Rosa, Dean A.
    1986 Trade and Protection in the Asian Developing Region. *Asian Development Review*
          4(1).
Dorian, James P., and Allen L. Clark
    1984 *A Geological and Mineral Assessment of Indonesia*. Honolulu: East-West Re-
          source Systems Institute, December. (U.S. Geological Survey contract no. 14-08-
          0001-a-0141.)
Fesharaki, Fereidun
    (forthcoming) Structural Change in the Asian-Pacific Oil Market. In *Pacific Energy
          Cooperation*. Tokyo: Ministry of International Trade and Industry.
Hill, Hal
    1984 Survey of Recent Developments. *Bulletin of Indonesian Economic Studies* 20 (2):
          32.
Hill, Hal, and Brian Johns
    (forthcoming) The Role of Direct Foreign Investment in Developing East Asian Coun-
          tries. *Weltwirtschaftliches Archiv*.
Japan External Trade Organization
    1986 *JETRO White Paper: Investment Edition, 1986* (in Japanese). JETRO Hakusho:
          Toshi Hen.

Kojima, Kiyoshi
  1985 *Japanese Direct Foreign Investment: An Economic Approach (Nihon Kaigai Cho-kusetsu Toshi: Keizaiteki Sekkin)* (in Japanese). Tokyo: Bunshindo.
McKinnon, R. I.
  1980 Financial Policies. In J. Cody, J. Hughes, and D. Welles (eds.), *Policies for Industrial Progress In Developing Countries*. London: Oxford University Press.
Naya, Seiji
  (forthcoming) Role of Trade Policies: Competition and Cooperation. In Shinichi Ichimura (ed.), *Development Strategies and Productivity Issues in Asia*. Tokyo: Asian Productivity Organization.
Naya, Seiji, and William E. James
  1986 External Shocks, Policy Responses, and External Debt of Asian Developing Countries. In Augustine H. H. Tan and Basant Kapur (eds.), *Pacific Growth and Financial Interdependence*. Sydney: Allen and Unwin.
Pangetsu, Mari
  1985 The Pattern of Direct Foreign Investment in ASEAN: The U.S. vs. Japan. Paper presented at the ASEAN-U.S. Economic Relations Workshop, Institute of Southeast Asian Studies, Singapore, 22–24 April.
Rana, P.
  1983 The Impact of the Current Exchange Rate System On Trade and Inflation of Selected Developing Member Countries. *Asian Development Bank Economic Staff Paper* 18. Manila: ADB Economics Office.
Richardson, J. D.
  1971 Constant Market Shares Analysis of Export Growth. *Journal of International Economics* I.
Tambunlertchai, Somsak
  1977 Japanese and American Investments in Thailand's Manufacturing Industries: An Assessment of Their Relative Contribution to the Host Country. Tokyo: Institute of Developing Economies.
Tan, Augustine H. H.
  1985 Singapore's Economy: Growth and Structural Change. Paper presented at the Conference on Singapore and the United States into the 1990s, at Tufts University, sponsored by the Fletcher School, the Asia Society, and the Institute of Southeast Asian Studies.
Thee, Kian Wie
  1984 Japanese Direct Investment in Indonesian Manufacturing. *Bulletin of Indonesian Economic Studies* 20 (2): 90–93.
Vyas, V. S.
  1983 Asian Agriculture: Achievements and Challenges. *Asian Development Review* 1(2).

The Renewable Natural Resource Base

JOHN A. DIXON

Naya presents a detailed discussion of a number of key elements responsible for the recent economic performance of ASEAN countries. The discussion is externally oriented and concentrates on trade issues, financial flows, and levels of borrowing and investment. The domestic economy and the natural resource base are largely discussed in terms of their external manifestations. There is very limited discussion of people, equity, or even structural changes between economic sectors within countries, all of which are issues relevant to economic performance.

In the context of these issues, I would like to comment on the renewable natural resource base of the ASEAN countries and the crucial role it plays in both the external and internal sectors. There is no doubt that agriculture and agriculture-dependent processing and services are the single largest source of jobs and income for people in all of the ASEAN countries, except Singapore and Brunei. Table 3.6 shows that agriculture provides employment to between 36 and 69 percent of the people in Indonesia, Malaysia, the Philippines, and Thailand, and that the agriculture sector generates about one-quarter of the GDP of the same countries. Trade also is dominated by primary commodities (although petroleum products have become increasingly important in Malaysia and continue to dominate Indonesian exports).

Agriculture is responsible for much of the present ASEAN prosperity. However, as shown by recent events in the Philippines, where poor management and low sugar prices have combined to create severe economic and social conditions on Negros, we cannot take for granted the continued "health" of the rural, renewable resource sector. Constant attention and work are required to maintain and improve productivity and income levels, and thereby help provide the basis for continued domestic and export-oriented growth.

As the ASEAN countries develop over the next 25 years, their urban, industrial sectors will continue to grow and become a larger source of jobs and GDP generation. The rural, agricultural sector, while decreasing as a percentage of the total, also will increase in absolute size. Therefore, the renewable resource base is and will continue to be important in terms of jobs, exports, and human welfare. I will briefly comment on three areas in which key management issues threaten long-term productivity of the resource base: staple food production, fish production, and the forestry sector.

STAPLE FOOD PRODUCTION

The ASEAN countries (or more correctly the ASEAN Four, since I exclude Singapore and Brunei) have been very successful in increasing agricultural production, especially of staple foods such as rice and maize, and also of export and plantation crops. The Green Revolution introduced new seeds and management techniques, helped make better use of irrigation investments, and led to a greater integration of farmers into the market economy. The successes in this area do not remove the need for continuing caution and work. Careful management of existing agricultural areas is required to maintain and increase productivity.

As agricultural production is intensified on existing cultivated land (and this is the likely route most countries will follow since new, undeveloped, prime agricultural areas are limited), greater management care is required. Pollution of surface- and groundwater by agricultural chemicals—fertilizers, pesticides, herbicides—is a growing concern. Erosion and resulting sedimentation from upland agriculture threaten downstream populations and infrastructure. Wide use of single plant varieties always carries the risk of drastic losses from new pest or disease outbreaks.

Most countries have developed widespread and quite sophisticated agricultural research and extension services. These systems will have to be maintained and strengthened to keep pace with the demands that will be placed on the agricultural sector.

FISH PRODUCTION

Marine fish resources are another type of renewable resource that have unique management dimensions. Fish products are the major source of animal protein in most ASEAN countries (even though staple foods are the largest single protein source in all countries) and fish exports are also important. Large numbers of coastal people depend on fish for food and income—either directly through catching fish or indirectly through services and processing. These people are also usually among the poorest groups in their countries.

Marine fish present a number of management challenges. Because access to fish is open, they are subject to overexploitation by coastal populations and others from outside the region. The breeding/spawning habitats of many species are threatened by pollution or destruction of coastal areas, especially mangrove forests and coral reefs.

In Thailand, for example, the creation of Exclusive Economic Zones (EEZs) by neighboring countries has resulted in Thai fishermen being restricted to a smaller area in the Gulf of Thailand and the Andaman Sea than was previously the case. The result has been some decrease in quantity of catch and a sharp reduction in quality. The percentage of more desirable fish—suitable for human consumption or export—is down, and the "trash fish" component—used for fish meal production—is way up. Management of the fish stock and the level of fishing effort is a complicated, thorny problem. And yet, if the resource is seriously degraded, all parties lose—consumers, exporters, and particularly the fishermen.

FORESTRY SECTOR

A last major renewable resource area is forestry. Forest products are a major export item for Indonesia, the Philippines, Malaysia, and to a lesser extent Thailand. Most of these countries started with large forested areas, both tropical hardwood and mangrove, which they have been depleting rapidly.

There are several sets of competing users of the forest resource: loggers, for domestic use and exports; fuelwood gatherers, for sale or own-use; and farmers, who clear forest areas for new farm land. A key management question is how to use the forest resource for sustainable economic development. Logging may be a rational policy, particularly if followed by careful conversion or reforestation. Unmanaged logging, however, often leads to heavy erosion, siltation, and rapid degradation of the forest lands. Grasses may enter and most productive uses are lost.

A related development question is what is done with forestry resources revenue. If these revenues are invested in productive assets, economic growth can be enhanced. If revenues are used to support pure consumption then the forest resources are being "mined." A recent draft World Resources Institute study of the forestry resources in Indonesia (Repetto 1985) concluded that the estimated value of resource depletion from forests (extractions net of regrowth and replanting) averaged from U.S. $1.6 to 3.0 billion per year. The ultimate use of this extracted rent—

whether for investment or consumption—is obviously an important question.

This discussion is meant to illustrate the complex renewable resource management problems faced by the four resource-rich ASEAN countries. Use of their resource base, wisely or not, has been a key element in the rapid economic growth that Naya has discussed. The continued economic growth of these countries and the well-being of a sizable share of their population will be in no small way dependent on the careful management of the renewable resource base.

Only Singapore has reached the stage where economic growth is primarily dependent on manufacturing or services. In Brunei, oil revenues are large and the population is small, and its economic development will be largely determined by how the oil "rents" are invested. In Indonesia, Malaysia, Thailand, and the Philippines, the renewable resource base demands greater attention as a growth factor in explaining the past economic performance of these countries, as well as in predicting future growth.

REFERENCE

Repetto, Robert
  1985 Natural Resource Accounting in a Resource Based Economy: An Indonesian Case Study. Draft, unpublished note presented at the UNEP–World Bank Natural Resources Accounting Meeting, Paris, October.

Human Resources and Economic Development

LINDA G. MARTIN

I would like to comment briefly on the role of human resources in the future economic development of the ASEAN countries. I will discuss first the positive implications of slowing population growth for the labor situations of the ASEAN countries and then focus on two labor issues: labor absorption into the modern sector and intra-ASEAN labor migration.

POSITIVE IMPLICATIONS OF SLOWING POPULATION GROWTH

Up to a point, one can argue that population growth and the resulting growth of the labor force make a positive contribution to economic growth. However, an economy may reach a point at which having more labor hurts rather than helps production. The challenge in the past for all the ASEAN countries has been to find enough jobs for their growing populations and to increase labor productivity and general well-being. That is, the challenge has been to keep ahead of a wave of population growth that can threaten to overwhelm an economy.

However, with declines in fertility and slowing of the population growth rates in the ASEAN countries, the task of finding productive jobs for the population—of absorbing more and more of the labor force into the modern sector of the economy—has become easier, though as I shall demonstrate and as Naya mentions in his conclusion, labor absorption remains an issue today in several ASEAN countries.

But first let me mention another benefit for the development of a more productive labor force that has resulted from the recent decline in fertility and family size in the ASEAN countries. With fewer children in a family, parents have had more resources to invest in the human capital, such as education, of each of their children. And with the decline in mortality

92

(the other component of the demographic transition) these children have grown up to live healthier, longer lives. Altogether, there has been an improvement in the quality of the population and of young workers entering the labor force in ASEAN each year, as indicated in Wong and Cheung's discussion of education (Chapter 2).

Another important contribution of the decline in fertility to the composition of the labor force has been the aging of the labor force—aging in at least its early stages. With the growth rate of the number of entrants into the labor force slowing down, the average *age* of the labor force has been increasing. Of course, with age comes experience, so on average the labor forces of ASEAN are more experienced today than they were ten years ago. One very rough measure of this phenomenon is simply the change in the proportion of the total population that falls in the 15–64 year-old group, from which most of the labor force is drawn. In 1960 only about one-half of each of the ASEAN countries' populations fell into this most productive age group. By the year 2000, however, each country will have approximately two-thirds of its population in the 15–64 age group—the situation of Japan in the 1960s and 1970s. Thus, aging, which comes as a result of slowing population growth, will in its early stages in ASEAN mean an aging of the most productive group. This is good news for now. After the year 2000, more and more of the ASEAN populations will fall into the 65 and over group, and that will raise another set of issues.

In the next twenty years, therefore, the age distribution of ASEAN's labor forces will be more favorable. Nevertheless, I do not want to paint *too* rosy a picture of human resources in ASEAN economic development. There are still some important labor issues facing the ASEAN countries.

LABOR ABSORPTION

For Indonesia, the Philippines, and Thailand, the problem of labor absorption into the modern sector is still not solved, though it may have been eased with slower population growth. By making some assumptions about future absorption rates, that is, the growth rate of employment in the modern sector, one can approximate the date in the future when the size of the agricultural labor force will stop growing, as I have done in Table 3.19. This date or year is the so-called turning point at which absorption into the nonagricultural sectors of the economy is keeping up with the growth of the total labor force. The agricultural labor force is no longer growing and one would expect agricultural productivity to be increasing.

Table 3.19 Projections of the year in which the agricultural labor force stops growing, assuming labor absorption rates into nonagricultural sectors of two and four percent per annum, selected ASEAN countries

Country and percentage of labor force (LF) in agric. in 1980	2-percent absorption rate			4-percent absorption rate		
	End growth year	Percent LF in agric.	Agric. LF size[a]	End growth year	Percent LF in agric.	Agric. LF size[a]
Indonesia, 58%	2020	55	196	1995	48	120
Philippines, 46%	2020	51	268	1995	36	118
Thailand, 76%	2030	73	227	2010	60	152

Sources: L'_t: United Nations, World Population Prospects: Estimates and Projections as Assessed in 1982 (1985). The growth rate of the population 15–64 is used as a proxy for the growth rate of the total labor force for each five-year period.

L_a/L_t for 1980: World Bank, World Development Report 1984 (1984).

Note: The calculations are based on equation 2 below, which can be derived from the identity in equation 1:

$$(1) \ L'_t * L_t = L'_a * L_a + L'_n * L_n$$
$$(2) \ L'_a = (L'_t - L'_n)(L_t/L_a) + L'_n$$

where L_t is the total labor force and L'_t is its growth rate,
            L_a is the agricultural labor force and L'_a is its growth rate, and
            L_n is the nonagricultural labor force and L'_n is its growth rate.

[a] Index of agricultural labor force size (1980=100).

For these projections, I have used two different scenarios: (1) that non-agricultural employment grows at only 2 percent annually and (2) that it grows at a 4-percent rate. (Actual rates in the 1970s were probably in the 2- to 5-percent range for the ASEAN countries.) Also shown in the table is the percentage of the labor force in agriculture at the turning-point year, plus an index showing how the size of the agricultural labor force in that turning-point year compares with 1980.

Obviously the 4-percent absorption rate leads to earlier turning points —25 years earlier for Indonesia and the Philippines and 20 years earlier for Thailand. Also significant are the differences in ultimate percentages of the labor force in agriculture and in the size of the agricultural labor force. The case of the Philippines, which faces the fastest growing population among the ASEAN countries in the coming years, is especially striking. If only a 2-percent absorption rate is achieved, there will be an increase in the proportion in agriculture from 46 percent in 1980 to 51 percent in the year 2020. In all other cases the proportion in agriculture declines from 1980. Furthermore, for the Philippines in the 2-percent case, in the year 2020 when the agricultural labor force stops growing, there will be over two-and-a-half times more agricultural workers than there were in 1980.

Of course, these turning points are just estimates, and agricultural productivity is certainly being increased without a cessation of growth of the agricultural labor force. Nevertheless, I think that the projection exercise underscores the importance of providing more nonagricultural employment opportunities, as Naya stresses. Labor absorption is largely a labor demand issue, now that fertility is being controlled and the population component of labor force *supply* is more predictable. So whether or not these turning points will be reached sooner or later hinges on trade and industrial policy and the operation of capital and labor markets.

Foreign investment also has a role to play in the pace of labor absorption into the modern sector. As labor forces of the more developed countries of the world have become more expensive, these countries have looked to the poorer countries as sources of cheap labor. Indonesia, the Philippines, and Thailand remain fairly inexpensive sources of labor, but certainly Singapore and to some extent Malaysia are beginning to lose their competitive advantage in this respect.

INTRA-ASEAN LABOR MIGRATION

This raises a second important issue with regard to the labor situation in ASEAN: that of labor *shortages* in Malaysia and Singapore. Singapore views Malaysia as a source of skilled labor, at a time when Malaysia is turning to workers from Indonesia, the Philippines, and Thailand. Recent estimates of the size of intra-ASEAN labor migration (Stahl 1985) indicate that Malaysia is the largest receiving country yet provides the largest amount of foreign labor of all the ASEAN countries to Singapore.

Malaysia faces labor shortages in agriculture, construction, and textile manufacturing. The shortage in the agriculture sector is the most serious, since workers are attracted to better opportunities requiring less physical effort in the cities of Malaysia, as well as being attracted to the higher wages in Singapore. Of course, with the current economic slowdown in Singapore, some of these Malaysians may return home, but no doubt there will be additional labor migration in the future.

There has been considerable talk recently about ASEAN–Pacific Cooperation under the auspices of a Human Resources Development Project. This project was proposed at the 6 + 5 meeting after the July 1984 ASEAN Foreign Ministers' meeting in Jakarta. If I could propose topics for consideration for this project, high on my list would be the issue of the costs and benefits of labor migration for the sending and receiving countries of ASEAN. In Chapter 2, Wong and Cheung raise questions about labor migration to the Middle East, but questions about migration within ASEAN should also be posed: Is there any way Singapore could compensate Malaysia for the human capital investment that Malaysia makes in its labor force, which Singapore subsequently uses? What should be done to regularize the situation of illegal Indonesian migrants in Malaysia? Does such migration simply delay needed adjustments in the receiving country, such as higher wages and shifts to more capital-intensive production? How can education and training programs be designed to meet the labor demand that exists in each country? These are just a few of the questions that could profitably be addressed in reviewing human resource development in the ASEAN countries.

REFERENCE

Stahl, Charles W.
  1985 Labor Migration Amongst the ASEAN Countries. In P. M. Hauser, D. B. Suits, and N. Ogawa (eds.), *Urbanization and Migration in ASEAN Development.* Tokyo: Nihon University.

CHAPTER 4

ASEAN ECONOMIC
COOPERATION

ASEAN
Economic Cooperation

NARONGCHAI AKRASANEE

The Association of Southeast Asian Nations is an economic grouping of considerable size. All of its members belong to the middle-income group of countries, with large foreign sectors by world standards, and until recently, they have experienced very high economic growth rates, averaging between 5 and 9 percent per annum. This impressive growth has been attributed to an orientation toward exports and a high rate of saving plus, for Indonesia and Malaysia, the high price of petroleum in the 1970s. The countries are therefore dynamic and relatively open, possess strong potential for attaining a high standard of living, and thus have an important role to play in the international economic community.

Impressive growth performance does not, of course, mean that the ASEAN countries are free of economic problems. In fact, in 1984 and 1985 there were signs of economic slowdown. Two basic economic problems underlie the development strategies of the six countries. First is the need for foreign exchange to finance imports of food, energy, and capital goods. Second is the need to raise the living standard of the people and to provide employment opportunities in all of the countries, though this problem has perhaps been solved in Singapore. These two problems have led to the adoption of export-promotion and industrialization policies, though sometimes with different approaches. In later sections it will be shown how these policies affect the viability of ASEAN ideas for regional economic cooperation.

More than nine years have passed since ASEAN took the first concrete steps toward regional economic cooperation, with the Declaration of ASEAN Concord in February 1976 (ASEAN 1977a:111–116). Since

---

This paper is an update of an earlier paper by the author published as *Asian Development Bank Economic Staff Paper* 23, November 1984.

then, various mechanisms to promote economic cooperation have been set up, including five economic committees and other task forces and agreements. In pursuit of economic cooperation, ASEAN activities have proliferated; but the measurable outcome has not been commensurate with the effort. This chapter assesses and analyzes ASEAN achievement in economic cooperation, and recommends new or improved approaches.

In degree as well as in form, ASEAN economic cooperation will have effects on the internal development and on the external relations of the ASEAN countries individually and as a group. In the following pages, it will be shown that ASEAN economic cooperation has an impressive record of performance in projects mainly requiring a pooling of resources. But when sharing of markets is at issue, the projects so far devised have not been effective, basically because no definite goals have been set. The findings suggest that ASEAN at this stage is only committed to building up the conditions and institutional infrastructure considered necessary for practical and efficient economic integration, without defining what such integration really means. A complete sharing of markets is still considered by ASEAN to be not practical at present, due to differences in the perception of the process of economic development and the limited degree of economic complementarity among the member countries.

This approach toward regional cooperation might once have been appropriate, considering the different stages of economic development of the member countries. But the rapidly changing international economic environment makes it necessary for ASEAN to accelerate the progress of economic cooperation. To do so, cooperation must have a target as well as a time frame; schemes need to be designed so that common interest is maximized and potential conflicts of interest minimized, all within the existing financial, human, and organizational framework.

The first section reviews the history of ASEAN economic cooperation; its objectives, instruments, and mechanisms. The results of cooperation are then assessed, and contributing factors are analyzed. The last two sections outline recommendations for future cooperation and possible new developments.

COMMITMENT TO ECONOMIC COOPERATION

While ASEAN regionalism could be said to have begun with the formation of ASEAN in 1967, the real commitment to regional cooperation, especially in economic areas, actually started after the summit of ASEAN heads of government in Bali, Indonesia in February 1976 (the Bali Summit). At the summit the following major decisions, which had implications for economic cooperation, were made (ASEAN 1977a):

1. To sign the Declaration of ASEAN Concord;
2. To establish an ASEAN Secretariat, including an economic bureau, in Jakarta;
3. To streamline ASEAN economic committees to promote economic cooperation; and
4. To assign individual countries to represent ASEAN in its dialogue with developed countries and international organizations.

These decisions could not have been reached without a certain degree of economic regionalism. The nature of the commitment, in terms of its objectives and the mechanisms set up to achieve them, is reviewed below.

Objectives

The main economic objectives of ASEAN since its inception have been to promote "prosperity and the welfare of the peoples of member states." These objectives are elaborated in several sections of the Declaration of ASEAN Concord as follows (ASEAN 1977a:11, italics added):

1. "The elimination of poverty, hunger, disease and illiteracy is a primary concern of member states. *They shall therefore intensify cooperation in economic and social development,* with particular emphasis on the promotion of social justice and on the improvement of the living standards of their peoples.
2. "Member states shall take *cooperative action in their national and regional development programmes,* utilizing as far as possible the resources available in the ASEAN region to broaden the complementarity of their respective economies.
3. "Member states shall *strive, individually and collectively* to create conditions conducive to the promotion of peaceful cooperation among the nations of Southeast Asia *on the basis of* mutual respect and *mutual benefit.*
4. "Member states shall vigorously develop an awareness of regional identity and exert all efforts to create a strong *ASEAN community,* respected by all and respecting all nations on the basis of mutually advantageous relationships, and in accordance with the principles of self-determination, *sovereign equality* and non-interference in the internal affairs of nations."

The objectives as spelled out in the declaration indicate intent to promote economic growth and development in ASEAN countries by means of mutual cooperation, on the basis of mutual benefit and sovereign equality. Economic cooperation is a means to an end; that is, economic progress in individual member countries. These objectives are also repeated in the Treaty of Amity and Cooperation in Southeast Asia, signed at the Bali Summit (ASEAN 1977a:119–120). The economic regionalism underlying these objectives exists to the extent that the member countries believe they have enough interests in common for cooperation to be of mutual benefit. The projects introduced at that time, and their subsequent record of achievement (or lack of it), also reflect the extent of economic regionalism of ASEAN.

INSTRUMENTS AND MECHANISMS

The ASEAN Concord officially established the *modus operandi* of subregional cooperation in all spheres including economics, in which four major areas of cooperation were defined:
1. cooperation in basic commodities, particularly food and energy;
2. industrial cooperation;
3. cooperation in trade; and
4. joint approaches to international commodity problems.

In addition, the concord established the Meeting of ASEAN Economic Ministers as the highest institution to implement economic cooperation programs, and the ASEAN Secretariat to facilitate all aspects of cooperation.

Since the declaration was signed, ASEAN has continued to develop and refine its instruments and mechanisms for economic cooperation, as summarized in the following sections.

Instruments for Industry, Minerals, and Energy

ASEAN members agreed to cooperate in the establishment of large-scale industrial plants to produce essential commodities, particularly to meet regional requirements. The instrument, known as the ASEAN Industrial Project (AIP), provides for the allocation of a project to a member country. In addition, an ASEAN Industrial Complementation scheme (AIC) was introduced to promote exchange of industrial products among member countries in order to facilitate an economic scale of production. And in 1982, the ASEAN Industrial Joint Venture (AIJV) was introduced to promote joint investment among the private sectors of member countries.

In energy, ASEAN has agreed to accord priority to an individual member's needs in critical circumstances and priority for the acquisition of exports from member states.

Instruments for Trade and Tourism

The Preferential Trading Arrangements (PTAs) promote intra-ASEAN trade through preferential tariffs, long-term quantity contracts, preferential terms for the financing of imports, preferential procurement by government agencies, and the liberalization of non-tariff barriers.[1] PTAs are intended to promote intra-ASEAN trade in basic commodities as well as in industrial products. They therefore complement the instruments in industrial cooperation and cooperation in basic commodities.

Cooperation in trade includes trade with non-ASEAN countries. The instrument used for this purpose is part of the dialogue with third countries, discussed later in this chapter.

ASEAN members have also agreed to cooperate in the area of tourism but no specific instrument has yet been formulated.

Instruments for Food, Agriculture, and Forestry

Besides an agreement to accord priority to member countries in food trade, a food security reserve scheme has been set up to provide food security to them. Other instruments for cooperation in food, agriculture, and forestry concern the supply and procurement of fertilizer and pesticides, the ASEAN Common Agricultural Policy (ACAP), a common stand on international agricultural matters, and cooperation in the fields of fisheries and forestry (ASEAN Secretariat 1982).

Instruments for Transportation and Communication

Agreements include the exchange of views and information; promotion of closer cooperation in and establishment and development of joint technical programs; review, reconciliation, and collation of the various projects under consideration by ASEAN; coordination of plans and activities; and recommendations on measures for cooperation, standardization, the development of training, and the exchange of experts.[2]

Instruments for Finance and Banking

Cooperation includes the financing of the AIPs and the promotion of financial instruments to expand ASEAN trade and investment. Some of

---

1. The Agreement on Preferential Trading Arrangements was signed by the ASEAN countries on 24 February 1977 in Manila. See Tan (1982).
2. Terms of reference for the establishment of the Committee on Transportation and Communications, 1977.

these have already been devised, e.g., instruments of the central banks and monetary authorities such as the ASEAN Swap Arrangement, tax and customs matters, insurance issues, fiscal and non-fiscal incentives for AIPs, and the establishment of the ASEAN Finance Corporation to finance ASEAN joint ventures.

Instruments for Relations with Third Countries and Parties

In order to promote more effective participation in international economic affairs, ASEAN has established a formal dialogue with third countries and has tried to adopt a joint approach to international economic problems and issues. A member country is assigned responsibility for the ASEAN dialogue with a third country and/or party. The original arrangement was: Indonesia—Japan and the European Economic Community (EEC); Malaysia—Australia and West Asian countries; Philippines—United States and Canada; Singapore—New Zealand; Thailand—United Nations Development Program (UNDP) and the Economic and Social Commission for Asia and the Pacific (ESCAP). These dialogues occur individually and jointly following the annual meeting of ASEAN ministers of foreign affairs.

Instruments for Participation of the Private Sector

The private sectors of ASEAN have been cooperating fully in trade and industry through the ASEAN Chamber of Commerce and Industry (CCI), established in 1972, and through numerous industry groups. The ASEAN CCI has several working groups that cooperate among themselves and work with ASEAN trade and industry officials.

Mechanisms

Since the Bali Summit, ASEAN has reorganized its economic cooperation mechanisms. The highest level is now the Meeting of ASEAN Economic Ministers (AEM), which takes place twice a year, hosted by a member country on a rotation basis. Below the AEM are five economic committees, each served by an interim technical secretariat (ITS) hosted by the member country appointed to be chairman of the committee. The present arrangement is as follows:

- Committee on Industry, Minerals and Energy (COIME)—Philippines
- Committee on Trade and Tourism (COTT)—Singapore
- Committee on Food and Forestry (COFAF)—Indonesia

- Committee on Transportation and Communications (COTAC)—Malaysia
- Committee on Finance and Banking (COFAB)—Thailand.

Below each committee are numerous subcommittees, expert groups, and working groups, which together with the ITS prepare issues and positions to be discussed and negotiated by the committee. The committee usually meets twice a year and the hosting is rotated. Thus, at all times there are several ASEAN economic meetings taking place, all culminating in their respective committee meetings and finally in the AEM. The committee meetings can be at ministerial or lower level.

As mentioned, the AEM is the highest institution for economic cooperation. But before a treaty or agreement is signed it must be endorsed by the ministers of foreign affairs at an ASEAN Ministerial Meeting (AMM).

In each member country all ASEAN-related matters are coordinated by an ASEAN national secretariat.

The ASEAN Secretariat in Jakarta is supposed to coordinate all ASEAN matters at the regional level. The secretariat is headed by the Secretary-General, assisted by the Economic Bureau Director and the directors of three other bureaus. Because of shortage of staff, the secretariat has not been able to coordinate ASEAN economic programs at the regional level, nor has it been able to provide technical inputs to the various committees. But recently ASEAN has approved the appointments of five additional economic officers and it is expected that the secretariat will gradually take over the role of the ITS of each committee.

AN ASSESSMENT OF ASEAN ECONOMIC COOPERATION

Since the establishment of ASEAN, and especially after the Bali Summit, a great deal of effort has been made to realize the objectives of economic cooperation as set out in the various declarations, particularly those in the ASEAN Concord. While the work of the different committees has varied in degree of achievement, certain common factors have influenced performance in all economic fields. The record of achievement is summarized below by area; the next section then analyzes the factors underlying ASEAN economic cooperation.

INDUSTRY, MINERALS, AND ENERGY

Work on cooperation in industry, minerals, and energy has been carried out by COIME, whose chairman and ITS are in the Philippines. Effort has mostly been in the area of industrial cooperation and has taken the form of making arrangements for AIPs, AIC, and more recently, AIJV.

The AIP concept was proposed as early as 1973 by a United Nations study (United Nations 1974) and officially adopted at the Bali Summit in 1976. To date, four AIPs have been identified and are at various stages of implementation. These are: the ASEAN Urea Projects in Indonesia and Malaysia, the ASEAN Rock Salt-Soda Ash Project in Thailand, and the ASEAN Copper Fabrication Project in the Philippines. Implementation of AIPs is governed by the Basic Agreement on ASEAN Industrial Projects (BAAIP), ratified in March 1980. AIPs are based on the principles of resource pooling and market sharing. The host country takes up 60 percent of the equity, with Singapore taking 1 percent and the rest shared equally by three other countries. The projects are based on the regional market, and thus market access is expected from all member countries.

Following the adoption of AIPs in 1976, it took four years for BAAIP to be ratified because of difficulties in reaching agreements on resource pooling and market sharing. The most advanced AIP is the ASEAN Urea Fertilizer Project of Indonesia, now completed. The ASEAN Urea Fertilizer Project of Malaysia is under construction. But the ASEAN Rock Salt-Soda Ash Project of Thailand has been scrapped. The Copper Fabrication Project of the Philippines was later adopted after a few other projects had been considered, but it is also unlikely to be implemented. Finally, Singapore has dropped the Diesel Engine Project assigned to it after the Bali Summit, and has not proposed a new Singapore AIP.

AIPs have been slow to be implemented, due to three major problems. First, it is difficult to identify a basic industry project that can be justified commercially and economically. Second, each government has different procedures for considering and approving actions needed for project implementation. Finally, every AIP requires a large capital investment, by ASEAN standards. Since most ASEAN countries have deficits in the government budget and current account, an AIP has to rely mostly on external sources of funds.

Unlike AIPs, the AIC and AIJV schemes initiated by the ASEAN CCI aim to provide opportunities for the private sector to undertake projects. The ASEAN private sector has been actively involved in the formulation and negotiation of the basic agreements governing the projects. Under the AIC scheme, firms in member countries are to produce complementary products in specific industrial sectors for preferential exchange among themselves. So far only the automotive sector has come under the AIC scheme. Of the two packages of automotive complementation products, negotiated over a period of more than three years, the first package covering existing automotive products has been implemented. The second package, covering new automotive products, was indefinitely deferred by the seventh COIME meeting in May 1982 pending a thorough review of the guidelines for product identification and allocation. In this respect, consultations have been conducted with leading car manufacturers on designing a brand-to-brand approach to automotive complementation.

The basic agreement on ASEAN industrial joint ventures as initialled by the AEM was finalized in October 1983. So far a number of projects have been identified but implementation has yet to be realized.

Cooperation in energy has been carried out by more than one ASEAN committee; at present reorganization is being considered. Starting with petroleum, the heads of national state oil companies at their meeting on 15 October 1975 agreed to set up the ASEAN Council of Petroleum (ASCOPE) to function as a forum and mechanism for regional cooperation in petroleum "in all its facets, including industrial and environment." Apart from ASCOPE, COIME takes care of cooperation in non-petroleum energy resources such as coal, geothermal, uranium, and nuclear power, and commercially nonconventional energy forms such as solar energy, biomass, and others.

However, another ASEAN permanent committee, the Committee on Science and Technology (COST), at its second meeting (Bangkok, February 1979) set up a working group on nonconventional energy research to focus on solar energy, bio-energy conversion, advanced coal technologies, wind energy, thermal energy, energy inventory and assessment, and micro-hydro energy. Again, to avoid duplication of COST's work with that of COIME (COIME 1978), it was later agreed that in the area of non-petroleum energy sources COST should handle energy sources still in the research and development stages.

This account of energy cooperation indicates that ASEAN is still in the process of devising effective arrangements. However, the energy crisis of 1979–80 was a test of the agreement to cooperate on basic commodities. At Thailand's request, Indonesia and Malaysia agreed to sell crude oil to Thailand at the rate of 10,000 and 5,000 barrels per day respectively at government contracted prices (i.e., without premium). Apart from this, the record of energy cooperation has mostly been in the form of conferences, consultations, and joint undertakings in research and development.

TRADE AND TOURISM

ASEAN cooperation in intra-ASEAN trade, carried out under the PTA reached at the third meeting of the AEM (Manila, 20–22 January 1977), has mostly been in the form of exchange of tariff preferentials (ASEAN 1977b). Since 1977, the tariff cuts have been deeper and wider. Starting with a 10 percent cut in tariffs for most products, the preferences are now generally 20 and 25 percent. In November 1982, the AEM agreed that they be raised to a maximum of 50 percent. Negotiations for tariff preferences started first with a product-by-product approach, and have since been complemented by across-the-board tariff reductions for imports below certain values, with a provision for an exclusion list of sensitive items. In April 1980, ASEAN agreed to make an across-the-board tariff reduction of 20 percent for imports with values less than U.S.$50,000 for each Brussels Tariff Nomenclature (BTN) classification in 1978 import statistics. In 1982, this ceiling was raised to include imports with values below U.S.$1,000,000 each. Subsequently, ASEAN agreed to raise the ceiling further. At present there is no ceiling, but items to be accorded preferential treatment have to satisfy various rules of origin specified in the agreement.

The record of performance in trade cooperation is one of tedious negotiations for tariff cuts, with little to show by way of actual intra-ASEAN trade expansion. First, the product-by-product approach in the form of "matrix" negotiation and "voluntary offer" lists has been found to be inefficient and time consuming. The recently implemented across-the-board approach has also met with the problem of the definition of "sensitive items," which in some country's lists has virtually eliminated all potentially tradable items. Thus, after eight years of PTA, the result has been growth in items accorded preferential tariff rather than in actual intra-ASEAN trade expansion. (The relative success in cooperation to promote extra-ASEAN trade is discussed in a later section.)

Cooperation in tourism has resulted from action taken in other areas. For example, the implementation of an "ASEAN Circle Fare" among ASEAN airlines has reduced the cost of intra-ASEAN travel. Permission to stay up to two weeks without a visa in a member country has made it easier for ASEAN tourists. Finally, related activities implemented by various ASEAN committees and organizations have certainly, as a by-product, promoted tourism in the region.

FOOD, AGRICULTURE, AND FORESTRY

The record of performance in food and agriculture may be seen in the activities of COFAF in general and in the establishment of the ASEAN Food Security Reserve (AFSR) in particular. COFAF has been implementing the following projects mostly with financial assistance from third countries or international organizations:

1. Regional seed technology program (New Zealand)
2. Plant quarantine training center and institute (PLANT 1) (United States)
3. Food-handling project (Australia)
4. ASEAN-EEC collaborative program on grains post-harvest technology (EEC)
5. Livestock and fisheries
6. ASEAN Agricultural Development Planning Center (United States)
7. Study on supply of and demand for food and other strategic agricultural products (UNDP)

In addition, COFAF has established the ASEAN Agricultural Research Coordinating Board to conduct research and development for crops and livestock. COFAF is also active in training and extension.

One of its major undertakings was the establishment of the AFSR, as detailed in the Agreement on the ASEAN Food Security Reserve signed on 4 October 1979 (ASEAN Secretariat 1981) under which member countries are to coordinate their food security policies. Rice, the staple food, was the first item to come under the scheme. A major component of the AFSR agreement is the ASEAN Emergency Rice Reserve of 50,000 metric tons, held by each member country as follows:

Indonesia	:	12,000 metric tons
Malaysia	:	6,000 " "
Philippines	:	12,000 " "
Singapore	:	5,000 " "
Thailand	:	15,000 " "

The AFSR agreement also includes a Food Information and Early Warning System for maize, soybeans, and sugar, in addition to rice.

All the activities of the AFSR are supervised by the ASEAN Food Security Reserve Board. The AFSR has been viewed favorably by other countries and organizations concerned with food security issues, such as the Group of 77, ESCAP, and the United Nations World Food Council.

TRANSPORTATION AND COMMUNICATION

Since the establishment of COTAC in 1977, a total of 114 projects has been identified, of which 26 have been completed. Work has been organized into four areas:

1. Shipping and ports;
2. Land transportation;
3. Civil aviation and related services; and
4. Post and telecommunications.

In each area the record of achievement varies. Several of the 34 shipping projects are under study, with financial assistance from UNDP. A priority project—the establishment of the ASEAN Liner Service or Joint Shipping Operations—is yet to undergo a feasibility study. A work program on land transportation for 1982–86 was designed to attain efficient use of existing land and inland waterways systems and improve auxiliary facilities, and to establish new land, inland waterway, and ferry links in the ASEAN region. Some projects, mostly institutional in nature, have been implemented under this program, while others are under study. In this area ASEAN has agreed in principle to the mutual recognition of domestic driving licenses.

Regional cooperation in civil aviation has a more impressive record. The ASEAN countries adopted common stands when confronted with discrimination in the Australian civil aviation policy in 1978, the Ho Chi Minh Flight Information Region (FIR) (former Saigon FIR), and West Germany's civil aviation policy. ASEAN also has several projects in civil aviation aimed at promoting safe and efficient air transport services.

Cooperation in post and telecommunications has an impressive record of achievement. Projects already implemented include the Business Reply Service, Inter-Country Remittance Services, use by other ASEAN countries of the Indonesian satellite, PALAPA, and ASEAN Cable Projects. ASEAN capitals are now connected by the submarine cable system, except for the Philippines–Thailand section, which is under construction.

FINANCE AND BANKING

Another active area of cooperation has been in finance and banking. As early as 1977, the ASEAN central banks entered into the Swap Arrangement whereby the member countries provide U.S.$200 million for short-term support. The private commercial banks have also been active in this field, having set up the ASEAN Finance Corporation (AFC) to finance joint venture projects. Besides ASEAN joint ventures, the AFC has established a joint venture with Japanese financial institutions to promote investment, finance, and trade between ASEAN and Japan. The AFC, together with the ASEAN Banking Council, is assisting in the development of other financial schemes to promote intra-ASEAN trade and investment.

In customs cooperation, an important achievement was the signing of the ASEAN Customs Code of Conduct in March 1983. This sets out the common basic principles and standards for customs valuation, classification techniques, and related matters.

In the field of insurance, the ASEAN Insurance Council, a private sector organization that works closely with ASEAN insurance officials, launched in January 1982 an ASEAN Reinsurance Pool to facilitate an exchange of reinsurance business among ASEAN insurers.

In taxation, agreements on the avoidance of double taxation have been concluded bilaterally between almost all ASEAN member countries.

JOINT APPROACHES TO INTERNATIONAL ECONOMIC PROBLEMS AND DIALOGUE WITH THIRD COUNTRIES

ASEAN countries have been cooperating in efforts to protect the commodity export earnings of members and to stabilize the prices of primary commodities. These efforts have been exercised internationally through the United Nations Conference on Trade and Development (UNCTAD) and the nonaligned movement, and through dialogue with Japan, the United States, and the EEC. In addition to addressing commodity problems, ASEAN has also adopted a joint approach to other world economic problems such as the reform of the international trading system, the reform of the international monetary system, and the transfer of real resources.

ASEAN's activities in the field of commodities have concentrated on the UNCTAD Integrated Programme for Commodities (IPC) and the Common Fund. ASEAN is known to have contributed significantly to a number of agreements under the IPC, but their implementation has been delayed due to lack of cooperation from some of the more developed countries. ASEAN cooperation has been effective in the Association of Natural Rubber Producing Countries and in the International Tin Agreement, but its efforts to persuade Japan and the EEC to enter into an arrangement to stabilize export earnings have not been successful.

Dialogues with third countries were originally designed to improve access for ASEAN products to markets in those countries. They began in 1972 with the establishment of the Special Coordinating Committee of ASEAN (SCCAN) to hold a dialogue with the EEC, and by 1976 formal dialogues were established with several other countries and international organizations. The scope of the dialogues has since been expanded to include securing assistance for ASEAN development projects and pursuing ASEAN concerns with regard to international economic and political issues. While the dialogues have been useful in providing a channel for ASEAN to receive technical assistance from third countries and parties, which had amounted to about U.S.$100 million as of early 1983, the ASEAN economic and foreign ministers have expressed concern that the diffusion of dialogue activities has had the effect of reducing the effectiveness of dialogue in terms of its original objective of improving market access for ASEAN products (ASEAN Secretariat 1983).

FACTORS AFFECTING COOPERATION

Factors that might explain the past record of ASEAN economic cooperation can be grouped according to certain general factors as well as factors specific to a scheme. We discuss these factors in turn.

General Factors

Economic Regionalism

Behind all aspects of economic cooperation lies the political will to cooperate. The political will of the member countries towards economic regionalism can be gauged by their degree of willingness to share markets and pool resources through special or preferential economic relations. Such arrangements imply a degree of discrimination against nonmembers of the regional group.

At present, ASEAN seems to favor closer cooperation rather than economic integration. ASEAN is willing to pool resources, but is ready to share markets only to a small extent. National priorities and sovereignty come before regional priorities, which become such only if they coincide with or are supportive of national priorities.

These priorities explain much about ASEAN's attempts at economic cooperation. Industrial cooperation involving only joint investment succeeds, but when markets have to be shared cooperation either breaks down or is subject to prolonged negotiation. The diesel engine project, one of the original AIPs, was dropped because certain member countries were not willing to share their markets. Negotiations on AIC were prolonged in the case of the complementation scheme for the automotive industry, for the same reason. Preferential tariff agreements have had very little impact on intra-ASEAN trade because member countries, in the process of negotiation, have attempted to protect their domestic producers from competition. Moreover, governments' reluctance to set final goals and a time frame for PTA made negotiations even more difficult.

On the other hand, cooperation schemes involving mainly a pooling of resources have found willing acceptance, as have schemes designed to bring member countries closer. Evidence can be seen in the various schemes for cooperation in food and agriculture, transportation and communication, and finance and banking, and in joint approaches to relations with third countries and international organizations. Some examples of successful schemes are the AFSR of COFAF, the AFC and ASEAN Swap Arrangement of COFAB, the policy on civil aviation of COTAC, and the economic cooperation agreement reached with the EEC. In addition, ASEAN citizens have been brought closer together by the formation of numerous nongovernmental organizations (numbering at least 30), all of which undertake multiple activities.

Economic Complementarity

Intra-ASEAN economic activities can be self-generating if member countries' economies are complementary to each other. But the extent of such complementarity is limited. When it exists, cooperation schemes have been found to be worthwhile and agreements easy to reach. The AFSR was possible because Thailand has a surplus of food, especially rice, while Malaysia, Singapore, and Indonesia have deficits. Oil for Thailand during an emergency was facilitated because Indonesia and Malaysia were in surplus.

Cooperation in industry and trade (especially in manufactured goods) has been slow to materialize, however, because the industrial output of member countries is similar. Singapore is industrially the most advanced, but the margin is not great compared with other ASEAN countries. In general, similar products are being manufactured in all ASEAN countries. If a product is not being produced in one member country at a given point in time, the chances are that it soon will be. At low levels of income this pattern of production does not lead to trade. The policy of import substitution followed by all ASEAN countries except Singapore further reinforces the noncomplementarity of industry. Since decisions to invest are based on the protection of domestic markets, any attempt to lower the protective level to allow competition from other ASEAN countries would generally be resisted by domestic producers and hence by the bureaucrats.[3]

Another facet of economic noncomplementarity is visible in economic policy. In principle, all ASEAN countries follow open-economy policies; trade and investment supposedly being based on market factors. Thus, the ASEAN economies are more complementary to the more advanced industrial countries, as evident in the extent of ASEAN's trade and

---

3. Bureaucrats and businessmen in individual ASEAN countries usually do not support each other. But when it comes to the issue of market sharing among ASEAN countries, the bureaucrats have been known to have gone out of their way to protect domestic businesses.

investment with these countries. In other words, ASEAN economic cooperation is not usually considered as a variable when ASEAN countries formulate their economic policies. It is not surprising to see that the ASEAN CCI has not been too successful in identifying projects of common interest, after several years of trying.

To the extent that there is economic complementarity, intra-ASEAN trade has taken place. The trade in petroleum and rice are examples, though they too remain subject to the existing trading system. On the other hand, sugar is not traded among ASEAN countries even though Thailand and the Philippines are major world exporters while the other ASEAN countries are importers of sugar.

The similarity of economic structure—or lack of complementarity— among the ASEAN countries has had positive effects on extra-ASEAN relations. Thus, ASEAN has found enough common interest to enter into joint approaches on international economic problems, as already noted.

Financial Constraints

Financial constraints act upon ASEAN cooperation at both public and private sector levels. With the exception of Singapore, all ASEAN countries rely on import tariffs as a major source of government revenue, and finance ministries have often argued against tariff reductions for fear of a loss in revenue. Thai budget constraints were the major factor in the cancellation of the ASEAN Rock Salt-Soda Ash Project, which would have reduced tariff revenue for that country.

Another form of financial constraint is the limited availability of funds for ASEAN projects—COTAC, for example. In fact, most ASEAN projects have been financed by contributions from third countries and/or international organizations. Failure to secure funds from those sources has caused project delay.

Within the private sectors there is still reliance on private capital flow from outside the region—mainly the advanced industrialized countries— in addition to locally generated capital. (The ASEAN private sectors do not possess enough surplus funds to invest in other countries, except in a few special cases.) Predictably, direct foreign investment in ASEAN fosters closer trade and investment ties with the investor countries.

Organization and Personnel

The ASEAN organization as it exists today makes meaningful economic cooperation difficult to achieve. Lack of technical staff to serve economic committees means that the committees must rely on a series of discussions, consultations, or negotiations by working groups, expert groups, or subcommittees, all of which involve international travel. Since most decisions are by consensus, all countries have to be represented. The difficulty in setting dates for ASEAN meetings is well known. In consequence projects inevitably experience delay.

When decisions are, finally, reached at committee level, they have then to be submitted to the AEM, which meets only twice a year. If a proposal is not approved by the AEM, it cannot be considered again for at least six months. Even after the AEM approves a proposal, speed of implementation will depend on processing at member-country level.

The ASEAN Secretariat has not been able to help much in the ASEAN decision-making process; its professional economic officers can do little more than monitor the work of the various economic committees.

SPECIAL FACTORS

Industrial Cooperation

Programs to promote industrial cooperation have been undertaken through AIPs and AIC; the agreement on AIJV has just been signed at the time of writing. I review here only the reasons for the difficulty in implementing AIPs and AIC.

The first problem for AIPs is that of identifying suitable projects that also meet the basic criterion of distributing benefits equitably among the member countries. Another difficulty is that a potential AIP may be adopted as a national project, thus limiting the scope of regional projects that can be identified without affecting the national projects. In other words, the lack of commitment to "share markets" fully limits the potential AIPs. Finally, ASEAN still does not have an institution capable of identifying AIPs, nor does it have adequate financial resources to fund feasibility studies for them.

Having identified an AIP, the procedures to implement it cause further delay. Experience in the first two AIPs shows a three-year average period of gestation for individual projects before they are finally implemented, i.e., construction begins. The procedures start from the submission of the AIP proposal by a prospective host country, and then go through several steps including negotiations for the supplementary agreement embodying, among other things, the specific commitments of member countries to support the project and negotiations for financing. Such lengthy procedures allow little flexibility for the host country to proceed immediately with a project and can eventually affect its viability.

Besides project-identification and procedural problems, the financing of an AIP has also been a serious problem. Financing options are currently very limited, having to rely only on the U.S.$1 billion pledged by Japan.

An AIC scheme is faced with a different set of problems, but it is also limited by the unwillingness to share markets. A complementation agreement is negotiated by the private sector, after which it requires government commitment in the form of investment promotion and tariff preferences. The first problem in the negotiations is product identification, which is not unlike the problem in identifying AIPs. Then the governments have to make provisions so that AIC projects are viable. This step too takes much time. In the meantime a government may change its policy concerning the AIC scheme. The long and tedious process of AIC has very much disillusioned the ASEAN CCI, whose members are the participants in the scheme. And despite the attempts to introduce flexibility, e.g., requiring that only two to three firms in two to three countries be involved, the schemes still have not worked.

The AIJV scheme is new and yet to be assessed. Its advantage is that it is based on limited market sharing and on mutual interest developed by the ASEAN private sectors, which should overcome some of the problems faced by AIPs and the AIC scheme. So far no AIJV project has been implemented, due to several problems including the unwillingness of certain non-ASEAN partners to participate. Furthermore, the member governments are still reluctant to grant preferential tariff rates for AIJV projects.

Intra-ASEAN Trade Cooperation

Preferential tariff arrangements were designed to encourage intra-ASEAN trade. In the negotiations the member countries also expect equitable benefit, which is difficult to achieve because of the most-favored-nation implications of according preferences. Thus, the member countries try to maximize the gains and minimize the losses expected to result from expanded trade, with the effect that the preferences finally given do not usually lead to trade expansion. The present across-the-board tariff cuts are also ineffective, because the potentially tradable items usually end up on the list of sensitive items and are thus excluded from the preferential list.

Other Areas of Cooperation

While industrial and trade cooperation requires a certain degree of market sharing, other areas of cooperation usually require only willingness to pool resources. ASEAN has clearly demonstrated that it is willing to pool resources, but this willingness is limited by members' resource constraints that are not always understood. As a result, most committees come up with more activities than available resources permit and there is delay in project implementation generally, but especially in COFAF and COTAC projects.

Cooperation in fiscal matters, finance, and banking has not been extensive because the COFAB host country, Thailand, has not been very active in promoting its activities despite keen activity by the ASEAN bankers themselves. In the areas of finance and banking, however, the ASEAN system is well linked to the global system and the need for a subregional financial system is thus less pressing.

ASEAN's joint efforts in the dialogues and its joint stand with regard to third countries and international organizations on international economic problems, particularly commodities, have produced some useful results, but the general feeling is that the efforts have been too dispersed and the dialogue unproductive of results in the areas most crucial to ASEAN, i.e., market access and improvement in export earnings. The inadequacy of preparations for both the dialogues and the joint stands have further limited their usefulness.

RECOMMENDATIONS AND NEW DIRECTIONS

Economic cooperation should continue to be one of the most important aspects of ASEAN cooperation, especially in light of the new economic development, which has to rely more on scarce resources, modern technology, and factor mobility, and has to face an extremely competitive world market. If cooperation can conserve ASEAN resources, maximize use of modern technology, and foster greater flexibility and resilience, it will be less at the mercy of a rapidly changing world market environment. This result will be very helpful to each member country's economic development program, but to achieve it, member countries must include ASEAN cooperation as a key factor in their economic development system, just as they have in the case of political development.

For cooperation schemes to be effective, they must be based on the reality of economic nationalism and regionalism, economic complementarity, global economic trends, and financial, organizational, and personnel constraints. These require member countries to appreciate each other's national problems and priorities, and to understand the extent to which each is willing to share markets and pool resources, to share views on global economic trends, and to set priorities for ASEAN projects.

Based on these principles, realities, and constraints, the following recommendations are made.

GENERAL RECOMMENDATIONS

1. ASEAN should closely monitor the economic development of member countries subregionally, regionally, and globally, with a view to identifying issues for cooperation, common stands, and common strategies, and to avoiding potential conflict. The appointment of an ASEAN Advisory Committee on Planning (AACP), on a term basis, consisting of two economic experts from each country, should serve this purpose. The AACP should report its views and recommendations to the AEM on a regular basis, and should be available for consultation at short notice.

2. An important ASEAN strategy should be to continue to strengthen the foundation for closer economic cooperation in the future. Regional economic cooperation does not necessarily imply economic integration but it is the essential first step towards some form of economic integration, which may gradually become ASEAN's ultimate aim. In other words, economic integration should not be imposed on ASEAN at this time, but ASEAN should continue to develop the conditions that would facilitate practical economic integration. Such conditions would build up a stronger degree of economic regionalism, so making it easier for cooperation schemes to be implemented.

3. A harmonization of economic policies, to the extent possible, is essential for the development of complementary economic structures—the prerequisite for market-sharing arrangements. A selective import-substitution policy would contribute towards a more complementary economic structure among the member countries.

4. ASEAN is now in a position to commit more finances to economic cooperation. Reliance on external sources of funds to finance ASEAN projects has been found unsatisfactory. Internally generated funds should be the main source of project finance and the agencies concerned should simplify procedures for the use of ASEAN funds.

SPECIFIC RECOMMENDATIONS

ASEAN economic cooperation schemes should be considered according to their requirement for resource pooling or for market sharing. Resource pooling is generally accepted but there are still some reservations about market sharing. Schemes based on resource pooling can be designed to have full participation from all member countries. Schemes that rely on market sharing need to take into account differences in the willingness of individual member countries to share their markets. Industrial and trade cooperation require both the sharing of markets and the pooling of resources, whereas cooperation in other areas requires basically only the pooling of resources.

Based on the foregoing, the following recommendations specific to cooperation schemes are made.

Trade and Industrial Cooperation

Schemes to promote cooperation in trade and industry should be designed to provide ASEAN industrial enterprises with a market and/or resource base so that economically scaled and internationally competitive industries can be established. The external tariff proposed for "market-shared products" is intended only to give ASEAN products an initial pricing advantage, not to enable ASEAN industries to pass on their cost penalties.

Because of differences in the readiness of individual member countries to grant preferential treatment to other member countries and to participate in projects, special arrangements need to be made for PTA and AIJV, and the procedure for the implementation of AIP needs to be modified.

PTA. ASEAN COTT is now moving towards the creation of a Free Trade Area (FTA) by making a broader and deeper across-the-board cut in preferential tariff rates. The sectoral approach to tariff cuts is also being considered, but ASEAN has not set a time frame for the exercise. The process is likely to take a long time because of the shortage of technical personnel and the time spent in pursuing the traditional approaches to tariff cuts, i.e., matrix and voluntary approaches.

It could be more productive if ASEAN would drop the traditional approaches and concentrate only on the across-the-board approach. To do so it is necessary to set targets in terms of products and sectors to be accorded preferential tariff treatment, and in terms of the rates to be cut or the maximum rates to apply, all within a certain time period. The exclusion list should be allowed, but there must be acceptable criteria or decision rules for items eligible to be on the list.

The approach outlined here is not unrealistic. In fact, COTT has already started the process. What is required is a study on target setting and program phasing for across-the-board tariff reduction. In order for ASEAN governments to decide on targets, and considering the present politics of economic cooperation, it is necessary to show the implications of targets on trade creation and trade diversion, and on import tax revenue. Again, the implications of different criteria need to be shown. The criteria may need to be flexible enough to accommodate differences among member countries.

So far, other instruments of the PTA have not been used very much. It is recommended that ASEAN investigate the feasibility of using long-term quantity contracts, purchase-finance support, preferences in gov-

ernment procurement, and liberalization of non-tariff measures to promote intra-ASEAN trade.

In addition to the regular PTA, ASEAN should consider allowing free
trade of raw materials among member countries.

AIJV. AIJV products should be specific only to the (two or more)
countries that agree to list them. AIJV coverage is product-specific and,
for a specified initial period, should be source-specific to prevent
mushrooming of enterprises with excess capacities. The intra-ASEAN
uniform tariff rate for AIJV products should be the lowest possible. The
tariff preference should be country source-specific for three or four years.
The participating member countries should aim at establishing a common external tariff for the same product from non-ASEAN sources.
Apart from these conditions, the host country should decide on ASEAN
ownership requirements and there should be no fixed value added
requirements. Finally, member countries that do not initially participate
in an AIJV project may participate subsequently as long as they adopt the
AIJV specified tariff rates.

AIP. AEM has recently adopted a new set of policies and procedures
for AIPs. Basically, the new policies and procedures entrust the propo-
nent country with assuming the major responsibility for implementing a
project as a possible AIP. Later on, other member countries, who may be
encouraged by the initial progress of the project, could participate in the
project. As for financial matters, AEM has agreed to give the member
countries substantial leverage in negotiating with third countries or international financial institutions.

The AIP is a useful concept and cannot be replaced by AIJVs. Thus,
the new policies and procedures on AIPs adopted by the AEM should be
fully supported. In this regard it is necessary for ASEAN to formulate a
new legal framework for the implementation of subsequent AIPs embodying the new policies and procedures.

Regarding the first set of AIPs, member countries should give zero tariff rate for the products of these projects so as to ensure their viability.

Food and Energy

Food production in ASEAN countries has substantially increased and
ASEAN should cooperate to sustain this momentum. COFAF's efforts
should receive continued support. But COFAF should also check the tendency to proliferate its subsidiary bodies. The AFSR is a novel and useful

idea, and should be developed further. The food information and early warning system under the AFSR, which has been expanded to include maize, soybeans, and sugar, in addition to rice, is a step in the right direction.

The existing arrangement on energy cooperation, which assigns responsibility on petroleum energy to ASCOPE, non-petroleum energy to COIME, and energy research and development to COST, is appropriate and should be formalized. Energy is such a broad subject that ASEAN should consider appointing an energy officer to the ASEAN Secretariat to monitor the various programs of ASEAN cooperation.

Commodities

Because of the significance of commodities to export earnings, ASEAN should intensify cooperation on commodity issues, including research and development, some measures of market sharing, and the realization of a common commodity policy. Since negotiating performance up to now has not had the desired effect, ASEAN should devise strategies that will be more effective in international negotiations on commodities issues. To pursue new approaches as complementary and supplementary measures to existing international arrangements, ASEAN should focus on the ongoing efforts within the Association of National Rubber Producing Countries, and on the early establishment of an Association of Tin Producing Countries.

Transportation and Communication

Efforts in this field of cooperation should be directed towards practical benefits, such as the promotion of intra-ASEAN trade through such measures as lowering rates for cable, telex, and telephone charges among member countries. Contacts between ASEAN peoples through COTAC should be encouraged. Greater efforts should be directed toward closer cooperation among the airlines of member countries, particularly in coordinating schedules and pooling arrangements. COTAC's schemes on shipping and ports and land transportation are useful to the process of building up institutional infrastructure for economic cooperation.

COTAC, like COFAF, should concentrate on a few projects that have greater likelihood of successful completion. COTAC should be requested to identify such projects. ASEAN should encourage self-reliance in the funding of transportation and communication projects and seek third-country support only as a last resort.

Fiscal Matters, Finance, and Banking

Priority projects in this area should be the ones that will promote trade and investment. Projects under customs and tax matters identified by COFAB are very useful in this regard and COFAB should be urged to put more effort into implementing them. The creation and activities of AFC are most welcome. The operation of AFC, however, should be made very flexible so that it can finance a venture that has either ASEAN ownership or ASEAN markets (in at least two countries).

To promote future trade in ASEAN capital goods, ASEAN should consider establishing as ASEAN Export–Import Bank as a joint venture among all member countries. ASEAN should also adopt a more liberal policy to enable more ASEAN commercial banks to operate in member countries.

Machinery for Economic Cooperation

ASEAN should reorganize its machinery so that economic cooperation schemes can be implemented more efficiently. In principle, policy decision work should be separated from technical work. While the former is dictated by national sovereignty, the latter should be based more on professionalism. A second important principle is continuity in this work.

The top policymaking body should remain the AEM, unless merged with the AMM to form an ASEAN Council of Ministers. There should be an Advisory Committee on Planning to advise the AEM or the council. The ASEAN Standing Committee should be replaced by a Committee of Permanent Representatives of ambassadorial rank, to be appointed by their respective governments and located in Jakarta. The establishment of this committee would end the problems created by the existing rotation system of the Standing Committee. Below this level, existing economic committees should receive technical support from the ASEAN Secretariat instead of from the interim technical secretariats. Under this arrangement it would be necessary for the ASEAN Secretariat to be staffed by a sufficient number of professionals with technical knowledge in each area of economic cooperation. Such an arrangement would cut down the number of meetings of the various subcommittees and expert groups of the present system, and hence facilitate and accelerate the cooperation process.

ADDITIONAL THOUGHTS ON FUTURE DEVELOPMENT

It is clear from the preceding analysis that achievement in economic cooperation has been limited. And if ASEAN continues along the same path, it is possible that interest in ASEAN economic cooperation will fade away.

One can be skeptical about ASEAN economic cooperation, but one should also admit that future development seems to require more of it. ASEAN has perhaps also attained a higher degree of readiness for economic cooperation, which, if certain actions are undertaken, will be a means for internal ASEAN development.

The need for greater economic cooperation could arise partly from the following developments:

1. The world economy has been growing relatively more slowly than before and is expected to continue to do so in the next decade. This slowdown has created two conditions unfavorable to ASEAN. First, prices of commodities exported by ASEAN have either fallen or have not increased as much as prices of industrial goods. Second, competition among the exporters of manufactured goods has become more severe; too many countries are fighting for the slowly growing market. The obvious consequence of these developments has been slow growth of export earnings for ASEAN, thus inhibiting growth potential.

2. Technological development is biased against ASEAN's comparative advantages of abundant labor, raw materials, and fertile land. At present, the most rapid technological development is in the fields that save labor through the application of microelectronics; that save material, as evident in the production of new materials such as optic fiber, graphite, and ceramics; and in biotechnology, which has made land less important for food production. These technological developments could result in ASEAN's exports becoming less competitive.

3. Because of the economic and technological trends outlined above and growing national development requirements, it is now more important for ASEAN to optimize the use of resources. Market size considerations thus become crucial.

4. Now and in the near future, foreign investment will be attracted into the production of intermediate goods and machinery, both of which require larger-than-national markets.

5. Finally, ASEAN may need tangible evidence of economic cooperation in order to maintain the level of international support for some of its political objectives and goals.

Is ASEAN ready for a more meaningful economic cooperation? The answer depends on both political consideration and changing economic and institutional conditions.

• In terms of politics, one must try to read what the power groups in each country think of regional cooperation. In Indonesia, the armed forces and the technocrats are most powerful. Both groups seem to see regional cooperation as an important means to elevate Indonesia's role in the region.

The Malaysian power groups are UMNO (United Malays National Organization) and the technocrats, both of which seem to be more interested in nationalism than regionalism.

Politics in the Philippines are still fluid. The new political forces have first of all to put the national house in order, rather than work on regional cooperation, but the Philippines has demonstrated its strong interest in regional cooperation with other ASEAN states.

Singapore's only political force is the People's Action Party, which accords a very high priority to ASEAN cooperation.

Thailand's power groups are the army and the technocrats. The army does not seem to pay much attention to ASEAN cooperation. But the technocrats have made use of ASEAN to strengthen their stand on the Kampuchea issue, which is the total withdrawal of Vietnamese troops from Kampuchea.

Thus on the whole we may conclude that politically ASEAN would seem to favor a higher degree of regionalism.

• ASEAN's economies appear to have potential for greater complementarity. This is due to the fact that industrialization in ASEAN has gone into the second phase of import substitution, into resource-based industry, and into production for export, all of which would benefit from markets larger than the individual markets. Moreover, in the service sector, development is now taking place more and more in second-phase infrastructure, which is more commercial. Examples are the development of transportation and telecommunications. This type of infrastructure would also benefit from regional cooperation.

• ASEAN domestic savings are up, and more ASEAN business groups have funds to invest in other countries.

• There have been some improvements to the ASEAN organization. The ASEAN Secretariat now has more technical staff, thus it is more capable of serving the technical needs of ASEAN. The term of the Secretary-General has been increased from two to three years, beginning in July 1986, which should allow the Secretary-General to take more initiatives in promoting ASEAN economic cooperation.

It may be concluded that, on the whole, development has been favorable to ASEAN economic cooperation. But much still needs to be done. For that reason, there should be another summit of heads of state as soon as possible to decide on a new program of ASEAN economic cooperation.

REFERENCES

Association of Southeast Asian Nations

1977a Declaration of ASEAN Concord. In *Ten Years ASEAN*. Jakarta: ASEAN Secretariat, August.

1977b *Agreement on Preferential Trading Arrangements*. Manila, 24 February.

ASEAN Secretariat

1981 Agreement on the ASEAN Food Security Reserve. *ASEAN Documentation Series*. Jakarta: ASEAN Secretariat.

1982 *COFAF Cooperative Programme to Increase Production in Food Communities*. Jakarta: ASEAN Secretariat, December.

1983 ASEAN Relations with Third Countries/International Organizations. Document ATF/III/49/k, prepared for the third meeting of the ASEAN Task Force, Kuala Lumpur, 2–4 February.

COIME

1978 *Report of the Fifth Meeting of COIME*. Manila, April.

Tan, Gerald

1982 Trade Liberalization in ASEAN. *AERU Research Notes and Discussions Paper* 32. Singapore: Institute of Southeast Asian Studies.

United Nations

1974 Economic Cooperation among Member Countries of the Association of Southeast Asian Nations. *Journal of Development Planning* 7.

Economic Structure, Trade, and Cooperation

GERARDO P. SICAT

The progress of ASEAN economic cooperation can be viewed from several perspectives. The first is that the progress is quite satisfactory. In other developing country regions, economic cooperation among neighboring countries has not proceeded as well. Therefore, by this standard, it is possible to say that ASEAN is a worthy example of growing economic cooperation.

A second, entirely different, perspective is that ASEAN is not living up to the high hopes for greater economic cooperation envisaged in the region. A decade after the Bali Summit of 1976, there has been a loss of momentum—even a standstill.

A third, possibly equally valid, proposition is that ASEAN's pace is slow because it was not meant to go fast to begin with. By starting economic cooperation slowly only in areas where common ground can be established, the member countries are really assuring a future solid basis for economic cooperation. Going fast risks exacerbating differences rather than cementing the common grounds for meaningful cooperation. Considering the diverse backgrounds of the ASEAN countries, an effort to cement ties and create a common experience is more important than going full steam ahead with stronger forms of economic cooperation.

The last probably represents a majority view inside the negotiating panels within the economic ministers' meetings. It would further be the viewpoint of many in the inner circles of decision making who prefer to slow down the process because to move ahead would clash directly with national economic interests as perceived by them, thereby causing resistance to and criticism of movement in the direction of greater economic cooperation.

It is perhaps confusing that all three contradictory perspectives could be reasonable ways of assessing the ASEAN situation. Those who want greater economic cooperation in ASEAN are disappointed at the slow progress. Those who see greater gains from economic cooperation the sooner it is achieved include academics and business leaders, who view the gains from quite different perspectives—national and regional in contrast to private. Economic decision makers and other actors, including those outside the region who await more direct signals of ASEAN cooperation, are sometimes disappointed at their weakness.

On the other hand, the ASEAN decision makers trying to forge ties of economic cooperation are working through the maze of what seems feasible at this time. Their perception is probably more limited and therefore they consider the timing still not ripe.

Personally, I share the second perspective, but I also have some appreciation of the third. My own assessment is that now more than ever ASEAN should set bolder goals. I will review the current state of economic cooperation revealing, in the process, some defects that might be related to the current machinery. Finally, I will cite the factors that could promote greater economic cooperation within the region.

CURRENT STATE OF ASEAN ECONOMIC COOPERATION

ASEAN economic cooperation began very auspiciously in the mid-1970s. In five years immediately after the Bali Summit, the machinery of new economic cooperation produced a broad array of economic agreements including: preferential trading arrangements (PTAs), under which tariff concessions are negotiated periodically; food and energy cooperation, involving some understanding on forms of security from supply disruption; industrial cooperation of various forms; cooperation in finance; and cooperation in settling issues with third countries and in tackling international issues at world forums jointly or in consultation.

In all areas some progress has been achieved. But the greatest has probably been in the last area, because ASEAN seems to find it easier to reach common positions with respect to third, non-ASEAN, parties than among its members in matters involving trade-offs of costs and benefits in negotiating economic cooperation. In any case, dealings with third countries meant establishing direct communications links with important countries with which serious common ASEAN concerns could be consolidated. This has resulted in the conduct of "dialogues" with the United States, Japan, the EEC, Australia, Canada, and New Zealand. As a bloc, ASEAN is better able to gain access to the official opinions and reactions of these countries on issues of mutual interest. These include bilateral issues of trade, investment, economic cooperation, energy and other resources, industry, and agriculture.

For instance, approaches to the Multifiber Agreement have been partly aired through discussions of ASEAN with the United States, the EEC, and Japan. One particular successful joint action was over the airlines dispute with Australia, when the latter tried to protect its national carrier against competition from ASEAN national airlines operating the Australia–Southeast Asia–London routes. Through these dialogues, ASEAN concerns have also been communicated on such issues as the general system of preferences (GSP), the United States initiative on special trade preferences with the Caribbean and Israel, and on protectionist policies of the industrial countries.

Despite the relative strength of these joint actions, one could ask whether the position of ASEAN can be taken very seriously by third parties when within ASEAN itself internal economic cooperation agreements have lacked vigor and clear forward direction. One could argue that ASEAN positions on issues would become stronger if the other parties in these dialogues could sense full unity within ASEAN. It could be considered a sign of weakness within ASEAN when the economic cooperation schemes do not show sufficient vigor.

It would therefore be worthwhile to review some factors that account for the current situation of economic cooperation within ASEAN.

ECONOMIC STRUCTURE

Much has been said about the relative economic structures of the member country economies and their lack of complementarity. Whatever specialization has existed in the past, it is being partly supplanted by import substitution, hence causing trade substitution and diversion. The best example is the complementarity between Singapore, Indonesia, Malaysia, and to some extent Thailand. A lot of intra-ASEAN trade has happened in the past because of the entrepôt character of Singapore's role. But the countries in the region are developing industries that reduce the intermediary role played by the entrepôt trader. To the extent that the growing industries require certain inputs from some countries, there are products being traded to feed the industries of each of the countries. The fate of the petroleum refinery in Singapore is partly a result of the import substitution happening in domestic refining capacity for petroleum products in the other countries.

The peculiar position of some countries with respect to the rest accentuates the problem. Singapore, for instance, has a much higher income and is especially oriented toward the world economy. Its domestic market is relatively limited compared to the others. One reason it was not viable to set up a large ASEAN industrial project based in Singapore is that its only market are the ASEAN countries. On the other hand, it could not offer a market share for the products of other ASEAN industrial projects since, for the same reason, it has no domestic market for these projects. Therefore, it was a difficult proposition to get protection raised for the product of that project based in Singapore. The same problem could arise in at least one other member country, but among the larger ASEAN countries, the potential structural complementarity exists.

DIFFERENCES IN TRADE REGIMES

There is a marked difference in the trade regimes of the ASEAN countries. The larger countries are protectionist in their trade regimes. The smaller countries have low, if not zero, tariffs. They rely heavily on excise taxation but not on import taxation. The smaller countries are much more integrated therefore with the world economy than the bigger ones.

Structurally, this poses a problem for the preferential tariff agreement, which is a keystone of the trade agreements. A deep preferential tariff cut does not help the countries with high-tariff barriers if another country has zero tariffs. In the same way, the country with the very low tariffs stands to gain nothing from any percentage reductions in the tariff rates. Thus, Singapore and now also Brunei are very different from the rest of ASEAN. Even Malaysia, with its low tariff rates overall, is different from the three larger countries, which have fairly high tariff rates.

This problem poses the question of what compatible economic arrangement, which enlarges the market of the ASEAN countries, is feasible. A country used to free trade, such as Singapore, would have to face the prospects of erecting tariff walls. On the other hand, the countries with quite different tariff walls will have to harmonize theirs, either by erecting community free trade, without compromising their unequal rates, or by adopting a common market framework. The agenda for doing this cannot be followed of course unless there is sufficient political will, engendered by a willingness to compromise among the domestic interests in each country, in favor of some regional goals.

One of the suggestions that has been made to solve the impasse on this large, future issue, is to introduce a two-tiered economic arrangement in which the countries with the high tariff walls agree to some future commonizing tariff framework. With respect to the no-tariff country, the arrangement would be for a free-trade concept with the rest of the common market. This arrangement could be feasible only if precise rules of origin are developed, assuming they can be implemented, so as to protect the common market from the free entry of goods outside the region.

Of course, the above is already going too far into the future. For the moment the major concern is to improve the size and coverage of the preferences under the PTA with emphasis on the coverage. ASEAN unfortunately has been led to the preferential tariff route for items of trade that are minimal in the hope that working on these would permit the later extension to products of greater trading significance. It should be recognized now that if the PTA is to be made more meaniningful, ASEAN should consider moving into the items of substantial trade. Efforts to negotiate only a limited list of food items in the early period of PTA negotiations did not succeed.

Need for Visionaries in ASEAN

It can be said that the ASEAN efforts of the last decade may have instilled visionary concepts for improved economic cooperation within the region. Yet, one could ask whether the parties in the region have made enough efforts to carry out the agenda for a program of action. There is still a strong element of domestic policy concern on the one hand and some open internationalism on the other in the approaches to policy within the ASEAN countries.

One can argue that if the ASEAN countries fail to enlarge their cooperation schemes, each member country will be forced to direct its energies to its domestic economic base and its own foreign markets. The consolidation of the regional grouping therefore still needs a great internal push within and among the countries themselves.

One institution that could carry forward the regional trend is a periodic summit meeting of leaders. It is to be noted that since the Kuala Lumpur meeting in 1977 there has been no such meeting. So the interest in regional issues is not stimulated enough, because the national leaderships tend to concentrate on affairs nearer to home. The danger is that ASEAN could, by default, fail to move forward. The economic ministers need a new mandate to move. Whatever mandate they had was stimulated by the 1976 and the 1977 summits. The last summit also catapulted ASEAN to international prominence, as the leaders of three other countries—Japan, Australia, and New Zealand—made the pilgrimage to the ASEAN+1 summits in Kuala Lumpur.

There has also been a noticeable reduction in the bilateral exchange of visits between ASEAN national leaders. If the sense of community is faltering, some effort at resuscitating it is needed. More than ever, there is need to examine the alternatives for breaking the stalemate that has arisen.

There is certainly the need to focus on the most important instrument for bringing ASEAN economic cooperation closer, which is through a more general trade agreement with the objective of commonizing or reducing tariffs. Trade arrangements that reduce the barriers among ASEAN countries is the clearest demonstration of the regional spirit. The realities of the trade regimes being as they are, ASEAN is faced with the critical choice of continuing the stalemate or moving towards a time frame for future cooperation, in which some definite target of cooperative framework is envisioned. The catalyst for the cooperative framework to move is a major trade agreement, in which there is some idea of whether ASEAN would move or not to some form of common market, a free-trade area, or some combination of both.

Finance and Banking

VINYU VICHIT-VADAKAN

It has been said often that the ASEAN group has performed relatively well in global terms, even during the recent bouts of recession, and has been quite successful in coordinating its membership's political stands, especially on international issues at global conferences. However, it is generally believed that economic cooperation has not progressed as much.

Evaluation of performance is relative and in many instances subjective. It largely depends on the target to be compared. Because my expectations have not been high, I feel that ASEAN has achieved quite a lot. In the recent past especially, we have witnessed substantial changes and improvements in economic cooperation among the ASEAN member countries. The economic ministers have been meeting regularly twice a year for a number of years now. The ASEAN Urea Project is soon to be completed in Malaysia, and the Indonesian project has been completed and is in operation. Another important accomplishment has been the dialogue sessions with the industrial countries. For example, since the signing of the cooperation agreement with the European Communities, economic and commercial links between the two regions have expanded quite substantially.

There is one area, however, within the scope of ASEAN economic cooperation that has not been very successful: the area of money, banking, and finance. Several notable initiatives have been made to promote closer financial cooperation among the member countries:

1. The ASEAN Swap Arrangement has been, probably, the most successful attempt at cooperation in the area of money, banking, and finance. The five-year arrangement entered into in 1977 was renewed for another five years in 1982.

2. The private sector initiated the setting-up in 1981 of the ASEAN Finance Corporation for the purpose of financing ASEAN joint venture projects, but very little progress has been made.

3. The ASEAN Reinsurance Pool was launched in 1982 to facilitate an exchange of reinsurance business among ASEAN insurers. Again, progress has been slow.

4. In the area of customs cooperation, however, significant progress has been made with the acceptance of the ASEAN Customs Code.

The potential for development in finance and banking is becoming more and more apparent. The delay in the past has been due partly to the fact that cooperation among member countries was not really needed, as other alternatives were available that provided the same services at lower administrative costs. But the global economic situation in the past few years has changed the picture. We are no longer in a period of rapid expansion, and we are all short of foreign exchange. The global market is becoming more competitive and at the same time restrictive. There is now a need to look for an alternative that would save foreign exchange.

I suggest that consideration be given to reviewing the collaborative situation among member countries in the area of finance and banking. It may be useful even to look at some of the earlier proposals that have been rejected, including, for example, recommendations for:

1. The development of new financial instruments, especially the ASEAN Bankers Acceptance Scheme;

2. A feasibility study of a limited ASEAN Payment Union;

3. The establishment of an ASEAN Export–Import Bank; and

4. Policies to enable commercial banks of ASEAN countries to operate in other member countries.

Certainly, reservations have been expressed about all of these proposals. It was felt that the ASEAN Bankers Acceptance Scheme would not be workable without strong support and concessions from member governments. It was argued that the benefits to be gained from the establishment of an ASEAN Payment Union were outweighed by its cost, as happened in the case of the ASEAN Preferential Trading Arrangements. The same argument was made against the proposal to establish an ASEAN Export–Import Bank, particularly in the light of the existence of similar institutions such as industrial development banks in most of the member countries. The opening of branches of member-country commercial banks would go against the overall policy of most, if not all, ASEAN countries of building up domestic banking strength *vis à vis* foreign banks.

I am not sure that these negative reactions are well founded. Because a payment union would allow the settlement of intra-ASEAN transactions in local currencies, member countries could save foreign exchange. This is becoming more important in a period of scarce foreign exchange reserves in most member countries. A union would liberate intraregional trade from the constraint imposed by the need to use convertible currencies and would divert some of the existing foreign exchange transactions between ASEAN countries and traditional financial centers such as New York or London to within ASEAN, and thereby develop further banking connections among the ASEAN commercial banks. The banking industry in the ASEAN countries is quite sophisticated and administrative stumbling blocks would not be insurmountable. An Export–Import Bank would also facilitate and therefore promote trade with non-ASEAN countries. On the proposal to allow commercial banks of ASEAN countries to establish branches in other member countries, other alternatives should also be explored, such as granting the establishment of one new domestic branch to each country not already represented, or setting up an ASEAN commercial bank on a consortium basis where each member country would have equal shareholding.

The economic situation in the ASEAN countries seems ripe for further cooperation in the subsector of finance and banking, which has been very much neglected in the past. But any cooperative arrangement can only succeed if the benefits are mutual and not outweighed by the costs, and such cooperative arrangements are not easy to come by. Experience in ASEAN should already have taught us the lesson that quick decisions do not necessarily lead to positive results. There have been enough cases of decisions being reversed or not implemented because they were not well thought out. I submit that this is an area that needs further serious and in-depth study.

In conclusion, it is true that economic cooperation among ASEAN countries has not progressed as far as cooperation in politics or international diplomacy, but a start has been made and it is going in the right direction. Cooperative arrangements in finance and banking have lagged behind because of the lack of interest in this particular subsector, because of the absence of serious studies, and because the economic situation in ASEAN countries, up to now, has not made cooperative arrangements necessary. But I see challenge and potential in this area. The domestic systems in member countries are sufficiently sophisticated to make use of new developments, but options have to be fully explored, understanding has to be increased, and research and studies need to be made. Such steps would certainly improve the performance and competitiveness of the ASEAN countries—something needed now more than ever.

A Malaysian View of Economic Cooperation

PENG LIM CHEE

Before the onset of the current global recession, the Malaysian economy achieved a relatively high rate of sustained economic growth over a period of 20 years. Between 1960 and 1980, the Malaysian economy grew at an average real rate of 8 percent per annum. Per capita income increased from U.S.$371 in 1970 to U.S.$1,639 in 1980, representing a rate of growth in excess of 12 percent per annum. In short, for most of the last 18 years since ASEAN was established, Malaysia achieved a very satisfactory level of economic success. However, all this success has been due entirely to Malaysia's own individual national achievements and owes virtually nothing to ASEAN economic cooperation.

ECONOMIC COOPERATION

This fact can be clearly seen when we examine the pattern of ASEAN economic cooperation and its impact on the Malaysian economy. Consider, for example, ASEAN cooperation in trade and industry, the two dominant forms of ASEAN economic cooperation. Despite the launching of the ASEAN Preferential Trading Arrangement (PTA), which has now expanded to cover about 20,000 items, it has not contributed to any significant increase in Malaysia's intra-ASEAN trade. In 1984, Malaysian exports to ASEAN countries under the PTA were valued at less than U.S.$8 million or less than 0.05 percent of total exports. Malaysian exports boosted by the PTA were mainly small-volume deliveries of deodorized palm oil, cocoa beans, phosphoric acid, rubber gloves, non-motorcar tires, welding wire, specialized aluminium products, and air compressors. Apart from the limited range of export goods (only 60 PTA items), there was only a small number (35) of exporters using the PTA facility. Considering the low volume of PTA exports, it is not surprising

135

that the ASEAN PTA has failed to boost Malaysia's intra-ASEAN trade, which was valued at less than $7 billion in 1984 or less than 25 percent of its total trade. As a matter of fact, Malaysia's intra-ASEAN trade as a proportion of its total trade was higher *before* ASEAN was established.

There are many reasons for the failure of the ASEAN PTA, but suffice it to say that the two major reasons are the inadequate range of PTA items on the one hand and the high non-tariff barriers on the other. Despite the inclusion of so many items, the PTA still covers less than 5 percent of the traded items among ASEAN members. Moreover, the reduction of tariffs under the PTA means very little in terms of the actual advantage it offers. For example, a 20-percent cut on a 40-percent tariff gives the ASEAN exporter no more than an 8-percent tariff advantage over his non-ASEAN rivals, mostly from the industrialized countries. Many of the latter are strongly entrenched in the ASEAN market and have the resources to hold on to their market share by cutting profit margins, offering better credit terms, and the like.

More significantly, non-tariff barriers in the ASEAN countries pose an even higher impediment to trade than tariff levels. For example, Indonesia's handbook on customs rules and regulations contains over 500 pages, enough to frighten any potential exporter. In addition, customs rules and practices are not uniform and are difficult to interpret in many ASEAN countries. A simple illustration is the procedure for payment of import duty. In four of the ASEAN countries, import duty is paid to the customs office. In the Philippines, import duty is paid to the bank and only additional duty found to be payable when the goods are examined is paid directly to customs. Although there is little variation between countries in the type of supporting documents required with import entries, in some countries (e.g., the Philippines) an invoice is required only with the first copy of the entry, while the other countries (e.g., Thailand) seem to require an invoice with each copy of the entry.

Coming to the other main area of ASEAN economic cooperation, we can be a bit more brief since ASEAN cooperation in industry has had even less effect on the Malaysian economy than ASEAN cooperation in trade. This is because, of the five ASEAN industrial projects mooted in Bali in 1976, only the two urea plants in Indonesia and Malaysia have been implemented. However, the Malaysian urea plant would most likely have been established even in the absence of ASEAN. Moreover, Malaysia's unhappy experience with the urea project has persuaded the government not to participate in any future ASEAN industrial project on a government basis.

The ASEAN Industrial Complementation (AIC) scheme has fared even worse. Under the scheme, an impressive range of locally produced automotive components was allocated among the ASEAN countries, but this scheme has now been relegated to the dustbin of ASEAN cooperative efforts. All the ASEAN member countries, with the exception of Singapore and Brunei, are now promoting their own independent automotive industries in collaboration with their traditional transnational manufacturers.

To sum up, ASEAN economic cooperation has not made any significant contribution to Malaysia's economic development in the last 20 years. Unfortunately the same is true for the other member countries of ASEAN. In short, whatever economic success the six ASEAN states have achieved in the ASEAN era has been due almost entirely to their own individual national achievements. ASEAN has contributed virtually nothing to the economic development of the region. In view of this poor assessment, it is not difficult to understand why Malaysia, like many other ASEAN countries, has paid scant attention to ASEAN in its economic planning. Thus the Mid-term Review of the Fourth Malaysia Plan almost completely ignores ASEAN economic cooperation, holding out instead "the possibility of an indigenous technology" via increased manufacturing for export beyond the ASEAN region. In line with this thinking, Malaysian economic policies—such as manufacturing investment decisions—are increasingly based on hardheaded assessments of national interests rather than on any hopeful regional economic cooperation scheme. This result will be clearly seen in the soon-to-be-published National Industrial Master Plan.

Reflecting the disappointment of Malaysian policymakers about ASEAN cooperation, the local business press generally has carried little specific guidance on new ASEAN cooperation schemes. For example, there was hardly any attempt to analyze the implications or to explore the opportunities for Malaysian companies of the recently signed ASEAN joint ventures agreement.

In view of ASEAN's dismal record in economic cooperation, Malaysia is now putting greater emphasis on bilateral cooperation. For example, during his recent visit to Indonesia, the Malaysian Prime Minister said that Malaysia was considering cooperating with Indonesia in the joint manufacture of aircraft. A few months earlier, Malaysia had discussed the possibility of exchanging automotive parts with Thailand. While these arrangements are still taking place within the ASEAN region, they are taking place outside the ASEAN cooperation framework. If this trend in bilateral cooperation continues, the future of ASEAN economic cooperation appears doubtful.

However, despite its disappointing experience, Malaysia has not given up entirely on ASEAN economic cooperation. Indeed, ASEAN still figures significantly in the minds of Malaysian policymakers especially on issues related to international trade negotiations. In addition, there has been considerable success in ASEAN economic cooperation involving the pooling of resources, such as cooperation schemes in the areas of food and agriculture, transportation and communication, and banking and finance. Unfortunately, such schemes have had only a limited impact on economic development in the region. Consequently ASEAN has not emerged as a significant factor in the economic planning of any of the ASEAN countries, especially Malaysia.

RECOMMENDATIONS

Whether the present situation will change will depend on the further development of ASEAN economic cooperation. It would appear that the future of ASEAN economic cooperation will in turn depend on the extent to which the ASEAN countries are willing to implement the major recommendations made by the ASEAN Task Force.[1] Among the recommendations, the most important one appears to be a change in the organizational structure of ASEAN. The present structure does not facilitate the development of any meaningful economic cooperation. What is urgently needed is to strengthen the existing ministerial gatherings and the ASEAN Secretariat. More specifically, an ASEAN Council of Ministers should be established to incorporate the ASEAN foreign ministers', the ASEAN economic ministers', and other ministerial meetings as the top policy- and decision-making body of ASEAN. In addition, the ASEAN Standing Committee should be replaced by a Committee of Permanent Representatives of no less than ambassadorial level to be appointed by their respective governments, with a view to providing continuity and a better-defined direction to ASEAN activities.

Following its reorganization ASEAN should try to expand intra-ASEAN trade not only by increasing the scope of ASEAN PTAs, but also by removing non-tariff barriers. Items in the preferential-tariff-exclusion lists should be kept to a minimum while other instruments of the PTA, such as long-term quantity contracts, purchase-finance support, and preferences in government procurement, should be more actively used. At the same time, ASEAN should standardize and harmonize its customs and tariff nomenclature. At present, the national tariff schedules of

---

1. The ASEAN Task Force, composed of an academic, a professional, and a government official from each of the five original ASEAN countries, was formed in June 1982. Its objective was to review ASEAN's progress and propose ways to encourage development in the region. Its report was published in 1983.

ASEAN countries are compatible only up to the four-digit level. Beyond that, traders have difficulty identifying and matching items for classification and valuation purposes. Problems can also arise as interpretation of the national codes is subject to the discretion of customs officers. A prime example is valuation practices. In all ASEAN countries (except the Philippines), duty is assessed on a base price called fixed or indicative values in the docket system. Consequently, if the quoted price for the imported product is lower than the base price for that particular product, the import duty charges will still be based on the base price, and therefore, they are often referred to by importers as supplementary charges. This practice, referred to as "uplifting of duties," remains a sensitive problem for traders who are not always sure about the circumstances in which customs officials may impose an uplift on the invoice value. Equally important, an attempt should be made to persuade national authorities to relax local-content requirements specified by them for joint ventures or assembly operations to ensure higher locally added value. By agreeing to treat imports from ASEAN sources as local content, they would give a fillip to interchange of components. Since this boost will presumably help in enlarging production, both the importer and exporter stand to benefit from the economies of scale. This trade-off, on which the ASEAN complementation program is based, may be possible in segments of industries other than the few now under consideration.

Apart from expanding intra-ASEAN trade, the member countries should also broaden the scope of the ASEAN Industrial Joint Venture program and search for new ways to increase ASEAN industrial cooperation. Joint economic ventures undertaken on a regional basis should not be restricted only to industrial projects but should be widened to include other business activities such as agriculture, forestry, trading, shipping, finance, and banking. New ways to increase ASEAN industrial cooperation could include the streamlining of procedures governing approved ASEAN industrial projects and a zero tariff rate for the product of these projects.

To sum up, as ASEAN approaches its 20th anniversary, it can look back with pride on its achievements in political cooperation. But it is the region's economic development that people in the region are eagerly anticipating. The speedy implementation of the major recommendations made by the ASEAN Task Force will enable ASEAN cooperation to make a significant contribution to the economic development of the region. Otherwise, what we will witness in the next five years will be an increasing trend towards bilateral rather than regional cooperation.

CHAPTER 5
POLITICAL DEVELOPMENT AND REGIONAL ORDER

Political Development and Regional Order

JUSUF WANANDI

This paper focuses on three main issues of great relevance to the future development of the ASEAN region: problems of political development in the ASEAN countries; establishment of a regional order and its necessary institutions; and the presence and roles of the major powers in the Asia-Pacific region, in particular in the Southeast Asian subregion.

These issues will be discussed separately, though each influences the others. The first section deals with the central problem of national development in the ASEAN countries and the main challenges they face in their political development. The next section discusses the desire of the ASEAN countries for the creation of a regional order for Southeast Asia, as embedded in the idea of the so-called Zone of Peace, Freedom, and Neutrality (ZOPFAN), and the obstacles to its realization—mainly the conflict in Kampuchea. Political developments in the Philippines, which pose some regional concerns, and ASEAN cooperation and its future prospects—upon which the success of ASEAN largely depends—will also be examined.

The third section discusses the role and influence of the major powers in the Southeast Asian region. It examines the regional implications of U.S.–U.S.S.R. rivalry, the influence of Japan and the People's Republic of China on Southeast Asia, the role of ANZUS (Australia, New Zealand, United States Pact), developments in the South Pacific, and prospects for Pacific economic cooperation.

The concluding section suggests the importance of the Asia–Pacific region for ASEAN and *vice versa,* in terms of both politico-security and economic affairs.

The quite wide range of issues discussed in this paper cannot all be dealt with extensively. Similarly, while trying as much as possible to provide an ASEAN perspective on those issues, in some instances I am limited to a view from an Indonesian perspective. However, differences that exist between the two perspectives will be made explicit.

POLITICAL DEVELOPMENT IN THE ASEAN COUNTRIES

Since the 1970s, remarkable progress has been made in the ASEAN countries, not only in the economic field, but also in the social, political, and security fields. These achievements are all the more pronounced if viewed in comparison with other developing regions in the world, namely Africa, the Middle East, and even Latin America.

A number of factors explain the favorable developments but two stand out as most important. First, and foremost, is the ability of the national leaderships to properly assess the nature of the threats their nations face. As a result, all ASEAN countries give top priority to national development. The ability to properly set national priorities results partly from the existence of longer-established and better-functioning social and political institutions and government apparatus than was the case two decades ago.

The second factor relates to the relatively stable regional environment that helps support national development efforts. The stability not only of the Southeast Asian subregion but also of the Asia–Pacific region as a whole has been greatly enhanced by favorable developments in both Northeast and Southeast Asia and by national development efforts in the ASEAN countries.

These two factors are closely interrelated. In accordance with the ASEAN Concord, adopted at the Bali Summit in 1976, the main preoccupation of ASEAN leaders is to cope with internal challenges arising out of growing desires and demands of the populations, both in quantitative and qualitative terms. These entail not only more food, more clothing, and better housing facilities, but also better education and health services as well as greater participation in the political process, greater freedom in the pursuit of social justice, greater assurance in the application of the rule of law, and the promotion of democratic practices in general. The ASEAN leaders understand this to be their priority task in response to the main threat to their nations, which is still perceived to be internal in nature.

Compared with the situation about a decade ago, the primary internal threat to the ASEAN countries is no longer from insurgencies and subversion or infiltration in support of internal rebellions by separatist, religious, or communist movements. Internal insurgencies may not have been entirely eliminated, but today they do not threaten to topple the legitimate national governments. Therefore, they are of secondary concern as an irritant that may result in some diversion of resources from national development programs.

Nonetheless, the challenges faced by the ASEAN countries remain complex, since problems of development have become more complex and wide-ranging, encompassing simultaneously the entire spectrum of life—economic, political, social, and cultural. In the initial stages of national development, priority was given to economic development as a prerequisite to further development. Economic development is also seen as an important element in providing legitimacy to national governments, especially in developing societies, and has led to postponement of development in other fields for the benefit of longer-term objectives.

Economic development in the ASEAN countries since the 1970s has been quite successful and the prospects remain bright, although they currently are under immense pressures, largely due to the protracted global recession. The very progress in economic development, however, brings with it new problems: traditional values need to give way and adapt to new challenges and external influences. The emerging middle classes no longer are satisfied with physical and material developments alone and demand higher quality of life, which *inter alia* implies greater political rights, greater participation in the formulation of development policies, and juridical warrant. Economic development can never satisfy the entire population, since some parts of society will gain more than other parts and some may even be deprived in the process. Thus, sooner or later, social and political developments will be called for to rectify the side effects of economic development.

Social development should aim at the provision of minimum basic needs for each member of the society in health, education, and the like. The objectives of political development should be a system of government and a political system in general that accommodate both indigenous national values and international influences. The system that evolves from this process will not be the liberal democratic system as practiced in the West but will harmonize (just as Western systems aspire to do) individual interests with the interests of the entire community. ASEAN governments and social leaders should recognize that a system so conceived will evolve continuously in response to changing demands by a better-educated population and by the growing middle class, as well as to more intensive international relations and communication. Trial and error are unavoidable, but proper management will guarantee the necessary support of a majority of the population for both the process and its outcome.

Political development also entails the building of political institutions: the legislative, executive, and judicial branches of government as well as political parties and other mass organizations. Development of government institutions that function properly constitutes the most important element in the development of the national political system. A strong executive branch is necessary for national development, but at the same time it has to be balanced by an equally strong legislative branch, responsive to people's aspirations, otherwise the system will become too rigid and repressive. In order that the legislative branch can play its role, political parties and other mass organizations must be given room to develop. The judiciary should function as a respectful arbiter between conflicting interests in society, including between the government and the people.

The ASEAN countries fare rather well in their political development efforts in terms of the responsiveness of the political system to the demands of the people. Without popular support it is unlikely that their respective political systems could have survived the last 20 years. Undoubtedly, each ASEAN country still faces a host of medium- and longer-term problems, but the prevailing systems are likely to survive. (Current problems in the Philippines will be discussed in a later section.)

As in the case of the Liberal Democratic Party (LDP) in Japan, it is expected that the system of one dominant political party will prevail in Indonesia (GOLKAR, the functional group Golongan Karya), Malaysia (UMNO, United Malays National Organization), and Singapore (PAP, People's Action Party). One will also see a continuation of the political role of the armed forces in Indonesia and Thailand. The recurring question raised by Western scholars as to when the respective armed forces will retreat from their political role is not a relevant one so long as they can perform a role in the maintenance of internal political stability. Even in the Philippines, greater reliance on the military may be necessary in the future in view of the fact that the armed forces have become the only remaining power in the maintenance of internal stability.

Sociocultural development seems to be the most difficult task for governments in developing societies. Preservation of indigenous values in an era of rapid changes is an enormous task. However, Southeast Asians can be quite optimistic in this regard since in the past they have successfully gone through acculturation processes in which they absorbed some influences from Hinduism, Buddhism, and Islam, as well as from Chinese and Western cultures.

Despite the many shortcomings, the achievements made in the ASEAN countries have been quite remarkable if compared with the many failures and national crises of the past. The abortive coup by the Indonesian Communist Party (PKI) in 1965 was a culmination of government mismanagement in almost all fields of life. There are other examples from other ASEAN countries, perhaps less traumatic than the Indonesian experience, that might have resulted in national crises with disastrous implications had they not been overcome in time. These include the 13 May 1969 racial incident in Malaysia and the 1973 student rebellion in Thailand. Apart from the situation in the Philippines, no serious mismanagement problems exist in the ASEAN countries. Overall, they have been quite successful in responding to the central challenge of developing in a balanced and comprehensive way to satisfy the rising demands and aspirations of the people.

Balanced development in the ASEAN countries implies, first of all, economic development that adequately addresses distributional issues so as to strengthen national solidarity in the process. Efficiency principles, however, should not be sacrificed in pursuing structural changes in the economy or in promoting a more equitable distribution of the gains of development. The ASEAN countries have increasingly given greater emphasis to export-oriented industrialization in order to increase economic efficiency at home and economic competitiveness abroad.

Balanced development also implies political development. Currently, political development in the ASEAN countries is being pursued more seriously than 10 to 15 years ago, but the results thus far are mixed. In Indonesia, for example, GOLKAR needs to develop a mechanism to become more sensitive to the aspirations of the people and to increase its ability to balance the power of the bureaucracy and the armed forces, and thereby perform its social control function more effectively. The main challenge faced by Malaysia is the development of a political system that can harmonize religious and race relations within the society. The challenge to the new generation of leaders in Singapore is to adapt the PAP to the attitudes and aspirations of Singapore's younger generation.

One related and relevant issue often raised in discussions of ASEAN political development is that of prospects for smooth leadership transitions; how a younger generation of leaders will affect member countries' foreign policy and outlook. Malaysia has had changes in national leadership without political turmoil and without reorientation of foreign policy. In Singapore, a new generation of leaders is being prepared by the generation in power to take over in a few more years. The PAP is likely to remain in power, although it may no longer receive the overwhelming popular support it presently enjoys. Singapore's foreign policy is therefore not likely to undergo dramatic changes with the change in its leadership.

Thailand has not been able as yet to institutionalize a democratic process of succession. The abortive coup of 9 September 1985 may suggest that such events will not be tolerated in the future, in part because of the existence of a growing middle class and the establishment of more diversified political institutions. The undemocratic changes of leadership in Thailand in the past, however, were not accompanied by drastic alterations in foreign policy. Nonetheless, it may be worth noting that the so-called "Young Turks" in the military seem to have adopted "populist" attitudes that could lead to the formulation of policies—including foreign policies—that are based on narrow nationalism or socialism.

In Indonesia, generational changes in the national leadership have taken place already, both in the military as well as civilian establishments such as the bureaucracy, GOLKAR, and the political parties. It seems to me that the next succession of the presidency will not take place until 1993, and that therefore the country still has some time to prepare for a successor. What has become clearer over the last few years is the mechanism for succession: the candidate will be proposed by GOLKAR, and the election will be through the general assembly of the People's Consultative Assembly. The coalition of sociopolitical forces that support the future candidate will be the same as that currently supporting President Soeharto, namely GOLKAR, the bureaucracy, the military, professional groups, and the middle class, as well as a large fraction of the rural population. Therefore, no fundamental changes in foreign policy orientation are to be expected. Changes may occur essentially as a response to changes in the international environment, and nuances in foreign policy may reflect nuances in individual leaders' personalities.

DEVELOPMENTS IN THE SOUTHEAST ASIAN REGION

Toward A Regional Order

The desirability of establishing a new form of regional order in Southeast Asia has been expressed by the ASEAN countries in the so-called ZOPFAN (Zone of Peace, Freedom, and Neutrality) idea. In essence, it is a regional order in which Southeast Asians themselves maintain regional peace and stability and determine their own future.

The ZOPFAN idea implies the structuring of relations among the Southeast Asian countries themselves as well as relations with countries outside the region, the major powers in particular. It implicitly proposes a structure of relations in which none of the major powers will have a dominant position in the region and as such will remove from the major powers any opportunity or justification to intervene. However, the realization of ZOPFAN rests primarily on the successful development of

ASEAN national and regional resilience and should not be based on a *de jure* recognition of the idea by the major powers.

Ever since the proposal of the ZOPFAN idea, questions have been raised within and outside the region as to whether it is realistic. A closer examination of the objectives of establishing such a regional order suggests that its implementation could be gradual, since the goals involve various dimensions.

The first dimension is the creation of a peaceful and stable environment conducive for development. In the ASEAN subregion this goal has been achieved and indeed has greatly contributed to its remarkable economic performance.

The second dimension is the prevention of conflict among neighboring countries. The establishment of ASEAN has greatly enhanced mutual trust, mutual understanding, and mutual assistance among its member countries, which contribute to their ability to manage crisis situations that emerge among them, such as the border problems between Malaysia and Thailand.

The third dimension is the structuring of relations between the ASEAN countries and other countries in the region, namely the Indochinese countries and Burma. The Kampuchea conflict has become an obstacle to the realization of regional order. The Vietnamese invasion of Kampuchea has shaken ASEAN's trust and confidence in Vietnam, which are necessary for the creation of regional order. The Kampuchea conflict is also a setback to the attempts to structure relationships with the major powers, because some countries in the region have found it necessary to rely on certain major powers to safeguard national security.

Nonetheless, the ASEAN countries remain determined to work toward the realization of regional order based on ZOPFAN. The annual meeting of ASEAN foreign ministers in July 1984 reiterated the commitment to the idea. In his keynote address to the meeting, President Soeharto stated that "ASEAN is determined not to let itself become an arena of rivalry among the great powers, which is not at all in the interest of ASEAN. That is why we cannot sit idly in the face of a situation that threatens the peace and stability of our region." In fact, this commitment to ZOPFAN has been an important motivation for the ASEAN countries to continue efforts to find a political solution to the Kampuchea conflict.

Another dimension of ZOPFAN, which is of more recent origin, is the proposal for the creation of a Nuclear Weapon Free Zone (NWFZ) in Southeast Asia. This proposal, sponsored by Indonesia and Malaysia, was also endorsed by the ASEAN foreign ministers' meeting in July 1984. Efforts to elaborate on that proposal were not pursued due to controversy over New Zealand's decision to refuse U.S. nuclear-powered and nuclear-weapons-carrying ships entry to its harbors. The formula recently developed by the South Pacific Forum may provide a model for ASEAN. It proposes to define a nuclear free zone as that where no nuclear weapons are being produced and deployed by or stored in the member countries, but where each of them has the right to allow or to refuse entry to its harbors of foreign nuclear-powered and nuclear-weapons-carrying ships.

Toward A Solution of the Kampuchea Conflict

As things stand today, in mid-1985, there are only two realistic options for solving the conflict in Kampuchea.[1] Both are far from ideal.

1. Kampuchea will develop a status similar to that of Finland, meaning that its internal affairs will be determined by the Kampuchean people themselves, but they will have to involve Vietnam in formulating policies in the areas of defense and foreign relations. This solution requires a personality of the Sihanouk type as the head of the government—a person acceptable to all parties concerned, the Kampuchean people in particular, who at the same time understands Kampuchea's position *vis-à-vis* Vietnam. Sihanouk was in a position to perform this role well into the 1960s, although he had to allow Vietnamese forces to build sanctuaries in Kampuchean territory along the border.

2. The status quo will be maintained, ultimately leading to a *fait accompli*. A consequence is a continued large presence of Vietnamese forces in Kampuchea for the next five to ten years; that is, until the Heng Samrin government becomes sufficiently strong to stand on its own feet and prevent a return to power of the Khmer Rouge.

The second option seems more likely to materialize than the first, primarily because there are no incentives for any one of the parties to the conflict to change the status quo. A change of the situation in military terms may also be too costly, even for the Vietnamese leaders, who seem better able to understand the language of war.

Some argue that China and Thailand are quite comfortable with the status quo because it does not pose a heavy economic burden on them, and they believe that its cost will be even higher for the Vietnamese, both economically and politically.

Counterarguments suggest that a Vietnam heavily dependent on the Soviet Union is not in China's interest, and that improvements in China's relations with the Soviet Union in the future may require some accommodation with Vietnam. Equally, it has been argued that for Thailand con-

---

1. For earlier assessments see, for example, Wanandi (1985).

tinued military pressures on its border may not necessarily be preferable to a political solution along the lines of the first option described above. For the time being, the present situation may indeed help to strengthen the position of the Thai military in the country's internal political scene, but the medium- and longer-term implications for the country and the military itself remain questionable.

It can be argued, therefore, that it may be better for ASEAN to opt for the first alternative. This alternative should also be attractive to Vietnam since this scheme would sufficiently guarantee its security from the Southwest. The problem is whether in the near future the parties concerned could start the process of negotiation toward such a political settlement. If this process can get underway, there is no reason why support for this alternative would not be forthcoming, from the United States or even from the People's Republic of China.

The first step in the negotiation would involve a regional conference between Vietnam, Laos, and eventually also representatives from the Heng Samrin government on the one side and ASEAN plus representatives of Democratic Kampuchea on the other side. This first step essentially is an extension of ASEAN's proposal for a "proximity talk" between the parties directly involved in the conflict. The idea of such a regional conference was proposed by former Malaysian Foreign Minister Tan Sri Ghazali to Vietnam's Foreign Minister Nguyen Co Thach at the summit meeting of the nonaligned countries in New Delhi in 1983. Other countries, in particular the major powers, would be kept informed about the negotiations during this first phase.

Only in the second phase, in which an international conference would be convened, could there be participation by other countries, specifically the permanent members of the U.N. Security Council plus Japan and India. The function of this conference would be to endorse the settlement agreed upon in the regional conference and to guarantee that it would be honored by the parties concerned.

The regional conference should focus its negotiations on the following issues:

1. If an "elimination" of the Khmer Rouge is part of the settlement, it needs to be clearly defined who is meant by the Khmer Rouge group or the Pol Pot clique by Vietnam. It seems that ASEAN and Vietnam could reach an understanding on the exclusion of the few Khmer Rouge leaders, especially now that Pol Pot himself has been formally discharged.

2. Whether or not Vietnam would accept the "Namibian formula," which implies that an election be administered by the Heng Samrin apparatus—the only administration that functions—under the control and

supervision of the U.N. Secretary General. ASEAN and Vietnamese forces could participate in the supervision. In the election itself, each group—including the Heng Samrin group—may not participate as parties; only individuals may run for election.

POLITICAL DEVELOPMENTS IN THE PHILIPPINES

Most writing on the Philippines during the past two years contains a prediction of doomsday. I personally do not believe that the Philippines is "going down the drain," with the Communist Party of the Philippines (CPP), together with the New People's Army (NPA) and the National Democratic Front (NDF) in power in three to five years. It has been suggested that a military coup is necessary to prevent that situation from emerging, even though the military may not be in a position—and will lack legitimacy—to run the country.

There are reasons for greater optimism than this, based on the resilience of the Filipino people. It cannot be denied that the Philippines is today in a crisis situation. But it can be argued that this situation may perhaps be necessary for the Philippines in the process of rediscovering its national character, personality, and self-confidence as a sovereign nation. It may also be a necessary—and the only available—instrument for bringing about corrective measures and policies in almost all fields of life.

Heavy protection of its domestic industries since the 1960s, "cronyism," and the heavy external debt incurred concurrently with falling commodity prices have all greatly weakened the Philippine economy. In the decade and more of martial law there was hardly any political development, and political institutions remain very limited. Meanwhile, the NPA has grown from an insignificant force to one of about 12,000 armed guerillas. In various regions these guerillas have reached a strategic stalemate with the Armed Forces of the Philippines (AFP). In addition, the threat posed by the Moro National Liberation Front (MNLF) has never been successfully dealt with by President Ferdinand Marcos. All these problems have been aggravated by the unwillingness or the inability of Marcos, due to his illness and the eroding support of the elite, to make fundamental changes.

Nonetheless, some hopeful signs can be discerned in the economic field. Recent monetary measures have successfully reduced the inflation rate and efforts to dismantle the heavy protection of industries continue to be pursued, though resistance remains strong because they threaten the economic domination of the cronies. Problems of employment, however, might become more serious and could lead to greater political unrest. At present there does not seem to be a better alternative to these liberalization efforts if the economy is to be turned around in the medium term. Pressures from outside, especially from international lending agencies, may be necessary to keep the momentum going. Some movements in the political field have also taken place, as illustrated by a freer election of the Legislative Council in 1984; a freer press since the assassination of Benigno Aquino; a more active and growing opposition outside parliament; the results of the Agrava Committee's investigation of Aquino's murder; the formulation of a better constitutional mechanism for succession; a more pronounced role of the church in matters of social welfare and social justice; the emergence of a new group of social leaders, from business as well as from politics, including the government party itself, the KBL *(Kilusang Bagong Lipunan);* and in general, greater political consciousness among the elite and the middle class as a result of Aquino's assassination.

The military also has undergone changes with the suspension of General Fabian Ver as Chief of Staff. Within the military itself, demands have been made for drastic changes in discipline and capabilities, as manifested in the "We Belong" movement comprising young officers, which has formed a pressure group within the AFP.

Where all these developments may lead is still far from certain. The opposition, which has grouped itself in the National Unification Committee and the Conveners' Group, has not yet become a unified and effective force. By the same token, it seems that President Marcos no longer holds absolute power, and even though under the sixth amendment of the constitution he still has the right to issue decrees, he can no longer exercise that right as he wishes.

Marcos maintains a large base of support within the armed forces as well as in rural areas. Be that as it may, it may be best for Marcos and the country if he would soon allow greater freedom for the development of political institutions to take place. It is clear that this process should be determined by the Filipino people themselves, and it is also in the United States' interest to let the political process in the Philippines take its own course. ASEAN should use diplomacy to discourage any intervention by the major powers in the domestic affairs of the Philippines, even though the Philippine crisis can have region-wide implications due to the regional significance of U.S. military bases in that country.

The United States should redress the overemphasis of the bases issue in its bilateral relations with the Philippines. The U.S. bases indeed have become an internal political issue in the Philippines that can easily be exploited and become an explosive issue, and at the same time there are many quarters in the United States that look at the bases issue only from a narrow U.S. national interest point of view. A new formula for the renewal of the agreement in 1991 will need to be examined. The successful conclusion of such agreements between the United States and Egypt and between the United States and Oman suggest that this issue can be resolved. In the event that the Philippines refuses to renew the agreement, the phasing-out of the bases can still be negotiated. A negotiated phasing-out of the bases would be acceptable to the ASEAN countries, granted that the overall balance of military forces can be maintained. After all, such a balance is necessary to the realization of regional order in Southeast Asia based on ZOPFAN.

The Future of ASEAN Cooperation

ASEAN, which so far has been regarded as an important cornerstone in the foreign policies of its member countries, now seems to be questioned in many quarters. Prime Minister Datuk Seri Mahathir Mohamad of Malaysia has been very blunt in his criticism of the slow progress in ASEAN economic cooperation. Recently, the same sentiments have been expressed in Thailand (Far Eastern Economic Review 1985).

Likewise, the general public in Indonesia remains supportive of ASEAN as one of the cornerstones of Indonesia's foreign policy, but criticisms and questions have been raised as to the advisability of following the Thai policies on the Kampuchea conflict for the sake of maintaining ASEAN solidarity.

The younger generation—and the next leadership—in Indonesia does not have the same commitment to ASEAN as the present leaders, who were closely involved in its establishment. Therefore, they also have been more critical in assessing concrete economic gains to the country, which are important for the continuation and strengthening of national commitment. The many achievements of ASEAN, especially in terms of relations among individuals and groups both governmental and nongovernmental, are not sufficient to justify a central and sustainable role for regional cooperation in the foreign policies of its members.

If ASEAN continues to be seen as vital to the future of Indonesia, it has been suggested that the various schemes for economic cooperation must be examined seriously and the necessary political commitment to make them successful must be renewed. The mechanisms for cooperation need to be overhauled and to be strengthened as suggested in 1983 by the ASEAN Task Force.[2]

---

2. The ASEAN Task Force, established by the ASEAN governments in 1982, consisted of 15 wisemen from the then five ASEAN countries and was assigned the task of reviewing ASEAN's progress and suggesting ways to improve its operation and enhance regional cooperation.

The various concerns about the future of ASEAN cooperation expressed in the ASEAN countries have led to serious efforts by its leaders to convene an ASEAN summit as early as possible. In view of the economic difficulties faced by many of the ASEAN countries, a new commitment towards more effective schemes of cooperation may more easily be mobilized. At the same time, however, some countries may find it more difficult, politically, to commit themselves to the regional cause under this circumstance. ASEAN, one could argue, is really at a crossroads.

THE ROLE OF THE MAJOR POWERS

SUPERPOWER RELATIONS

Developments in the Asia–Pacific region, including Southeast Asia, are to some extent influenced by developments in the relationship between the two superpowers, the United States and the Soviet Union. The heightened confrontation following the Soviet invasion of Afghanistan in late 1979 seems less tense now. Competition between the two superpowers appears to have become more controlled, as manifested in the negotiations on strategic arms, joint efforts to fight terrorist activities, and even in the promotion of bilateral economic relations. This development was made possible by changing attitudes on both sides. The American public seems to perceive that a stable balance, in strategic terms, in superpower relations is being reached. The new Soviet leadership appears to give priority to internal economic development and progress.

The attainment of strategic stability, however, does not automatically reduce competition between the two different ideologies and value systems. Such competition may continue to manifest itself in the efforts by both sides to gain influence in various regions of the world. Thus, the superpower relationship will always involve some degree of confrontation and some degree of cooperation depending on developments in their respective countries, the nature of problems being faced, and the regions in which their interests meet.

The support of the American public for President Ronald Reagan's firm policies *vis-à-vis* the Soviet Union has been an important factor in regaining U.S. confidence and strength in international affairs. Critics have pointed out that Reagan's success has been based more on rhetoric than on concrete actions. But this can also be seen as Reagan's strength: he has been able to rebuild America's power without the use of extreme means—such as intervention, as often proposed by the ideologues around him—which would not be acceptable to the American public at large or to world opinion. In addition to the firm stance toward the

Soviet Union, U.S. foreign policies in general have become unilateralist. These attitudes, which are in great contrast to the indecisive and uncertain policies of the early 1970s, are likely to characterize the U.S. international outlook for a number of years to come, even beyond 1988, independent of who will become the next U.S. President.

The change of leadership in the Soviet Union will open up new opportunities for the improvement of relations with the United States. It appears that the new Soviet leadership is primarily concerned with internal problems, in particular with overcoming economic difficulties. Being a superpower, however, the Soviet Union will continue to show considerable interest in its foreign relations. But changes in orientation seem to have been signaled by the reform in the foreign policy establishment, where Mikhail Gorbachev himself assumes an active role, particularly in initiatives toward the West.

Despite the improvements in Soviet relations with the West, the Soviet Union is likely to continue to increase its military presence in a number of regions over the years to come. Being an Asian country as well, the Soviet Union will maintain or increase its military power in the Asia–Pacific region, because it is the only dimension of power in which it has strength there, political and economic relations being unlikely to improve.

In view of the increase in Soviet military power in the region, one could expect the Reagan Administration to continue to build up American military capabilities also, to enhance military relations with Japan, and to improve political and economic relations with China, in order to have a dominant influence in this increasingly important region. Be that as it may, the level of tensions is not likely to surpass that in Europe or the Middle East.

JAPAN AND CHINA

Japan has become an important economic partner of the ASEAN countries, and its economic role in the Asia–Pacific region is likely to continue to be dominant. Japan's economy will continue to be affected by regional developments. In spite of the great progress achieved in strengthening relations with the ASEAN countries over the past 10 to 15 years, there is need for Japan to extend its relations to the field of science and technology as well as culture and to be more open and international in its dealings, especially with its neighbors.

The United States hopes that Japan, its most important ally in the region, will play an increasingly significant military role in their alliance. For now, Japan's self-defense capabilities are confined to defense of the homeland and surrounding waters, and are considered sufficient by the

United States. However, new leaders in both countries, who may not get along as well as Prime Minister Yasuhiro Nakasone and President Reagan, could result in stronger political pressures by the United States for Japan to do more in this field. Further deterioration of bilateral U.S.–Japan trade relations could also increase such pressures. This possibility suggests the importance of intensive dialogues and consultation between Japan and countries in the region on security issues, including its defense efforts.

The future of Japan's defense capabilities will also depend upon its relations with the Soviet Union and upon its public's perception of the Soviet threat. The new leadership in Moscow is likely to pursue the recent efforts by both sides to improve Soviet–Japan relations.

An important factor in Japan's relations with the world is its ability to adjust to the challenges of internationalization, which in a fundamental way has been started by Prime Minister Nakasone. It remains to be seen whether the increased reliance of the Liberal Democratic Party on urban, middle-class voters, as compared to its traditional power base in rural areas, will smooth that process.

China, another major power in the Asia–Pacific region, will always be seen as posing a challenge—positively and negatively—to the countries in the region, especially the Southeast Asian countries. There are many reasons for the Southeast Asian ambivalence towards China. Historically, the Southeast Asian region has always been considered by China as part of its sphere of influence. The South China Sea, for example, is still seen by the Chinese as a Chinese sea.

Of irritation to the Southeast Asian countries is the ambiguous Chinese policy on the citizenship of overseas Chinese. This policy allows Chinese who have taken up citizenship in another country to enter China without a visa and to regain Chinese citizenship if they move back to China. The Chinese call for overseas Chinese to invest in China has also caused great misgivings in Southeast Asia.

China is also seen as a future competitor of the Southeast Asian countries, politically and especially economically, as well as a military threat if its development efforts succeed and enable China to build up its military might.

The efforts of Deng Xiaoping to modernize and develop China could have positive implications for the entire region, including Southeast Asia. Successful modernization may bring China into the world community as a responsible member that observes "the rules of the game." This should be manifested, among other things, by a discontinuation of China's support for communist parties or movements in the ASEAN countries. In this way, China could become a stabilizing force for the Asia–Pacific region. China's economic progress could also provide new economic opportunities for the region and the Southeast Asian countries.

Whatever the challenges posed by China to Southeast Asia, a China that becomes a responsible member of the international community and is close to the West and ASEAN is definitely more conducive to regional peace and stability than a China that returns to radicalism as a result of failure of its current development.

The Southeast Asian countries, Indonesia in particular, need to structure a "positive" relationship with China in the sense that the positive elements in the relationship can be promoted and the negative ones suppressed. However, some ambivalence towards China will always be present because China is a big country situated in Southeast Asia's immediate neighborhood.

The present government and party leadership in China can be seen as the most stable since 1949. The majority of the population—the farmers —has gained considerably from the economic reforms introduced by Deng. Progress in the urban centers still lags behind, and the government still faces considerable challenges from extremist members in the party and the People's Liberation Army.

China's foreign policy has stressed a more independent position in relationship to the United States and the Soviet Union. The more China needs technology and other economic inputs from the United States and the West, the greater is its awareness of the need to adopt a more independent posture in international affairs. Normalization of its relations with the Soviet Union can be seen in this light, as can reducing tensions along its borders and reducing the need for increased defense spending.

There is mutual attraction between China and Japan due to the common elements in their history and culture, as well as to economic complementarities. Since normalization of relations in 1974, the Japanese euphoria over the prospect of greater cooperation with China keeps recurring, notably in 1979 and 1985. However, geopolitical factors and differences in economic and political systems will likely make Japan and China competitors in the Asia–Pacific region. Developments in the region will also determine the degree of competition or cooperation in Sino–Japanese relations.

THE SOUTHWEST PACIFIC

Australia, New Zealand, Papua New Guinea, and other South Pacific island countries, constituting the Southwest Pacific region, increasingly have become an important factor in the affairs of Asia and the Pacific. ASEAN, which is an immediate neighbor, is interested in the stability of this region. That is to say, instabilities in the Southwest Pacific would be detrimental to developments in Southeast Asia. ASEAN's growing interest has been shown by its efforts to strengthen cooperation with the South Pacific Forum, and by inviting Papua New Guinea as a special observer to ASEAN meetings. Indonesia, for example, has focused its economic and technical cooperation with countries outside ASEAN— within the framework of ECDC and TCDC (Economic Cooperation among Developing Countries and Technical Cooperation among Developing Countries)—on those in the South Pacific, Papua New Guinea in particular.

Indeed, among the ASEAN countries perhaps it is Indonesia—due to its geography—that has given greatest attention to this region. Its relations with Papua New Guinea remain delicate due to the nature of the border and differences in the patterns of development on the different sides of that border.

Recent developments in the Southwest Pacific suggest that its importance to other countries in the Asia–Pacific region is based on more than just ASEAN's interest as an immediate neighbor, for two primary reasons. First, ANZUS, the pact between Australia, New Zealand, and the United States, is in crisis as a result of the New Zealand government's refusal to allow U.S. warships to visit New Zealand ports without sufficient assurances that they do not carry nuclear weapons.

The reasons behind this policy may be mixed; the firm stand of the Labour Party on the issue is one reason, but Prime Minister David Lange appears to have used it to get a deal from his party on measures to reform the New Zealand economy that do not accord with the party platform.

The government may have underestimated the Reagan Administration's reaction. In fact, the Reagan Administration has been concerned with similar issues, namely the Nuclear Free Zone in the South Pacific, the proposal for a Nuclear Weapon Free Zone in ASEAN, U.S. bases in the Philippines, and the continuing debate in Japan about the placement of U.S. nuclear weapons in its bases in Japan. The United States preoccupation with the Soviet threat has not allowed the Reagan Administration to give proper regard to domestic considerations in the various regions and countries that have led to these issues.

There is every reason to hope that New Zealand and the United States will be able to settle their differences in the near future, most likely on the basis of a formula similar to the one used by Japan, but put into law in New Zealand to avoid continuing pressure from the left wing of the Labour Party.

Second, the South Pacific island countries are also unhappy with the United States. Not only have they not been given proper U.S. attention but they have even been hurt by U.S. disregard for their Exclusive Economic Zone (EEZ). This irritation may have led some countries to look to the Soviet Union, Cuba, and even Libya. Kiribati, for example, has signed a fishery agreement with the Soviet Union, which unlike the United States has signed the new Law of the Sea Treaty and thus recognizes the EEZ. Vanuatu has opened diplomatic relations with Cuba, although this has little practical meaning as yet. The Kanak Party in New Caledonia is reported to have sent cadres for military training in Libya. These developments have no serious implications today but may suggest areas of future concern.

PACIFIC BASIN ECONOMIC COOPERATION

A lot has been written and discussed about the idea of economic cooperation among Pacific Basin countries.[3] Over the years those discussions have led to a more explicit formulation of the specific features that any meaningful form of Pacific cooperation should possess.

One important feature is its consultative nature, and another is its tripartite participation, namely a forum for government officials, academics, and business representatives to exchange views. Still another feature is its pragmatic orientation, implying that areas of cooperation be defined on the basis of unfolding mutual interests rather than on the basis of a blueprint. These features suggest that Pacific regional cooperation as such would not involve the establishment of a formal, intergovernmental institution.

A consensus seems to have been reached about those desirable features and at the same time concrete steps have been taken to put the idea into practice. One form of cooperation is a series of tripartite consultative meetings, called the Pacific Economic Cooperation Conference (PECC). Government officials attend those meetings in their private capacities, along with businessmen and scholars. A consultative arrangement that is more formal, in the sense that it is attended by government representatives, is the newly established dialogue forum involving the six ASEAN countries and the five Pacific Organization for Economic Cooperation and Development (OECD) countries, following the annual ASEAN foreign ministers meeting. The first 6 + 5 meeting (also referred to as the ASEAN–Pacific Forum) took place in July 1984 in Jakarta, at the instigation of Indonesia's Foreign Minister Mochtar Kusumaatmadja. This

---

3. See, for example, Japan Center for International Exchange (1980); Crawford (1981); Joint Economic Committee, Congress of the United States (1981); and Soesastro and Han (1983).

meeting agreed to continue the dialogue on economic development in the Pacific on an annual basis. The ASEAN Secretariat was given the task of preparing the background paper. In addition, participants in the dialogue agreed to explore the possibility of setting up concrete schemes of cooperation among Pacific countries, in particular in the area of human resources development (HRD).

Many do not yet recognize that the 6 + 5 meeting is the form of Pacific cooperation most feasible for the rest of the 20th century. This lack of recognition may be due in part to the involvement of only 11 countries, thus leaving out some countries or regions (including South Korea, the Pacific island states, and some Latin American countries) that are considered to be part of a Pacific regional cooperation arrangement, and in part to public expectations that such Pacific cooperation must involve the establishment of a new regional institution. Indeed, the Pacific Basin cooperation idea still suffers from the image that its original proponents (in Japan in particular) had an institution in mind. Such a proposal was rejected because it was feared that it could easily be transformed into a political alliance structure. This politically sensitive problem has not been removed from current discussion on the subject of Pacific Basin cooperation.

Government officials in Indonesia and other ASEAN countries took note of the PECC idea only in 1978, when Prime Minister Masayoshi Ohira of Japan announced his support for it. Earlier proposals, such as PAFTA (Pacific Free Trade Area) and OPTAD (Organization for Pacific Trade and Development), have been ignored, partly because they were discussed in non-official circles, but also because they were seen as reflecting the interests of the more developed countries in the region to "dominate" the region's economic development. The Pacific Basin Economic Council, a forum of regional business representatives, has been pointed to as an example of self-centered interest on the part of the developed countries. Questions were also raised concerning the place and role of the developing countries in any scheme for broader Pacific regional cooperation.

ASEAN governments remain very concerned about the political aspects of broader Pacific regional cooperation even if it is confined to the economic, social, and cultural fields. Questions of membership and leadership are at the heart of the matter.

It is important to recognize that the various obstacles to the realization of the idea cannot be overcome easily in the near future. However, it is equally important to recognize that the necessity for cooperation among Pacific Basin countries remains valid—perhaps even more so. Global economic development in the years to come is likely to be more complicated than in the 1960s and 1970s. Such an environment would necessitate greater regional or international consultation and cooperation in trade, in monetary and financial matters, on public and private resource transfer to less developed countries, on the idea of an international division of labor in industrialization, and on the deteriorating terms of trade for countries producing primary commodities.

The global recession has highlighted the growing economic interdependence of the ASEAN countries, especially with the other Pacific economies. Therefore, it is important for the ASEAN countries to be able to effectively seek solutions on many international economic issues within a broader Pacific regional framework involving their main economic partners. In a Pacific forum, ASEAN countries could make a more effective case for a kind of regional division of labor in industrial activities and the accompanying access to markets in the more developed part of the region. More consultation might also prevent serious effects upon the developing economies of monetary and other policies adopted by the developed countries. The Pacific economic cooperation idea can evolve into something useful and can be perceived as a necessity only if those issues can become its central concern.

There would be further gains to the ASEAN countries from a regional mechanism so conceived. First, in view of ASEAN's success in dealing with its dialogue partners, a broader regional forum for cooperation could enhance ASEAN's effectiveness in its economic diplomacy toward those countries, rather than dilute it, as is often believed. Second, in view of the stalemate in the global North–South dialogue, it is likely that regional approaches could become more effective and workable, although ultimately global solutions must be found. There are reasons to believe that the Pacific region is in a better position than other regions to formulate those regional approaches, such as in the areas of raw materials and commodities trade, including agreements on the stabilization of export earnings, expansion of GSP (general system of preferences), the implementation of the new Law of the Sea, as well as in the areas of direct foreign investment and resource transfers in general. Most of these issues can and should be linked to the fundamental problem of industrial structural adjustments in the Pacific Basin countries in order to produce fruitful results.

Present circumstances dictate that efforts to realize broader Pacific regional cooperation cannot be pushed too fast and too far without risking a serious backlash. The present movement, as manifested in the PECC, already shows remarkable progress, which many observers would not have dared to imagine a few years ago. It is noteworthy that two of the first four PECC were held in the ASEAN region.

The above examination suggests that the idea of Pacific cooperation already has taken shape, both in a series of tripartite consultative meetings under the coordination of an international standing committee, and a more formal series of dialogues among Pacific foreign ministers as well as efforts to implement programs for cooperation in the area of HRD.

ASEAN's involvement and role can be found in all those activities. They have not been insignificant. In fact, ASEAN took the lead in the latter form of activity. The question now is whether ASEAN can be relied upon to further the development of those activities, especially of the ASEAN-based "Pacific dialogue" and the forthcoming Pacific HRD programs.

There are three main points for further deliberations in attempting to answer the above question.

First, official ASEAN attention to the development of Pacific economic cooperation in the foreseeable future will likely be confined to the ASEAN–Pacific Forum and the Pacific HRD programs. However, the progress of these activities is likely to be slow if ASEAN's resources devoted to them remain limited.

Second, in view of the above, the momentum can be sustained only if Japan (in particular, but other Pacific countries as well) will cooperate more actively with ASEAN in further developing these initiatives.

Third, ASEAN's preoccupation with the above activities does not mean that PECC has lost its relevance. In fact, due to the many limitations on ASEAN's part, PECC can be of assistance. Indeed, PECC should be invited to assume an active involvement in the ASEAN–Pacific Forum in the same way the ASEAN CCI (Chamber of Commerce and Industries) is involved in official ASEAN economic meetings, primarily as a source of information and suggestions. This action should also pave the way for a greater involvement—and eventually full participation—of South Korea and the Pacific island states in the ASEAN–Pacific Forum.

CONCLUSIONS

It has become customary to speak and think of the Asia–Pacific region as "one region," either from an economic point of view or on the basis of strategic considerations. Developments in Northeast Asia affect developments in Southeast Asia (and the Southwest Pacific) and *vice versa*. What happens in the Korean Peninsula, for example, will definitely have some repercussions for the Southeast Asian region. Similarly, developments in the Philippines are felt in Japan.

In economic terms, there are indeed strong links between the two subregions. Japan is the most or second most important trading partner of the ASEAN countries, and a large portion of Japan's Official Development Assistance (ODA) is directed to the ASEAN countries.

However close the links are between these two regions, the problems each of them face are different and responses are likely to differ also. Therefore, U.S. policy towards the Asia–Pacific region needs to clearly distinguish between these two regions: U.S. policies in the military-strategic and political realms as applied to its relations with Northeast Asia cannot be valid for structuring its relations with Southeast Asia.

There is a strong tendency in the Reagan administration to apply simplistically its global policies to regional situations. For instance, the U.S.–U.S.S.R. rivalry in East Asia certainly manifests itself differently than the superpower competition in Europe. Furthermore, the Soviet threat in East Asia is not perceived by countries in that region to be as great as perceived by Europeans. Similarly, in spite of the presence of Soviet military facilities in Danang and Cam Ranh in Vietnam, the threat from the Soviet Union in Southeast Asia is not considered as great as that in Northeast Asia.

China to the United States is different from what Japan is to the United States; the former is a friend and the latter is an ally. Similarly, China to Southeast Asia is certainly different from what China is to the United States. Therefore, U.S. policies towards the Asia–Pacific region can be successful only if they harmonize U.S. global interests with the regional interests of friends and allies.

In the area of trade relations, an area that has assumed an equally important position, the mood in the United States is far from encouraging. This "ugly mood" has wide-ranging implications for the future stability and development of the Asia–Pacific region, which depends to a large extent on sustained economic growth and development. It is not clear as yet how this problem can be resolved, for its resolution requires a longer-term perspective, a virtue that the American public lacks.

This fact suggests that the Asia–Pacific region will be faced with great uncertainties in the future, because U.S. policies do not seem to appropriately take the regional situation into account. In the realm of politics and security its global approach dominates, whereas in the economic field its actions are primarily unilateralist.

REFERENCES

Crawford, Sir John (ed.)
   1981 *Pacific Economic Co-operation: Suggestions for Action.* Singapore: Heineman Educational Books (Asia) Ltd.

Far Eastern Economic Review
   1985 New Cement for the Bloc. *Far Eastern Economic Review.* Hong Kong: F.E.E.R. Ltd., 5 September.

Joint Economic Committee, Congress of the United States
   1981 *Pacific Region Interdependencies.* A compendium of papers submitted to the Joint Economic Committee. Washington, D.C.: U.S. Government Printing Office, 15 June.

Japan Center for International Exchange
   1980 *The Pacific Community Concept—Views from Eight Nations.* The proceedings of the Asian dialogue at OISO, Japan, January 1980. Tokyo: JCIE.

Soesastro, Hadi, and Han Sung-joo (eds.)
   1983 *Pacific Economic Cooperation: The Next Phase.* Jakarta: Centre for Strategic and International Studies, October.

Wanandi, Jusuf
   1985 ZOPFAN and the Kampuchea Conflict. *The Indonesian Quarterly* 13(2).

ASEAN and Malaysian
Political Development

ZAKARIA HAJI AHMAD

I join Wanandi in the belief that, in contrast to other developing regions, ASEAN has been able to cope with the problems and challenges of socio-economic and political modernization in large part through the quality of political leadership and the support, generally, of the populations of member states. There is no doubt also of a strong element of both national and regional resilience that explains the relative success of ASEAN even as it faces the difficult economic times of the 1980s and the concomitant and increasingly salient problems of political participation, a thesis first proposed in the 1970s by Indonesia, the country that Wanandi represents.

REGIONAL ORDER

It may be provocative, but still worthwhile, to ask if ASEAN has become too "small" for an Indonesia seeking a bigger role extending beyond Southeast Asia to the Western Pacific and befitting the large nation that it has long been; a sort of "middle power" in the making. One sees, in effect, ASEAN–Pacific Cooperation (APC), first officially recognized in 1984, as but a manifestation of Indonesia's desire to play a leading role in the Asia–Pacific region. In this context, too, I find it most poignant that Wanandi has touched little on the challenge that Vietnam, or perhaps more correctly an Indochinese federation, poses for the region. Please do not misunderstand me. I am an optimist, albeit a cautious one. But I daresay we neglect Vietnam at our own peril when assessing Southeast Asia's regional order.

The challenge to regional order in Southeast Asia is the Kampuchea problem and Vietnam's role in it. Over time, I have become "hard-line" toward the Vietnamese. I do not discern any real desire on their part to

166

allow Kampuchean self-determination, nor do I see any evidence that they are really desirous of coexistence with ASEAN.

This raises a host of problems for the Zone of Peace, Freedom, and Neutrality (ZOPFAN) concept. Although there is supposedly ASEAN agreement in principle on ZOPFAN, there exist ambiguities toward the concept—inside and outside of ASEAN. Given what I see as Vietnam's intransigence, ZOPFAN must be viewed in pragmatic terms. In principle, as a long-term objective, it is an ideal based on:

1. "Coexistence" in Southeast Asia between noncommunist ASEAN, communist Indochina, and "neutral" Burma;
2. The external and major powers not being interventionist; and
3. The non-existence of foreign military bases.

In practice, and for ZOPFAN to be workable, there has to be a regional balance of power both between the indigenous powers and between foreign military powers, but with the (unstated) ASEAN proviso that the balance of power be tilted in favor of the United States. In the interim— between the desire and the reality—there should be tacit acceptance of foreign military bases and presence, and enough transition time should be allowed for the buildup of full military capability (self-reliance) in the ASEAN states. The bottom line on ZOPFAN will depend on the solutions to two conundra: whether Hanoi believes in ZOPFAN or wants to subjugate Southeast Asia militarily, and whether the Soviet Union and the People's Republic of China will want to dominate the region if and when the United States "withdraws."

I believe Wanandi is correct about the roles of the major powers in Southeast Asia, but there is also the problem of a Vietnam supported by the Soviet Union. In a different vein, the role of the United States is sometimes benign, but often it tends to dismiss Southeast Asia as only a minor factor in its global strategies. Indeed, at times the United States is more damaging in its policies, especially in the economic dimension.

MALAYSIA

On Malaysian political developments, I find little to disagree with Wanandi's treatment of the subject. A strong factor in ASEAN political stability has been the high premium on "strong government" as a basis for national development. But increasingly this notion is being questioned by a more politically aware citizenry benefiting—ironically for those in power—from the dramatic socioeconomic progress. Wanandi is evidently conscious of this dilemma. But the process has also made more salient the deleterious effect of government and political party corruption —the whole question of "money politics" that has besieged UMNO

(United Malays National Organization) of late. A parallel development, which is a concomitant of socioeconomic progress and arises from the need for a "strong" Malay say in government affairs in the aftermath of the May 1969 racial riots, has been that the strength of UMNO has soared to new and dizzying heights, highlighting in effect Malay political hegemony in multiracial Malaysia.

Have Malaysian politics become synonymous with Malay politics? And with the resurgence of Islamic consciousness are the battle lines being drawn between those who seek heaven on earth and those who seek paradise in the hereafter? Religious extremists cannot disrupt the political system, but the quest for the absorption of Islamic values does present difficulties, indicated by official reference, no less, to deviationist interpretations and the dwelling on trivia instead of on the positive effects of learning from secular experiences.

Can Islam play the role of promoting good work ethics *à la* Protestantism as the country pushes for socioeconomic advancement? In terms of racial politics, it is more likely that non-Malay political demands and aspirations have become submerged but retain the potential to explode if the assertion of Malay political power becomes intolerable. But it is interesting to ponder if in some sense the Malaysian Chinese Association leadership crisis suggests that Chinese interests could be represented, after all, by UMNO as a national movement.

Fortunately, the need to "harmonize racial and religious relations" (in Wanandi's words) has also meant an understanding of the need for moderation, so that the assertion of Malay political power cannot be pushed too far nor can ethnic (both non-Malay and Malay) chauvinism be left unbridled. Nonetheless, the coming to power of a state government in Sabah that is seemingly non-Malay (and non-Moslem) earlier this year has caused some concern among those who hold power at the center.

One can expect of course that further socioeconomic progress will lead to increasing demands on the political system, but it is more than likely that the high degree of political institutionalization will enable the system to accommodate such pressures. Having said that, however, Malaysia's major challenge will still be its effort in nation building.

Malaysia and the rest of ASEAN face serious challenges as they head toward what many of us believe to be a "Pacific Era." Malaysia's modernization represents the quest to achieve a place in the sun that equates to having arrived at an economic well-being on a par with the developed world. In Malaysia, a strong and vigorous leadership is striving for this status through industrialization but at the same time allowing for a modicum of political rights and liberties. A fair balance has to be struck between the ideals of liberal democracy on the one hand and avoiding, as much as possible, authoritarian tendencies as the country pushes for discipline in attempting to become a newly industrialized country on the other. In ASEAN, the Marxist model has long since faded into the background, but often those very countries that should provide the climate for noncommunist Southeast Asia's prosperity are committing acts contrary to that objective. In that sense, Malaysia's and ASEAN's performance in regional order and development are contingent as much on internal dynamism as on the actions of others in the Asia–Pacific region.

The Philippines: Implications for Regional Order

CAROLINA G. HERNANDEZ

The current (mid-1985) situation in the Philippines has caused anxiety among countries that have a stake in the preservation of regional order in ASEAN and in the larger Pacific area. Host to strategic American military facilities, notably those at Clark Air Base and Subic Bay Naval Base, the Philippines is presently faced with the most serious economic crisis in its postwar history. A growing communist insurgency, a perceptible distancing of the people from a government that has lost much of its credibility and popular confidence, and serious social polarization only serve to compound the economic crisis. This crisis may indeed have serious implications for regional order. Instability and uncertainty make the future of the bases equally uncertain. The American military presence in the region, made credible by its facilities in the Philippine bases, has for many years provided a security that, in no small measure, has contributed to the economic development and prosperity of several countries in the region.

The implications of a disruption of that order could be far-reaching, especially given the unprecedented Soviet presence in both mainland Southeast Asia and Afghanistan, the phenomenal expansion of its Pacific fleet, the deployment of intermediate-range nuclear forces in Soviet Asia, Soviet deployments on three of the four northern islands claimed by Japan, and its close and friendly ties with India. It is in this light that the Philippine situation assumes strategic significance.

This short discussion will highlight the major elements and consequences of political "development" in the Philippines during the last fifteen years and its implications for regional order in ASEAN.

POLITICAL "DEVELOPMENT": 1970–85

The past 15 years saw the transformation of the Philippine political system from a democratic to an authoritarian one. This transformation was effected through martial law, imposed throughout the country on 21 September 1972. The rise of the Communist Party of the Philippines (CPP) and its military arm, the New People's Army (NPA), the growing tension and conflict in southern Philippines, and the general breakdown of law and order following the urban ferment of the late sixties and early seventies became the excuse for martial law. To be sure, the imposition of martial law was legal since the old constitution empowered the president to exercise emergency powers under certain specified conditions.

Martial law laid further assault to already weak political institutions. As soon as it took effect, hundreds of persons, including leading politicians from both the Liberal and the Nacionalista parties, were arrested. All political activities were prohibited; cases pending before civilian courts were transferred to newly created military tribunals; the legislature was disbanded; and the media were muzzled. In one clean sweep, martial law further weakened—if it did not destroy—these institutions. The executive was the only institution spared. In fact, it was strengthened and made preeminent.

A new constitution, in the process of being drafted by the Constitutional Convention elected in 1971, was quickly completed and submitted to special citizens' assemblies (in violation of the old constitution's amendment provisions) for ratification in January 1973. When this process was challenged, the Supreme Court could not muster enough votes (or courage) and declared that although these provisions were not followed, there were no longer any legal impediments for the new constitution to take full effect (Supreme Court of the Philippines 1973).

The new constitution installed a parliamentary system of government with a weak president as head of state and a strong prime minister as head of government. In 1976, a series of amendments was ratified by the people in a referendum, preparatory to the holding of the first elections under martial law in 1978. Amendment 3 authorized President Ferdinand Marcos to become both president and prime minister, while Amendment 6 empowered him to exercise decree-making powers even after an interim legislature had been elected, even beyond the duration of martial law, and even after a regular legislature was elected. The latter took place in May 1984 and Marcos, by virtue of Amendment 6, continues to play the preeminent rule-making role.

Just before the 1978 parliamentary elections, Marcos allowed the revival of political parties. He organized his own party, the *Kilusang Bagong Lipunan* (KBL or New Society Movement). An alliance of various political groups formed the *Lakas ng Bayan* (LABAN, or People's Power) in Metro Manila, *Pusyon Bisaya* in Cebu, Bicol *Saro* in southern Luzon, and the Mindanao Alliance in central Mindanao. Predictably, the KBL won an overwhelming majority of the seats, with opposition parties winning a token few. Electoral rules and institutions were loaded in favor of the government party and—with martial rule as the environment— opposition chances were virtually nil. Opposition groups did not have access to media, a situation that further handicapped their electoral performance. But perhaps more important was the fact that they did not have any organizational structure at the local level to assist them in getting votes. The disruption of political activities during the previous six years exacted a heavy toll on the opposition.

While civilian political institutions declined, the military, under the president as commander-in-chief of the armed forces, was developed into a partner of government. It was made to assume essentially nonmilitary responsibilities, including judicial, administrative, management, and even political. Officers replaced politicians as dispensers of political patronage and in some cases became political executives of local government units (Hernandez 1979: Ch. V). The assumption of these responsibilities exposed the military to a wider public and provided opportunities for the abuse of power. To some extent this change eroded popular confidence in the military and prompted allegations by civilian groups of "militarization" in the Philippines.

The concentration of political power in the hands of a few people also affected the economy. The free enterprise system evolved into a command economy where decisions tended to favor those close to the leadership. Monopolies in traditional agricultural exports were formed and "crony capitalism" developed. On the positive side, during the early part of martial law the foundations for export-oriented industrialization were laid, the country achieved its goal of self-sufficiency in rice, and export growth was robust. However, unsound economic policies and excessive government intervention in the economy reversed these early achievements. Infrastructure development was replaced by the development of showcase projects of the first lady, Imelda Marcos, such as the Manila Bay reclamation and building complex, the University of Life complex, expensive medical centers, and the building of government-financed five-star hotels. The negative effects of these costly, nonproductive investments were aggravated by poorly conceived business enterprises of the Marcos cronies, which the president had to bail out at the expense of public economic welfare.[1] Economic mismanagement on such a scale would not have been possible had political power not been concentrated in so few hands.

THE CONSEQUENCES OF POLITICAL "DEVELOPMENT"

Events following the murder in August 1983 of Senator Benigno S. Aquino, Jr., Marcos' chief political rival, indicate some hopeful possibilities. For one, there is a noticeable letting up of media constraints. An "alternative press" has developed, and it provides the other half of what the people should know. The 1984 parliamentary elections also gave the opposition parties 61 seats out of 173 total. Although the National Assembly remains a rubber stamp legislature, there are many more opposition voices that can be heard and that can publicize issues and perhaps stimulate enough public opinion against unsound measures. There has also emerged, since August 1983, the "parliament of the streets" composed of cause-oriented groups, many of them unconvinced that electoral struggle under an authoritarian system can bring about meaningful change. This "parliament" uses pressure politics to dramatize popular demands. It includes businessmen, church people, professionals, students, workers, and farmers from many shades of the political spectrum. Many do not have any definite political orientation. They are simply tired of being dictated to and manipulated by a command society. And a reform movement, called "We Belong," has arisen within the military. The movement is interested in restoring professionalism and redeeming the tarnished image of the military in order to bridge the chasm between the military and the people it is sworn to defend and protect.

Yet amid these bright spots, certain consequences of the past 15 years continue to plague Philippine society. These are Moro secessionism, the communist insurgency, and political and economic uncertainty.[2]

MORO SECESSIONISM

Moro secessionism erupted shortly after the declaration of martial law, although its roots can be found in earlier Moro–Christian conflicts over land rights, which began in the 1950s when parts of Mindanao, the

---

1. See de Dios (1984) for a thorough analysis of economic policies that led to the present crisis.

2. A fuller discussion of these problems may be found in Hernandez (1985).

Moro's ancestral home, were opened up for settlement from more heavily populated areas of the Philippines. Martial law crushed the hope of young, better-educated Moro elites that the Constitutional Convention would frame a federal government that would provide a safeguard against Christian incursions on Moro dominance in Mindanao. The confiscation of all privately owned firearms in the early part of martial law was seen as a prelude to genocide.

The Moro National Liberation Front (MNLF) and its military wing, the *Bangsa Moro* Army (BMA), launched a secessionist movement that subsequently brought the Marcos government before an international conference table in Tripoli, Libya in December 1976 to negotiate a settlement of the secessionist problem. An agreement was forged leading to a short-lived ceasefire and the establishment of two autonomous regional governments in Mindanao. Important members of the old Moro elite were won over to the government side by the creation of these autonomous governments. Support for the MNLF was consequently eroded. The MNLF leadership also suffered from division due to generational gaps, ideological differences, styles of leadership, and apparent unequal distribution of Libyan aid.

The Marcos government also has introduced other policies geared to solve Moro secessionism. These include the adoption of infrastructure development projects in Mindanao, extension of credit for agriculture, fisheries, and industry, establishment of a bank based on Islamic principles, selective amnesty for MNLF leaders and men, recognition of Islamic holidays, promulgation of a code of Muslim Personal Laws, establishment of *Sharia* Courts and *madrasah* schools, and the creation of an Office of Muslim Affairs.[3]

However, these policies have not really solved the fundamental problem of Moro inequality with Christians. Nevertheless, most Moros have apparently given up armed struggle against the government for various reasons: terrible destruction of their land and their people; cessation of foreign assistance, especially from Libya; weariness over the long-drawn-out war; and cooptation into the government. Consequently, while Mindanao remains a trouble spot, the trouble comes primarily not from the MNLF–BMA, but from the CPP–NPA.

---

3. The Office of Muslim Affairs was integrated with another government agency for cultural minorities, the PANAMIN, after the latter's head fled from the Philippines shortly after the Aquino murder. This integrated office is now called the Office of Cultural Communities. The Moro Filipinos are apparently not too happy with this arrangement as they are lumped together with other cultural communities perceived as having less numerical (and therefore less political) importance.

THE COMMUNIST INSURGENCY

The Philippines is not only host to American strategic military facilities; it also hosts the only significant communist insurgency in Asia at present. The CPP–NPA is a splinter of the old *Partido Komunista ng Pilipinas* (PKP) and its military arm, the *Hukbong Magpapalaya ng Bayan* (HMB or Huks). The CPP was established in December 1968 as a result of generational and ideological differences between the old PKP leadership and young, middle-class intellectual cadres largely from the University of the Philippines led by Amado Guerrero.[4] The NPA, on the other hand, was formed by a group of Huks under Commander Dante that broke away from its mother unit when the latter, after falling outside the control of the PKP, degenerated into a crime syndicate. Thus, "The inevitable marriage between Dante's army in search for a party and Guerrero's party in search for an army gave birth to the NPA on 29 March 1969 (Nemenzo 1984:30)."

The phenomenal growth of the CPP–NPA must have surprised even the most optimistic of the student radicals who formed the core of the party in 1968. From a handful of firm believers in Marxism-Leninism-Mao Zedong Thought assisted by Commander Dante's small but experienced guerilla group, the CPP–NPA grew by 1985 to an estimated 10,000 to 12,000 regulars.[5] The CPP–NPA has challenged the ability of the government to rule by spreading its political and military activities throughout the archipelago. It is estimated that 20 percent of all the villages *(barangays)* in the Philippines have been infiltrated by the NPA,[6] and some military officers believe that NPA activities have been organized in all of the country's 74 provinces.[7]

I believe that the hard-liners in the CPP–NPA are a minority. Most of its membership is drawn from among those who have given up on government after years of poverty, oppression, and frustration. In many rural *barangays,* especially those with an NPA presence, the most visible symbols of government are the soldier and the civilian paramilitary personnel known as Civilian Home Defense Forces (CHDF). When they misbehave they create enemies for government among their victims.

---

4. An interesting and insightful account of this split is told by Nemenzo (1984:71–101).

5. See Yan (1985:1). Some estimates go as high as 20,000 to 24,000, probably because the NPA guerillas share their arms at the rate of two guerillas for every gun.

6. This estimate is made by Richard L. Armitage, U.S. Assistant Secretary of Defense for International Security Affairs, as cited by Gatbonton (1985:84). See also Center for Research and Communication (1985: Introduction, p. v).

7. From several interviews conducted by the author in September 1985.

Because the *barangay* government has no power over them and civilian institutions including the courts are weak and/or have little credibility among the people, the victims are left with little or no recourse within the political system. Consequently, they (the victims) are left to the NPA for the picking.

In the course of the government's counterinsurgency operations, military abuses have taken place, probably committed by only a small portion of the military but damaging enough to distance the victims and their sympathizers from both the military and the government. Aware of the importance of winning the hearts and minds of the people, the military adopted motivational programs like TANGLAW,[8] a counterinsurgency strategy called OPLAN KATATAGAN,[9] and, since the assumption of General Fidel V. Ramos to the Office of Acting Chief of Staff, several reforms intended to upgrade the morale, discipline, and operational effectiveness of the military at the same time that the people's faith and confidence in the military is strengthened or restored.

Unfortunately, even granting that these reforms are yielding positive results in reducing abuses and increasing NPA and MNLF casualties, their effects can at best be piecemeal, long-term, and uneven. The government may not have time on its side because of the presence of a multidimensional crisis pushing people to fewer and fewer alternatives. What may be required in addition to the reforms being currently undertaken are impact-oriented changes in the military that can bring dramatic results in the near term and convince the people about the sincerity and credibility of the government. Then, an atmosphere more conducive to the effectiveness of current reforms can be created for the longer term.

Moreover, as astutely pointed out by one analyst (Nemenzo 1984), it would be wrong to equate the capacity of the NPA to challenge regime security with the number of NPA regulars, for the military activities of the communist movement are essentially propaganda tactics. The real test of CPP–NPA strength is the ability to conduct mass actions nationwide, an objective that the Philippine communist movement may attain by the end of the eighties if present trends continue.

---

8. TANGLAW stands for *Tanod at Gabay ng Lahi at Watawat* or Guardian and Guide of our People and Flag.

9. OPLAN KATATAGAN is an operational plan for stability, of which the key elements are: (a) prevention of insurgency from taking root in threatened areas; (b) gaining popular support and involvement of the people in the counterinsurgency plan; (c) neutralization of insurgent leadership and political infrastructure; (d) denial of insurgent's access to manpower and material resources; and (e) development of the military into a well-motivated and people-oriented counterinsurgency force.

POLITICAL AND ECONOMIC UNCERTAINTY

Another consequence of the policies undertaken by Marcos over the past decade or so is the present political and economic uncertainty. On the political front, succession remains a problem because of the inadequacy of present rules on succession. The reported ill health of Marcos creates apprehension that his sudden incapacity might be used by power-seeking individuals and groups to jockey for position and thus undermine the constitutionally mandated succession process. The strongest contenders are the left and the right, because both possess organizational and positional advantages over other groups. Although the military has traditionally observed the ethos of civilian supremacy, in the event of disorder it would most probably perform its responsibility of restoring order even if that would mean holding power in the transition. The problem arises where the transition becomes semipermanent, as transitions go by Philippine standards.

The loss of credibility of the legislative, judicial, and administrative institutions contributes to the present state of uncertainty. Many people are becoming cynical, if they are not already so, about the ability of these institutions to discharge their proper functions. They are seen as extensions of the executive ego.

On the economic front, while it is true that many of the Philippines' current economic difficulties predated the Marcos era,[10] it cannot be denied that much of the responsibility for the present economic crisis rests with the Marcos regime, which has been in authoritarian control for 13 out of its almost 20 years at the political helm. This appears to be the judgment of Filipino professional economists who trace the present economic crisis more to domestic than to international sources, more to political than to economic factors, and more to factors in the government sector than to those in the private sector (Philippine Economic Society 1984). It is in this light that the perception of many Filipinos regarding the priority of political reforms over economic recovery should be viewed.

The murder of Senator Aquino merely exacerbated the Philippine crisis, which had been years in the making. Massive capital flight characterized the days following the murder, and the Philippines declared its first debt moratorium in October 1983. Since then, the people have faced chronic economic difficulties. Double-digit inflation became the rule: in

---

10. A penetrating analysis of these difficulties may be found in Sicat (1985:6–10, 15–20).

1984 inflation was estimated at between 50 and 63 percent; in 1985 the government claims it is down to 20 percent (while some economists claim the real figures should be higher). The economy deteriorated with GNP growth in 1984 at minus 5 to 6 percent. It is expected to remain negative in 1985. Traditional agricultural export industries, notably sugar, have declined, and the monopolistic control of the sugar industry by a Marcos crony has aggravated the problem.

When is the economy expected to recover? The most optimistic of the country's economists predict in four to five years, if things go right. Agricultural development, sacrificed in favor of industrial development, will take the rest of the present decade to put back on track—again, if everything goes well.[11] However, some fiscal reforms have been undertaken and deregulatory policies adopted that should help eventual recovery. But for the present, economic survival remains a problem for the ordinary Filipino, who is more vulnerable than others to radical propaganda.

IMPLICATIONS FOR REGIONAL ORDER

The situation in the Philippines is alarming from a regional viewpoint because of the future of the bases that have served to promote regional order and stability and, in no small measure, enabled the ASEAN economic miracle to take place. During the 1970s and the early 1980s ASEAN experienced rapid economic growth. It did not have to commit large amounts of resources to defense expenditures because regional order was made possible by a balance of forces favorable to the American side (with which ASEAN countries, albeit in varying degrees, identify). Even the U.S. withdrawal from mainland Southeast Asia following its defeat in Vietnam was somewhat moderated by its continuing presence in the region through its military facilities in the Philippines. The other ASEAN countries without exception welcome this presence, provided they themselves are not hosts to American military facilities.

This arrangement may be affected by events in the Philippines that will make an American military presence there no longer tenable. One such situation would be an escalation of communist insurgency, with mass uprisings all over the country organized by the CPP–NPA. Some believe that the CPP aim can be achieved before the end of the 1980s (Nemenzo 1984:93). Another would be a takeover by the left itself, which could

---

11. An analysis of the present economic crisis and proposed solutions may be found in Ongpin (1985:106–108, 112).

likely result in the expulsion of the United States from the bases. If this happens, the regional balance of forces will be upset and, if we are to believe what some American strategists claim, the American absence will impel the Soviet Union to fill the vacuum. While I do not necessarily subscribe to this argument, I believe the psychological effect of a reduced American presence would be great.

The United States may also choose to pull out from the Philippines if the costs of remaining there far outweigh the benefits. Already, the United States has reportedly leased some land in the Marianas for alternative base sites. It could choose to return to Thailand if the Thais agree, although this arrangement would not give it the strategic vantage point the Philippines provides. In fact, realistically speaking there is no exact alternative to the Philippines for global and regional strategic purposes.

Without the American security umbrella, or even with a reduction of the size of the umbrella, ASEAN states would have to find alternative protection. Because the creation of an ASEAN security grouping is far from their intentions, they would have to rely on bilateral agreements to secure their borders and unilateral increases in their defense expenditures to simulate even a portion of the security they enjoyed before. They would have to normalize relations with countries with whom ties are not presently desirable. In this regard, Indonesia has a long-range vision of opening up to Vietnam. At any rate, investment in their defense capabilities would mean a reduction of resources that could otherwise be invested in social services or productive economic activities.

Equally alarming would be the establishment of a socialist regime in the midst of ASEAN. It is doubtful if Philippine membership would continue under a socialist regime because the other ASEAN countries have market economies. The advantage of radical groups *vis-à-vis* liberal democratic forces in the Philippines is gradually being conceded by some liberal analysts even as they continue to cling to a liberal democratic ideal, on the basis of present political alignments, quality of organizational and leadership capabilities, and relative performance of political forces. The chances of a liberal democratic restoration are dim, in the view of some analysts.[12] If this is so, then there remain the radical and the "constitutional" authoritarian options. A prolongation of the latter can only benefit the former, so that in the end the radical option may triumph in spite of strong liberal democratic hopes nurtured in the hearts of many Filipinos. At any rate, regional order will be transformed. Its new shape will

---

12. This view is reflected in unpublished papers of the recently held series of colloquia on "The Nation in Crisis - Part II," University of the Philippines, 20 September 1985.

depend largely on initiatives taken by ASEAN states in collaboration with whichever non-ASEAN states happen to respond to the requirements of their national interests at that time.

On the other hand, Filipinos have a long track record of resilience. The present situation may continue indefinitely or until they stumble into a compromise solution that would allow the American presence to continue. If, for example, moderate opposition groups can agree to pressure their leaders into temporarily freezing their feverish political ambitions in order to forge a unity so essential to defeating Marcos at the polls, and if vigilant civic groups can assure relatively clean elections after the fashion of the National Citizens Movement for Free Elections (NAMFREL) during the 1984 parliamentary elections,[13] then it is possible to have an orderly constitutional transition. This is assuming that Marcos continues until the end of his term in 1987 and the military continues to support the constitution. If the moderate opposition wins, the bases will most likely remain accessible to American use, but depending on which moderate opposition group exercises a majority voice in the government the existing bases agreement will have to be modified to suit prevailing nationalist and political sentiments. This may be a long shot, but it may be the only moderate shot left.

REFERENCES

Center for Research and Communication
   1985 *The Philippines at a Crossroad: Some Visions for the Nation (A Summary Report)*. Manila: Center for Research and Communication.
De Dios, Emmanuel S. (ed.)
   1984 *An Analysis of the Philippine Economic Crisis: A Workshop Report*. Quezon City: University of the Philippines Press.
Gatbonton, Juan T.
   1985 The Year in the Philippines. *1984–85 Fookien Times Philippines Yearbook*. Manila: Fookien Times Publishing Co., Inc.
Hernandez, Carolina G.
   1979 The Extent of Civilian Control of the Military in the Philippines: 1946–1976. Unpublished Ph.D. dissertation, State University of New York at Buffalo. Ann Arbor, Michigan: University Microfilms.
   1985 Security Issues and Policies: The Philippines in the Mid-1980's. Paper presented at the First Pacific Workshop on Regional Affairs. Manila, 27–28 September.
Monsod, Christian S.
   1985 NAMFREL-Testing Democracy at the Grassroots. *1984–85 Fookien Times Philippines Yearbook*. Manila: Fookien Times Publishing Co., Inc.

13. An analysis of NAMFREL's contribution to the 1984 parliamentary elections is made by Monsod (1985:76 and 78).

Nemenzo, Francisco
   1984   Rectification Process in the Philippine Communist Movement. In Joo-Jack Lim
          and S. Vani (eds.), *Armed Communist Movements in Southeast Asia.* Hampshire,
          England: Gower House Publishing Company Limited.

Ongpin, Jaime V.
   1985   A Report on the Economic Crisis. *1984–85 Fookien Times Philippines Yearbook.*
          Manila: Fookien Times Publishing Co., Inc.

Philippine Economic Society
   1984   Report on the Survey of Opinions of the Membership of the Philippine Economic
          Society on the Current Economic Crisis. July.

Sicat, Gerardo P.
   1985   A Historical and Current Perspective of Philippine Economic Problems. *PSSC
          Social Science Information* 12(4).

Supreme Court of the Philippines
   1973   Javellana *vs.* Executive Secretary. GRL-36142, 31 March.

Yan, Manuel T.
   1985   Communist Insurgency in the Philippines. Paper presented at the Hotel Horison,
          Ankol, Indonesia. 6 September.

Political Development in Thailand and the Kampuchea Problem

SARASIN VIRAPHOL

POLITICAL DEVELOPMENT IN THAILAND

Over the past five decades, Thailand has had no fewer than 15 military coups or attempted coups, which may rank it in the top echelon of countries with such political phenomena. Notwithstanding the frequent changes of government, Thailand's political institutions, ideology, and practices have shown unusual resilience and continuity. Some political observers have likened the frequent occurrence of coups to the process of "changing of hats." In other words, they are merely a manifestation of the sharing of administrative power among top-echelon military leaders of the country; just another way of changing governments.

For years, the military has been the most visible and influential power broker in the Thai political setup. The fledgling experimentation with parliamentary democracy, with its attendant problems, has in one respect maintained a crucial role for the military, with the traditional ideology of "Nation, Religion, and Monarch" providing ideological legitimacy for its continued involvement in politics. The military has persistently claimed that its role in politics is to defend the country's democracy.

The coups have basically reflected an interplay of personalities and factions within the military, and have been acknowledged and accepted as an inevitable part of the national political life by politicians, the bureaucracy, and the people at large, especially when they have not been seen as disruptive of the normal process of life and the pursuit of happiness in general.

The Thai political institutions (monarchy, military, parliament, government, and bureaucracy) have gone through an orderly evolution influenced by a somewhat conservative ideological orientation. There has been no major violent political upheaval or change in the Thai political system in recent times. And certainly the coups cannot in most cases be described as anything approaching a violent—albeit forcible—overthrow of the government of the day.

It is true though that it is in the nature of coups that a degree of violence may sometimes be unavoidable. As in the latest coup attempt in September 1985, brief and limited acts of violence were committed. But as one participant later admitted, "Soldiers know when to give up like gentlemen."

Nevertheless, it seems that the days of personalized politics are numbered. Political institutions, though developing in a conservative environment, are becoming more broadly based and thus less personalized. In addition, issues and problems, particularly in the economic domain, are becoming too complex for the simple solutions invariably advocated by coup makers. The requirement for greater expertise and participation affects the power base of the military, which occasionally admits its own lack of ability to cope with all exigencies in the national political life. Increasingly, one hears of the military speaking out on the desirability of tackling various problems through so-called democratic means, which implies admission of the need to manage national affairs in a broadly based consensual fashion involving more than just the military.

It is true that the military has played a crucial part in preserving national security. Over the past decade, it has successfully handled a serious communist insurgency problem of the sort that has plagued nations of Southeast Asia. It has also served as a bulwark against the security threats stemming from the Vietnamese invasion and occupation of neighboring Kampuchea. Hence, its prominence and participation in the national political processes are undeniable.

Political development in Thailand is fraught with uncertainty; democratic experimentation continues to face mounting crises and problems of a political and socioeconomic nature. Personalities continue to figure importantly in the Thai political scene, but there is hope that parliamentary democratic institutions and ideas are gaining in strength. Rules and regulations are becoming more established. Generational changes, including those within the military, are also having an effect on political perceptions and behavior. All such developments are breaking down the traditional belief in and practice of personalized politics based on familial ties. This change cannot but affect the future function and role of the *coup d'état* in Thai politics and result in further refinement of the political processes.

THE KAMPUCHEA PROBLEM AND REGIONAL ORDER

The Kampuchea problem is vastly complicated and deeply affects regional order and security in Southeast Asia. The problem involves several countries as well as several sets of intentions and interests. It is an indigenous conflict that has become externalized, with root causes and implications that are varied. The immediate principal protagonists are Kampuchea, Vietnam, China, and the Soviet Union. The major concerned and affected parties are the ASEAN states, particularly Thailand, which has a long common border with Kampuchea and hence invariably is referred to as the "front-line state." At the most basic level, the Kampuchea conflict is one between the Kampuchean and Vietnamese regimes. But their falling-out has had to do with the rivalry between two other principal communist powers, namely the Soviet Union and China, together with the differences between China and Vietnam. The Soviet Union figures in the conflict primarily as Vietnam's supporter, to balance the Chinese role as Vietnam's adversary and major backer of Kampuchea. Amidst these complex relationships, the ASEAN states are caught up in the drama, their security and other interests gravely affected by the ongoing conflict.

Given the large number of protagonists, it is inevitable that their motives and interests are also varied and complex. The Vietnamese invasion and occupation of Kampuchea was due to a combination of Hanoi's perceived security concern, territorial aggrandizement, and a historical plan for an Indochinese federation comprising Vietnam, Laos, and Kampuchea under the Vietnamese suzerainty. Kampucheans have traditionally rejected radical nationalism and harbored strong ethnic animosity against Vietnam, which the Democratic Kampuchean regime expressed in extreme anti-Vietnamese policies. China, on the other hand, has actively opposed Vietnam and supported Kampuchea to counter Hanoi's attempts, with the help of the Soviet Union, to upset the existing power balance in Southeast Asia and exert pressure on China along the latter's southern flank. Consideration must further be given to Beijing's continuing strong ties with the Democratic Kampuchean faction in the Kampuchean coalition government, as well as the Chinese interest in forming an anti-Vietnamese front with ASEAN on the Kampuchea problem. For the Soviet Union, involvement on the Vietnamese side has meant the entrenchment of Soviet influence in Southeast Asia. In exchange for its military support of Hanoi's venture in Kampuchea, Moscow has gained access to Vietnamese facilities, notably the massive former American base at Cam Ranh Bay.

The acquisition of such bases has led to a dramatic strengthening of Soviet air and naval power in East Asia and has made the Soviet military presence in Southeast Asia a crucial factor in the regional power equation. The ever-increasing numbers of Soviet aircraft and warships give Moscow a louder voice in regional affairs (as well as more clout to Soviet global military might). Moscow more than ever before can now threaten China from the latter's southern flank both on land and at sea, as well as the U.S. air and naval installations in the Philippines—base of operations for the U.S. Seventh Fleet covering the Pacific and the Indian Oceans. The intimidating effects of growing Soviet military might in the whole Indochina region pose a worrisome problem for the noncommunist ASEAN countries. Furthermore, the Soviet role in the Kampuchea problem increasingly figures in the global rivalry between the Soviet Union and the United States, as well as in the ongoing dialogue between the two superpowers on disarmament and the lessening of world tensions caused by regional conflicts.

The interests of ASEAN in promoting regional order have been two-fold: to seek and develop cooperation among the indigenous states of Southeast Asia, and to minimize adverse external power influence. The Bangkok Declaration (1967), the ASEAN Concord (1976), and the Treaty of Amity and Cooperation (also 1976) contain the principles advocated by ASEAN for forging intra-ASEAN cooperation and promoting close collaborative relations among the states of Southeast Asia in general. ASEAN's Declaration of the Zone of Peace, Freedom, and Neutrality (ZOPFAN 1971), on the other hand, reflects a desire to remove adverse outside influence from Southeast Asia by eliminating foreign-induced conflict and strife. Hence, ASEAN's subsequent involvement in the Kampuchea problem has been rationalized as conforming with ASEAN sentiments as expressed in these written statements. Most importantly, ASEAN envisages that the Southeast Asian countries must resort to peaceful methods in settling differences and must try to promote mutually advantageous relations between one another based on respect for differences existing in their respective political, social, and economic systems.

Anxious to settle the current Kampuchea problem, which presently threatens regional peace and order, ASEAN has all along been spearheading an international effort to bring about a comprehensive settlement. The broad outlines of ASEAN's advocacy, as well as practical recommendations for action, are contained in the Declaration of the International Conference on Kampuchea (ICK), the ASEAN Joint Appeal, and most recently the proposal for proximity talks, which address such issues as the Vietnamese military withdrawal from Kampuchea, the establishment of an independent, neutral, and nonaligned Kampuchea, and self-determination for the Kampuchean people. Only when these conditions are fulfilled can a settlement be reached that takes into consideration the security and other interests of all the protagonists.

The main obstacle to such progress remains Vietnam, which continues to insist on acceptance of its domination of Kampuchea as a *fait accompli* in spite of Hanoi's recent peaceful protestations and apparent show of flexibility. Faced with the prospect of continued international sanctions and isolation, long-term domestic economic stagnation, and a stalemate in the struggle inside Kampuchea against Kampuchean nationalist forces, Hanoi desires to become unburdened of the Kampuchea problem. Hence, it has advertised several tactical proposals, including negotiations with China to settle their bilateral problems and bloc dialogue between ASEAN and Indochina to discuss regional issues including Kampuchea, as well as proximity talks between the nationalist forces represented by the Coalition Government of Democratic Kampuchea (CGDK) and the Hanoi-installed Heng Samrin regime in Phnom Penh. As a further attempt to demonstrate its seriousness in settling the problem, Hanoi has declared its intention to unilaterally withdraw its armed forces from Kampuchea by 1990 regardless of whether or not a settlement between ASEAN and Vietnam will have been found.

Obviously, Hanoi is counting on the possibility of weakened resolve over the long run by those opposed to its occupation of Kampuchea, including ASEAN. More importantly, it is determined to eliminate the Kampuchean resistance forces, to the extent of violating Thailand's sovereignty and territorial integrity. There is thus little prospect that Vietnam will agree in the short run to any arrangement short of a Vietnam-dominated Kampuchea, which is a far cry from what ASEAN and the majority of the international community deem an acceptable solution.

In the final analysis, given the complex interplay of issues, interests, and actors in the Kampuchea problem, ASEAN alone cannot hope to "settle" the problem with Vietnam, desirous as it may be of coming to terms with the communist states of Indochina. The most feasible scenario for an effective solution would be for Vietnam to propose a *modus vivendi* arrangement, with the consensus of the other protagonists, whereby a neutral Kampuchea posing no security threat to its neighbors would come into being under a freely elected indigenous government, which at the same time could see Vietnamese political influence at play, albeit without Vietnamese military presence. Hanoi is apparently trying to accelerate the process of strengthening the Heng Samrin regime and liquidating the opposing Democratic Kampuchean regime, thus effecting a *fait accompli*. But its prospects of success are not particularly high. Even if Hanoi were to succeed eventually in this undertaking, it would find little or no acceptance by ASEAN, China, or most other concerned parties. Such a prospect of course would not augur well for regional peace and order, as the region would continue to face the uncertainty of conflict resulting from the continued imbalance of regional power.

CHAPTER 6

RELATIONS WITH CHINA, JAPAN, AND THE UNITED STATES

China

BIFAN CHENG

The ASEAN countries are China's close neighbors, and between the Chinese and ASEAN peoples there exist time-honored friendship and intimate economic relations. ASEAN holds a significant position in China's external relations with the Third World, and China gives priority to its relationship with ASEAN. In recent years, more and more Chinese scholars of international affairs have engaged in research on ASEAN, and many scholars in other countries are taking greater interest in Sino–ASEAN relationships. A common question is "What is China's main interest in Southeast Asia?" Our answer has been very simple and clear: First, China hopes that there will be lasting peace and stability among its close neighbors. Second, China hopes that its economic cooperation with the Southeast Asian countries, especially with ASEAN, will lead to common prosperity.

I am sure the ASEAN countries share China's concern about obtaining lasting peace and stability in our region. Both, for example, maintain that Vietnam must withdraw its troops from Kampuchea, and consider that the United States and the Soviet Union must downgrade their military rivalry in the Western Pacific region. China is the first among the great powers to support ASEAN's proposal for a Zone of Peace, Freedom, and Neutrality (ZOPFAN). Inevitably, however, there are issues upon which we disagree, such as the problem of overseas Chinese, the relationship between the Chinese Communist Party and local communist parties, and so on. On these issues, the viewpoints held by both sides are well known, and since space is limited, I focus my remarks on the Kampuchea War.

This war not only directly concerns ASEAN security interests but also may be crucial to ASEAN's future political relations with China. Proposals for a political settlement of the Kampuchea problem have been well publicized. I would like to concentrate on one problem that seems to me vitally important to future relationships between ASEAN and China. The problem is: What kind of political configuration will have been shaped in Southeast Asia when the Kampuchea War ends? One of two possible scenarios is that all the countries will respect each other's sovereignty and national independence, and will gradually establish a harmonious neighborhood. All countries will refrain from seeking a sphere of influence. No rival alliances or semi-alliances will emerge. I think this scenario is in conformity with ASEAN's ZOPFAN idea. In that case, the future of the region would be a bright one. Of course, differences would exist among nations, but peaceful solutions and stability would be achieved.

In the second scenario, some nations might judge the situation by the prevalent theory of power politics, believing that countries—big ones in particular—cannot avoid seeking a sphere of influence. They would like to see any resolution of the Kampuchea problem that would help contain this or that bigger country. Under such circumstances, there would most probably be new political rivalry and tension, and new turmoil would be fostered.

Which scenario does China prefer? I think it is wise for China to choose the first one, because it will benefit all the nations in the region and will enable the development of the Chinese economy. China estimates that another 45 to 65 years is needed to catch up with the Western developed countries in terms of per capita income. Some people think that a more powerful China would not want peace, but in my opinion China would place even greater value on peace.

As a result of its open-door policy, China's economic interdependence with its neighbors will grow. This basic economic factor will have an even greater influence on China's policy direction. There are some who wonder if Chinese leaders after Deng Xiaoping will continue to implement the present policy. Their worries are understandable, given that many great changes have taken place in China during the past three decades or so. An American friend from Columbia University once said to me, when he was talking about China's future, "The behavior of big powers is unpredictable." But in fact, he was always trying to predict it! Anyone with an opportunity to visit Chinese leaders should, besides Deng Xiaoping, also call on those who are much younger than Deng, because personal contacts with the new leaders will be helpful in judging Chinese policy trends.

On the question of economic cooperation between China and the ASEAN countries, the open-door policy provides opportunities to both sides. China and the ASEAN countries differ in the structure of their economies, consequently there is complementarity between them in primary and manufactured goods. Also, there is an evidently great potential for technological exchanges. Of course, the other side of the coin is that there is some competition between the two sides in the sale of manufactured goods, particularly the products of labor-intensive industries. But this is only a secondary issue, one that exists even within ASEAN. Generally speaking, the complementarity of trade between China and the ASEAN countries may be greater than exists among the ASEAN countries.

Trade between China and the ASEAN countries (except Brunei) in 1984 was U.S.$2.4 billion. But for both sides, the proportions in foreign trade are still small, roughly about 2 percent for the ASEAN countries and 5 percent for China respectively, and there is room for the development of trade between the two sides. The trade deficits on the ASEAN side have been relatively high for many years. To solve this problem both sides must explore energetically the possibilities for increasing the quantity and variety of ASEAN exports to China. At the same time, it seems necessary and desirable for the ASEAN countries to invest more in China, especially in areas that will promote the export of resource products. China should also explore the possibilities for investment in the ASEAN countries. In the course of the Four Modernizations, China needs to import not only capital goods but also primary products and manufactured goods in quantity. China has already made some investment in resource-intensive industries in several countries, including Thailand and Singapore, and should explore such possibilities in other ASEAN countries.

Strengthening economic cooperation between China and the ASEAN countries needs great efforts from both entrepreneurs and governments. But, first of all, various necessary governmental arrangements should be improved step by step. The strengthening of economic relations between the two sides will certainly be helpful to the further improvement of political relations and *vice versa*. Clearly, the general trend is for relations between China and the ASEAN countries to grow better and better.

Japan

MOTOFUMI ASAI

This section focuses on Japan's economic relations with ASEAN, although political, military, cultural, racial, and religious elements also play significant roles in the life of the ASEAN countries and in Japan's relations with them. A reason for the economic focus is given by Wong and Cheung in Chapter 2, where they point out: "[B]y far the most serious implications for ASEAN's future development and stability lie in the problem of income inequality . . . Income inequality may be tolerated by the population during times of economic expansion (i.e., so long as the cake is getting bigger); this may not be the case if the economy stagnates." Indeed, according to Wanandi (Chapter 5), the recent success of the ASEAN countries is due in part to "the ability of the national leaderships to properly assess the nature of the threats their nations face. As a result, all ASEAN countries give top priority to national development." The experiences of Japan and Asian newly industrializing countries (NICs) manifest the validity of these arguments. In my remarks, I will discuss first challenges for the ASEAN countries and second challenges for Japan in its relations with the ASEAN countries.

CHALLENGES FOR THE ASEAN COUNTRIES

Rapid economic growth in the ASEAN region has become possible through the adoption of firm and bold policy initiatives to link national economic development with the expansion of trade, especially exports. Such a policy mix is sometimes labeled as an "export-led development strategy." ASEAN cannot be complacent though. However successful they have been, the economies of the ASEAN countries—or indeed of any country—cannot be immune from problems, and at least some of those problems are inherent in the strategy itself.

The ASEAN economies' big success is in large part due to increasing demand for their products by an expanding world market. A rising protectionist mood has already clouded prospects for future exports from these countries. High interest rates in the United States, together with uncertainty about the future, have caused investment flows into the ASEAN countries to stagnate. Of course, economic performance, resilience, and prospects vary from country to country, but no country can afford to neglect or dismiss the gravity of the international economic situation.

It is a rule of political life that when a country's economy runs satisfactorily, few people can openly challenge the rationale of relevant policies. However, once the economy falters or shows signs of stagnation, latent problems are certain to surface, and so are criticisms against the policies and the government.

Maybe I am drawing too gloomy a picture. The recent depreciation of the U.S. dollar in foreign exchange markets may be a good sign for ASEAN countries, whose currencies are more or less pegged to the dollar. Strong and continued growth of the Chinese economy is another factor for encouragement. Furthermore, Japan has been requested to play the role of economic "locomotive," and the Japanese government fully recognizes the need to do so.

The prevailing feeling in many of the ASEAN countries, however, is one of caution, if not pessimism. And that may be commendable. As one Japanese proverb says, you will not be taken by surprise if you are well prepared for the worst.

Thus, the basic problems facing ASEAN economies are: First, it is seriously questioned for the first time whether the export-led development strategy of the ASEAN countries can still demonstrate its validity both in resolving domestic socioeconomic and political problems and in countering adverse international economic trends.

Second, while it may be very easy to pick holes in an export-led development strategy, no alternative stategy has ever succeeded. No country has ever been content to remain an agro-economy. A heavily protected, import-substituting industrialization strategy was once dominant in the early phase of development but soon encountered unsurmountable obstacles and was abandoned in many countries. The only possible exception may be Japan's postwar economic performance under heavy protectionist policies in the early 1950s, but the policy mix may be difficult to repeat in or transplant to other countries in different circumstances.

Socialist economies are seriously handicapped by problems of quality and efficiency, two prerequisites for any modern economy. China's economic reform is exactly aimed at removing these problems and, through imaginative policy initiatives, achieving healthy growth. As Chinese leaders themselves say, theirs is a bold experiment. Nevertheless, the idea of socialist construction is out of the question in the ASEAN countries anyway.

Indeed, the spectacular economic development of the ASEAN countries has only been matched by the comparable performances of Asian NICs, which have also vigorously pursued similar strategies of export-led development. For practical purposes, therefore, and in the absence of any viable alternative strategy, the question for the ASEAN countries may be how to adapt the existing strategy to changing circumstances.

The third problem is that with the increasing difficulty of expanding access for their products in the developed world market, export-led economies of the ASEAN countries have to look elsewhere to market their products. The relatively small size of the domestic market in each ASEAN country is a physical constraint. If taken together, naturally, the potential of the ASEAN countries as a group with a total population of almost 300 million and a combined GNP of U.S.$200 billion cannot be neglected. If economic cooperation and regional integration develop gradually, it may not be impossible for the ASEAN countries to form an independent economic unit—the goal the ASEAN countries are jointly pursuing, although there is still a long way to go.

CHALLENGES FOR JAPAN IN ITS RELATIONS WITH THE ASEAN COUNTRIES

The ASEAN countries and Japan have highly complementary economies, and our economic exchanges have steadily increased in both trade and investment. The two sides have become major economic partners. The ASEAN countries are rich in resources, including minerals, energy, and agricultural and fishery products, and Japan is in a position to offer capital and technology. Moreover, some of the ASEAN countries sit astride crucial international maritime transportation routes leading to Japan.

In trade, the ASEAN countries are Japan's second-largest partner after the United States and accounted for about 12 percent of Japan's total trade in 1984. About 19 percent of Japan's overseas investments went to the ASEAN countries during the period 1951 to 1984. Japan is the six ASEAN countries' largest trading partner, accounting for about 24 percent of their total trade in 1983. Japan is also the largest or second largest investor for each member country, depending upon country and year. The ASEAN countries as a group are also the biggest recipient of Japanese technology transferred abroad. For instance, from April 1982 to

March 1983, the ASEAN countries received 23.9 percent in value terms and 25.6 percent in volume terms of all the technologies exported from Japan. These figures fully illustrate the economic interdependence of the ASEAN countries and Japan.

The maintenance of close and friendly relations with the ASEAN countries has, therefore, consistently been a major component of our foreign policy, and Japan has paid special attention to the ASEAN countries in the conduct of its foreign policy. I would like to cite a few examples to illustrate this point.

In economic and technical cooperation, Japan has accorded a high priority to the ASEAN countries. In 1983, for instance, about U.S.$727 million of Japanese ODA (Official Development Assistance) was disbursed to various projects in the ASEAN countries in such fields as human resource development, energy development, rural development, and small-business promotion. This amount was about 30 percent of Japan's total ODA extended on a bilateral basis, and the ASEAN countries have consistently received about one-third of Japan's bilateral ODA. The same pattern is also seen in other fields of Japanese cooperation with the ASEAN countries' nation-building efforts. In 1983, for example, the number of students in Japan on government scholarship from the ASEAN countries accounted for about 30 percent of the total number of foreign students with Japanese government scholarships.

In trade, in response to ASEAN countries' requests that Japan improve access to its market for tropical products as well as manufactured and semi-manufactured goods, we have instituted several series of market-opening measures for products from the ASEAN area. These measures include tariff reduction for products of major interest to ASEAN, advance implementation of tariff reduction agreed upon as a result of multilateral trade negotiations, a ten-year extension of the preferential tariff system from 1981, and larger quotas for the manufactured goods coming into Japan under its generalized preference scheme. These measures, which were taken despite the difficulties they cause for domestic Japanese producers, did not, however, entirely satisfy the ASEAN countries. I will come back to this subject later.

I would like next to touch briefly upon the political aspect of the Japan–ASEAN relationship. Japan and the ASEAN countries have common interests and concerns in the international community, and we have been cooperating inside and outside of the United Nations. The most immediate and serious problem that Japan and the ASEAN countries are facing in Asia today is, of course, the Kampuchea situation. We fully support ASEAN's position, and we are cooperating with the ASEAN countries in search of a peaceful solution.

Another important area of common interest for ASEAN and Japan is in cultural and personal exchanges to contribute to mutual understanding. The ASEAN countries are the highest-priority region for Japan's cultural grant aid, about one-third of which is extended for ASEAN cultural development projects.

Having reviewed briefly Japan's relations with the ASEAN countries, I now would like to touch upon problems in our economic relations and the challenges these problems pose for Japan. An immediate issue is the problem of market access for ASEAN products. Many of the products of traditional interest to the ASEAN countries are agricultural products, and agriculture is the least competitive sector in Japan's economy. The problem is that it is impossible for any country to totally give up agricultural production.

Another issue concerns energy and non-ferrous metal resources. The bulk of ASEAN countries' foreign earnings has been derived from the exportation of such natural resources—with Japan one of the biggest importers. Now that international market conditions have deteriorated, the earnings of the countries concerned have been adversely affected, and Japan is facing mounting demands to behave as a good customer as before.

Furthermore, of common and increasing interest for the ASEAN countries is market access for their manufactured and semi-manufactured products. As Naya points out in Chapter 3, "Trade relations between the ASEAN countries and Japan . . . have maintained the typical 'North–South' pattern, with Japan importing energy and raw materials and exporting manufactures . . . Japan's large trade surpluses reflect the difficulty that manufactured exports, from both developed and developing countries, have in penetrating the Japanese markets."

Second, and no less important, are the demands of the ASEAN countries for increasing rather sluggish Japanese investment in the region. As is clear from the above, the region's continued prosperity, and thereby political stability, is largely determined by the strength or validity of export-led development strategy, and the success of the strategy has been, in significant degree, attributed to foreign investment. It is not anticipated that this situation will undergo substantial changes in the foreseeable future.

Japanese investment is strongly urged for the following (sometimes contradictory) reasons:

- Japanese investors have been keen to understand and quick to pick up locally preferred areas of investment;
- Partly as a result of the above, Japanese investments have been

balanced between the two major sectors, manufacturing and mining, to the satisfaction of local governments;

- Under strong pressure of increases in population and labor force, some densely populated ASEAN countries desire investment in labor-intensive industries, and Japanese investments in the manufacturing sector have actually had some positive and alleviating effects;
- It is widely believed in developing countries that foreign investment is a source of new and advanced technology, and here again Japan is regarded as one of the major contributors. Nevertheless, there have been growing complaints from all quarters in Asia that Japanese contributions in technology transfer and especially that of advanced technology have been limited and insufficient, quantitatively as well as qualitatively, and that Japanese investors have feared "catch-up" or "boomerang" effects. There have also been related criticisms such as the expense, language barrier, slow manner of teaching, lack of manuals, etc. Unfortunately, reliable statistics on these issues are difficult to obtain.

From my limited conversations with colleagues in the ASEAN countries, I cannot escape from feeling that Japanese investment is regarded as an economic panacea in ASEAN countries, and I cannot but ask myself if the Japanese economy can meet all these requirements.

ADDRESSING THE CHALLENGES

This review of the challenges facing both the ASEAN countries and Japan highlights basic issues: the need of the ASEAN countries for further industrialization, and the inescapable need for structural changes in Japanese industries to meet the demands of the ASEAN countries. The question is whether both sides will be able to hammer out acceptable compromises within the narrow margins of maneuverability.

For Japan, the challenges perhaps are even more serious, because demands come not only from the ASEAN countries but also from other Asian, North American, and West European countries. Although the demands vary from country to country, the message is too clear to be misunderstood: Japan, being the biggest beneficiary of the international market economy system and most dependent on free trade for its existence (needless to say prosperity), should shoulder more economic responsibility in helping to cure and revitalize the ailing international economy as a whole and to assist developing countries in their efforts to escape from poverty and to share prosperity.

The various demands on Japan can be classified into several categories. A few of them are obviously ill-founded or even groundless, to be
very frank. Some of them are products of either misunderstanding caused
by a lack of information, contacts, reliable statistics, and so on, or by
analyses from different data. The latter is true, to some extent, of Japanese investment in and technology transfer to the ASEAN countries, and
also in the case of the balance-of-trade problem. There also exist situations in which one-sided and emotional accusations obscure the nature of
problems involved and increase mutual distrust.

It will not be easy, but these problems can be dealt with if the parties
stop blaming each other and sit down to talk seriously and in earnest. But
as mentioned earlier, there certainly exist problems that command special
and serious consideration. Some of the U.S.–Japanese trade conflicts are
one example. A few of the ASEAN–Japanese, Korean–Japanese, or
Sino–Japanese economic dealings are another. On our part, there has
been growing recognition that Japan is now on the verge of "the second
opening of our country" after the first in 1868.

The Japanese have come to realize the significance and profundity of
Edwin O. Reischauer's observations (1981:369–375) noting Japan's
increased dependence on the global economy in the postwar period and
arguing that although wars and disasters are unlikely for Japan, the
decline or stagnation of world trade is all too likely a catastrophe. But the
process of realization seems intolerably slow in the eyes of the affected
countries. The feeling of frustration can only be amplified by the shrewd-
ness the Japanese demonstrate in adapting to rapidly changing economic
environments.

As a diplomat, I recognize that much needs to be done by the Japanese. But, at the same time, I sincerely hope that due regard will be paid
to the Japanese character and the difficulties derived from it. Once again
Reischauer (1981:37,335) observed correctly that the suddenness of
Japan's reinvolvement with the world has been upsetting and that Japan's
uncertainty and lack of confidence about its position in the world in part
stems from some of its strengths, such as strong self-identity and homo-
geneity.

Whereas some ASEAN–Japanese economic problems can be solved in
the context of bilateral relations, we have to recognize that many others
can be properly dealt with only in a broader context, with each side having regional and even international perspectives. And we need patience
and due regard for each other's difficulties. I have touched upon the Japanese character and difficulties in meeting our challenges, in order to
invite the attention of the reader to the danger of driving the Japanese

into a tight corner. Without being allowed time to learn and adapt, the Japanese can react only in a desperate and counterproductive manner.

Japan's case is raised only as an illustration. Each country has its own difficulties. Patient and friendly consultations based upon mutual understanding and trust are the only way for all members of the international community to avoid repeating historical follies and for achieving long-lasting, worldwide prosperity.

REFERENCE

Reischauer, Edwin O.
  1981   *The Japanese.* Cambridge, Massachusetts: Harvard University Press.

The United States

ROBERT G. TORRICELLI

The United States and the ASEAN nations are linked by political, economic, and, in some cases, military ties. Trade relations are widespread and expanding continuously. The U.S. military commitment to certain of the ASEAN states is an important component in assuring regional security. Our social and cultural connections are growing stronger. Immigrants from Southeast Asia have enriched American life, and Americans are becoming increasingly aware of the cultural traditions their new neighbors have brought.

The United States is reaching maturity in its dealings with the rest of the world. We have at last overcome the trauma of our involvement in Vietnam. We realize that withdrawing into isolation from the world's problems is impossible, but that we must not return to a simplistic cold war mentality that sees the hand of international communism behind every upheaval.

The United States and ASEAN share two basic common interests: economic growth and national and regional security. These interests are complementary, since without economic growth our people cannot hope for a better life and without security economic growth is impossible. Because of their strategic location and growing economic importance, the ASEAN countries have a role to play beyond their immediate neighborhood. The volume of trade between ASEAN and Japan, Australia, and the United States dictates a concern for regional stability and the security of sea lanes.

The United States realizes that ASEAN is not a homogeneous bloc, but an association of states with different languages, cultures, religions, and traditions. Singapore, with a population of 2.5 million people, is in a far different position from Indonesia with over 160 million. Nonetheless, ASEAN leaders understand the benefits of solidarity. The United States welcomes this cohesion, for it is in our mutual interest and it allows us to deal with the ASEAN nations individually and collectively.

The United States does not seek an alliance with ASEAN as a whole. The era of constructing a worldwide network of pacts is over. Rather, the United States seeks productive, multilevel ties, based on regional circumstances, with friendly countries. ASEAN is the fifth-largest trading partner of the United States, and the United States is ASEAN's second-largest trading partner. The United States is committed to maintaining its foreign assistance program for the benefit of the ASEAN states. In 1986, Indonesia will receive almost U.S.$135 million; Thailand, U.S.$135 million; Malaysia, over U.S.$6 million; and the Philippines, almost U.S. $180 million.

ASEAN AND REGIONAL TROUBLE SPOTS

THE PHILIPPINES

The problem areas of chief concern to ASEAN—the Philippines and Kampuchea—are also worrisome to the United States. In the Philippines, economic and political instability threaten the livelihood of millions of citizens and, from the U.S. point of view, the viability of an ally of long standing. We cannot place any faith in the continued assurances of President Ferdinand Marcos and his advisers that everything is under control when we know that things are out of control. Real gross national product declined by 5.5 percent in 1984. No growth is expected in 1985. The communist New People's Army (NPA) is estimated to number as many as 15,000 guerillas. The success of the government in suppressing the insurgency in Mindanao in the 1970s cannot be duplicated today. The Marcos government has mismanaged the economy and alienated important sectors of the populace.

If the Philippines were to fall under the control of elements unfriendly to the United States, the consequences for our allies in Southeast Asia—and the entire Western Pacific—would be quite severe. The loss of access to Clark Air Base and Subic Bay Naval Base would complicate our efforts to secure the vital trans-Pacific trade routes. It would heighten the concerns among Southeast Asian nations about subversion both from within and without.

The crisis in the Philippines highlights a problem widespread in the developing world. From our point of view, it is not enough that a country be allied with the United States and engage in the rhetoric of anticommunism. A state must also work to provide its people with economic opportunities and with the basic human rights of self-expression. It must seek a society in which social and economic privileges are available to more than just a privileged few. Inordinate concentration of wealth and the choking-off of legitimate disagreement are a sure prescription for mounting instability and even revolution. These conditions provide fertile ground for subversion by outside powers.

U.S. Senator Paul Laxalt has recently conveyed U.S. President Ronald Reagan's concern over events in the Philippines to President Marcos. The U.S. Congress has approved the Philippines aid package for 1986, but has conditioned future aid on progress in instituting reforms. There is a clear consensus in both the U.S. House and the Senate that the Philippine government should undertake wide-ranging economic, political, and military changes in the very near future.

This is not a case of the United States trying to impose its political morality abroad; rather, it is an attempt to aid the existing democratic forces in the Philippines. We are saying that the United States supports the Philippines and its people, not the Marcos government. Of course, when a government is in power, the distinction is not always clear. The U.S. Congress sees no other way, however, to clarify its position.

KAMPUCHEA

Because of its involvement in the Indochina War (and it is important to remember that the fighting in Vietnam spread to Laos and Kampuchea as well), the United States bears a special and continuing responsibility in that area. Our objective, and the objective of the ASEAN nations, is the establishment of a free and independent Kampuchea. We oppose Vietnamese imperialism just as we oppose the return of the genocidal Khmer Rouge regime. We in the United States are gratified that ASEAN has taken the lead on this issue; it is an example of the kind of regional cooperation necessary to counter the forces of instability and expansionism.

In order to further these purposes, the U.S. Congress has approved U.S.$5 million in assistance to the noncommunist Kampuchean resistance. It is important that noncommunist elements be strengthened against the onslaughts of Vietnam now and, perhaps, the Khmer Rouge later.

Vietnam is an integral part of the Southeast Asian region and as such should play a role in that area's political and economic life. We cannot accept, however, Vietnam's attempt to dominate all of Indochina, a drive that has caused further warfare in Kampuchea after the bloody years of the late 1970s and whose repercussions have reached Thailand as well.

The behavior of the Vietnamese regime within its own country is also cause for concern. It is not for nothing that thousands of desperate families have embarked in small boats to escape their native land. Nonetheless, our initial focus must remain on Vietnam's international behavior.

The United States has rightly been criticized for its role in the Vietnam War. We are at least partially responsible for setting into motion the train of events that produced the ongoing violence. This in no way provides an excuse for the current behavior of the Vietnamese regime and does not mean that the United States should wash its hands of the area's problems. On the contrary, we must now recommit ourselves to working with the countries of the area to ensure that all states can determine their own futures within secure and recognized borders.

The United States has accepted the fact that Vietnam is reunified and functions under its current government. We do not accept, though, Vietnam's thirst for conquest, which undermines its own economic base and threatens the security of the entire region.

This concern is based not only upon Vietnam's role in Kampuchea, but also on Vietnamese acquiescence in the growth of Soviet military activity in the area. The Soviets have transformed Cam Ranh Bay naval base into one of their largest military installations abroad. The Soviets have brought two floating piers to Cam Ranh to add to the existing facilities. On an average day, the base hosts between 20 and 25 surface ships and between four and six submarines. MiG fighters and medium- and long-range bombers have flown reconnaissance missions out of the base. Soviet air and naval projection into the South China Sea and the Indian Ocean cannot be overlooked by either the United States or ASEAN. Our mutual concerns dictate continuing attention to developments in this area.

JAPAN AND ASEAN

In World War II, the peoples of Southeast Asia suffered conquest and subjugation by the Japanese empire. Today, Japan is a peaceful state, seeking prosperity through trade rather than war. As Prime Minister Lee Kuan Yew of Singapore told the U.S. Congress in October 1985, the maintenance of peace is partly due to the ability of formerly militaristic states to prosper through trade. This prosperity also brings responsibility to make it possible for others to follow the same path. It is right that Japan should contribute to the world prosperity it has so richly benefited from. "America has the right," Mr. Lee stated, "to ask that those who have benefited from America's market open up their own." The same applies to Japan and the Asian market.

The U.S. Congress is now considering legislation designed to signal concern over Japan's trade policies and restrictions, both formal and informal, on imports. American legislators recognize that this issue is of great concern to ASEAN as well. The proposed U.S. legislation will ensure that Japanese exports held back from the American markets will not be shifted to other parts of the world. In addition, the United States applauds ASEAN's efforts to sell more finished products to Japan. Currently, Japan relies on ASEAN for almost all of its imports of natural rubber and tin, and substantial percentages of its lumber, metals, and crude oil and gas needs. It is time that Japan also increase it purchases of ASEAN manufactures. Japan has set an example for the rest of Asia; let it not block others on the road to prosperity.

There have been numerous calls in the United States, both by administration and congressional figures, for Japan to increase its defense spending. These pressures are misguided. The Japanese people have been right in rejecting the militarism and thirst for dominion that brought them and half the world to grief. In the last 40 years, Japan has concentrated on developing the economic machine that has produced an amazing quantity and variety of goods for the global marketplace. Now is the time for Japan to reciprocate for the benefit of a benign international trading system guaranteed by the United States. It must upgrade its participation in bilateral and multilateral development assistance. Japan is already active in such programs in ASEAN. This trend is to be encouraged.

U.S.–CHINA RELATIONS AND THE IMPLICATIONS FOR ASEAN

U.S. ties with China are strong and growing stronger. As in any relationship, certain problems remain outstanding—in this case, the Taiwan question. This should not obscure, however, the enduring friendship and expanding cooperation between the two countries. U.S.–China links are developing in both economic and military matters.

The American government realizes that the military aspects of the relationship cause concern among the nations of Southeast Asia. It should be emphasized, therefore, that U.S.–China links will not come at the expense of ASEAN. On the contrary, Southeast Asia is probably in less danger of direct or indirect Chinese subversion since the Sino–American rapprochement. China is no longer the wild card of world politics that it was during most of the rule of Mao Zedong. China now shows greater awareness of the responsibility conferred on it by its vast population and territory and awareness of Southeast Asian security concerns. U.S. policy is designed to promote this awareness.

China is beginning to realize, through the application of free-market economic policies and more enlightened social measures, the benefits inherent in its enormous human potential. A secure and prosperous China will concentrate on its own development, not on international adventurism. This is why the United States has sought to draw China into a mutually beneficial network of relationships.

The United States and China are not about to enter into a military alliance. This would be not only unwise but also unnecessary. The United States sells China defensive weaponry only, weaponry that will modernize the Chinese armed forces and deter Soviet intimidation. The United States will continue to encourage China to play a constructive role in the settlement of the Kampuchea conflict. It should be quite clear that ASEAN should not hope to play China and Vietnam against each other; the longer the conflict lasts, the greater the danger of an expanded conflict that will threaten ASEAN in general and Thailand most directly. Rather, ASEAN must persist in its effort to reduce tension between Vietnam and its neighbors.

THE UNITED STATES IN THE PACIFIC

New Zealand

In the South Pacific, nuclear issues have come to the forefront. New Zealand's Labour government shows no sign of reconsidering its decision to ban American warships on the presumption that they are nuclear-capable. Prime Minister David Lange has stated that he intends to make this issue a matter of law. If this should happen, ANZUS (Australia, New Zealand, United States Pact) naval exercises in the area will be disrupted. More importantly, a loyal ally of long standing will be seen to have broken ranks with the United States.

The U.S. Congress and the Reagan Administration are united on this issue. Those that would benefit from defense ties with the United States must also accept the burdens. In this case, the burden is extremely slight, and in no way compares to the responsibility the Australians have undertaken by hosting American communications facilities.

We continue to hope that Prime Minister Lange's government will find a way to resolve this matter without unnecessary strain between our two countries. It would be a great shame if these incidents were allowed to disrupt the traditionally friendly relations between New Zealand and the United States at the very time when we all must be seeking greater security in the Western Pacific. And although this affair does not concern ASEAN directly, it should be noted that the security of Southeast Asia does not rest on a single component. Trouble in ANZUS can only be harmful to ASEAN as well.

THE PACIFIC ISLANDS

In August 1985, the eight members of the South Pacific Forum, including Australia and New Zealand, met in Rarotonga to establish the South Pacific Nuclear Free Zone (SPNFZ). This is a matter of concern to France, which, as can be seen from the *Rainbow Warrior* affair, will go to some length to preserve its nuclear testing capabilities in Polynesia.

The United States understands the French desire to maintain an independent deterrent force and to continue nuclear testing. At the same time the establishment of the nuclear free zone must be applauded as a further step toward restricting the areas of nuclear competition, and a welcome companion to the Treaty of Tlatelolco in Latin America and the Antarctica Treaty. It is to be hoped that both French interests and the maintenance of the zone can be reconciled by the negotiation of a worldwide comprehensive test ban treaty.

The nuclear free zone, whose western border coincides with that of Papua New Guinea, is not of immediate concern to ASEAN. Nonetheless, as in the case of ANZUS, the nations of Southeast Asia will profit by consulting with the United States on matters of wider concern. The growth and prosperity of ASEAN will impel its members to look beyond their immediate neighborhood and cooperate in the effort to ensure stability in the wider Pacific region.

The island states of the Pacific are a part of this broader neighborhood with a unique set of challenges. Burgeoning populations and the transition from colonialism have the potential to cause upheaval among some of the islands. Not all of the new countries are as well endowed with resources as Fiji, Papua New Guinea, and Vanuatu; new states such as Kiribati and Tuvalu possess limited resources and few prospects for growth, except for the exploitation of fishing rights. The United States has entered into a Compact of Free Association with the Federated States of Micronesia, the Republic of the Marshall Islands, and the Republic of Palau, and has signed a covenant with the Commonwealth of the Northern Marianas, thus undertaking continuing responsibility for aiding the parties involved.

We are concerned about the growing Soviet interest in the South Pacific. The recent Soviet fishing agreement with Kiribati and unsuccessful attempt to establish one with Tuvalu are not in themselves worrisome. We must, however, be alert to Soviet moves in this area. Their overtures to the newly independent states, coupled with the substantial growth of the Soviet Far East fleet, bear close watching.

Americans realize that their particular political system is not necessarily a desirable model for all countries. Nevertheless, the growth of democracy and the commitment to human rights are desirable goals for all states. We commend the upholding of democratic institutions where they exist among the ASEAN states and would welcome further moves in this direction. Authoritarianism is no guarantee of stability; rather, it stifles the individual initiative so necessary to economic growth and social development. The United States and its friends must work toward the fulfillment of a common outlook and a shared commitment to political participation, human rights, and respect for the dignity of all members of society. It is these factors more than any that bind the United States to its close allies in Europe and elsewhere, and the U.S.–ASEAN partnership should also be characterized by these qualities. A strong relationship is one that continually becomes stronger. It must not become stagnant; it must always be infused with fresh content and the expansion of shared values and interests.

The United States has gained significant experience in its worldwide activities since the end of World War II. We have erred at times by pursuing simplistic solutions to complex problems and by drawing inappropriate historical analogies. The advocates of rigid and reflexive policies are still touting their theories. Yet at the same time, a new realism is taking hold in American policymaking—a realism that seeks a sophisticated understanding of conflicts by considering local and regional, as well as international, factors.

The United States has always praised moderate leaders around the world. We must now put this rhetoric into practice in more cases. We must reject the extremes of repression and anarchy, and the excuses that are made in the name of each. Where children go to bed hungry and disease strikes them down before their prime, political participation becomes irrelevant. And where government stifles the aspirations and initiatives of the individual, prosperity is hollow. The United States hopes that the nations of ASEAN will continue to share the endeavor of political and economic development to improve the lives of all our peoples.

CHAPTER 7
CONCLUSION

ASEAN:
The Challenges Ahead

LEE-JAY CHO

Prior to the formation of the Association of South East Asian Nations in 1967, the individual countries of the group stood alone. With the possible exception of Indonesia, none was regarded as economically or politically significant on a global or even a regional scale. In the previous chapters, the individual and collective successes of the ASEAN countries in meeting the social, economic, political, and foreign policy challenges of the past 18 years have been discussed. These chapters and the discussions at the East–West Center's 25th Anniversary Conference on ASEAN and the Pacific Basin point out, however, that the countries of the region and their association will face difficult tasks ahead. It is fitting, therefore, to conclude this volume with a brief overview of ASEAN's future challenges.

DEMOGRAPHIC AND SOCIAL CHALLENGES

Demographic and social change in the ASEAN countries has been remarkable. The rapid reduction in mortality and extension of life expectancy are undeniable indications of significant progress. Impressive achievements also have been made in extending the scope and quality of education. The improved health and increased skills of the ASEAN populations have no doubt played an important role in their countries' economic growth. There is debate, however, about how well these and other

The author is very grateful to Charles Morrison for his review of the draft of this paper and for his valuable suggestions.

improvements have been distributed throughout society. Because data on income distribution are of poor quality, some economists argue that one should simply look at aggregate indicators of the fulfillment of basic needs, such as life expectancy and per capita income. Besides, they argue, inequality usually first increases before it decreases in the course of economic development. Although differentials in access to services and opportunities in the ASEAN region appear to be less than in most developing countries, the governments recognize that serious disparities do exist and they are pledged to increase equality of opportunity in their countries. Fulfilling these pledges is a long-term task.

The ASEAN countries have also not had to face so rapid a rate of urbanization as some of the other developing countries of the world. Nevertheless, the absolute growth of urban populations and of the major cities in ASEAN is cause for concern. Not only is the quality of life affected by the excess demand for public goods and services in the cities, but it is also very basically linked to the excess demand for jobs and the resulting urban unemployment.

Ironically, it is the success of the ASEAN countries in reducing fertility and population growth that presents one of the greatest long-term challenges—aging of their populations and labor forces. Although the issue is of immediate concern only to Singapore with its below-replacement fertility, the ASEAN Heads of Population Programme are to be congratulated on their foresight in sponsoring the current ASEAN-wide study on aging. Of particular concern are the future roles of the family and the government in caring for the elderly who are unable to care for themselves. With fewer adult children for each elderly parent, urbanization and tighter housing space, separation of families through migration, and increased labor force participation of women who are the traditional caretakers, the ability of the family to care for the elderly in their extended later years may be severely circumscribed.

There are economic implications of aging beyond the possible need for greater public assistance. One of the ASEAN countries' greatest competitive assets over the last 20 years has been a young, abundant, increasingly skilled, and low-paid labor force. For Indonesia, the Philippines, and Thailand, absorption of these workers into the modern sector of the economy remains a challenge, but Malaysia and Singapore experienced labor shortages in some industries in the late 1970s and early 1980s. Malaysia has recently instituted a pro-natalist policy, which, if successful, could slow aging and stimulate further growth of the labor force, but Singapore will be faced with making the best use of an older, more expensive labor force and in this regard will lose some of its comparative advantage relative to Japan and Western countries.

ECONOMIC CHALLENGES

The outstanding economic success story of the ASEAN countries has its foundations in their rich resource bases (excluding Singapore) and in outward-looking economic policies that have sought to exploit opportunities in expanding world markets. Trade has accounted for from 40 to 300 percent of gross domestic product of the member countries and has been an engine of growth for the modern sectors of their economies. In the years ahead, ASEAN's primary-product resources, such as petroleum, tin, and natural rubber, may be less in demand in world markets, and the ASEAN countries may have to depend more upon internal sources of growth, as well as continue to shift their economic structures toward manufacturing and services. The member countries' ability to meet successfully the social challenges of providing employment and ameliorating socioeconomic inequalities will depend in part upon their ability to sustain aggregate growth rates.

In the first half of the 1980s, there have been sharply reduced growth rates for the group as a whole, and two members (the Philippines and Singapore) are experiencing negative per capita growth in 1985. It is impossible to tell whether this economic downturn represents a short-term cyclical problem or a more fundamental change in economic conditions, but there are reasons to believe economic growth in the future will not come quite so easily as in the past. The technological success of the developed countries in conserving energy and raw materials in manufacturing industries has depressed demand for a wide range of primary products, including petroleum and tin, which account for high proportions of the export earnings of Indonesia, Malaysia, Brunei, and (indirectly) Singapore. The successes of many developing countries, including those of the ASEAN group, in increasing agricultural production, together with agricultural overproduction in some advanced countries resulting from high subsidies, have depressed the markets for ASEAN agricultural exports such as rice (affecting mainly Thailand) and sugar (principally affecting the Philippines). The manufacturing sectors in all of the ASEAN countries have been growing rapidly, but may be affected over the longer term by slower growth in demand for these products in the advanced countries, by technological change undercutting ASEAN's labor-based competitive advantage, and by protectionism. Moreover, the ASEAN countries will be facing increased competition in these markets from other, cheaper-labor industrializing countries including China and India.

The basic ASEAN policies of promoting exports in world markets, especially of those products in which the member countries have an advantage because of their labor or resource endowments, are sound. To maintain high growth and strengthen their competitiveness, however, the countries will need to supplement these policies with stronger efforts to reduce internal economic distortions and inefficiencies. These include a number of internal monopolies, many of them protected from external competition through high tariffs, quotas, and subsidies. The ASEAN countries may also need to increase domestic savings to compensate for reduced foreign aid, investments, or borrowing from abroad. At the present time, saving rates (aside from Singapore's exceptionally high rate) are only modestly above those of other middle-income developing nations.

Though the most significant economic tasks facing ASEAN involve individual governments, the potential for regional economic cooperation should not be neglected. ASEAN economic cooperation has made only slow progress; the highly publicized internal trade preference schemes, for example, so far have involved only marginal reductions of tariffs and many of the more significant trade items have been excluded. Some participants at the October 1985 East–West Center conference argued that because of bureaucratic delays the ASEAN large-scale industry projects and industrial complementation schemes slowed, rather than hastened, industrial development. There appears to be growing interest in the private sector of the ASEAN countries to improve the quality of regional cooperation principally by reducing artificial barriers among the countries. The history of other regional associations indicates that there are formidable political obstacles to trade liberalization, even among friendly countries.

POLITICAL AND FOREIGN POLICY CHALLENGES

In the political and foreign policy sphere the ASEAN countries also face difficult challenges on the road ahead. Perhaps at the head of the list of these challenges is what Wanandi in Chapter 5 calls "the building of political institutions." Such institutions, which include governmental agencies, political organizations, and widely accepted rules or norms for the resolution of issues and leadership transitions, have been evolving slowly but by and large remain untested. For example, of the ASEAN countries only Malaysia consistently has had peaceful transitions of political leadership.

These challenges are illustrated by the current leadership crisis in the Philippines; a crisis aggravated by serious economic difficulties and by the failure of President Ferdinand Marcos to promote younger leaders among his supporters or countenance alternative leadership through a fair electoral system. Although Indonesia and Singapore have maintained the same top political leadership as long as has the Philippines, no such leadership crisis has developed. In both countries there has been a conscious effort to build political institutions and promote generational change within these institutions. President Soeharto of Indonesia and Prime Minister Lee Kuan Yew of Singapore, however, have played the critical role so far in developing the new institutions, of which the supreme test will come when these able political leaders retire.

There is a daunting array of other political challenges that lie ahead for the ASEAN countries—accommodating demands for ethnic autonomy in some countries, developing a consensus on the proper role for religion, and striking an agreement on the appropriate roles of civilian and military institutions. All the ASEAN countries maintain some restrictions on what Westerners would regard as political freedoms; the scope of such restrictions is frequently a matter of domestic contention.

In the foreign policy sphere, the ASEAN countries advocate as an ultimate goal the creation of a Zone of Peace, Freedom, and Neutrality (ZOPFAN) in Southeast Asia. The challenge they face is to maintain a safe regional environment in the near term, while developing a workable strategy for the realization of ZOPFAN in the longer term.

ASEAN has already achieved one remarkable foreign policy success—for almost two decades there have been close and generally harmonious relations among its members. This is remarkable because prior to the creation of the association, there was considerable tension among the countries of the region, including Indonesia's two-year "confrontation" opposing the creation of Malaysia. Today it is almost taken for granted that foreign policy differences among the members will be settled peacefully. Even where problems persist, as in the case of the failure of the Philippines to renounce completely its claim to the Malaysian state of Sabah, these differences have not been politicized. A recent example is the quiet way the Philippines and Malaysia dealt with a retaliatory raid by Malaysian authorities against a Filipino-based group that had terrorized a Sabah town.

Reaching an agreement with Vietnam on a common definition of an acceptable regional order is a further daunting task on the road ahead. In the mid-1970s, ASEAN made considerable headway in establishing a dialogue with Vietnam, but the 1978 Vietnamese invasion of Kampuchea stymied further progress. Kampuchea may remain a stumbling block until there is a significant change in the leadership in Vietnam or in the international support Vietnam is receiving for its aggression.

The ASEAN group has important relations with all the larger powers —China, Japan, the Soviet Union, and the United States. In the cases of the United States and Japan, there is a qualitative as well as quantitative difference in ASEAN foreign policy tasks. The relations of the ASEAN countries with these two economic giants is basically friendly and based on many shared interests and values. Partly because the relations with Japan and the United States are so multifaceted, there are many more specific issues, some of which, especially in the economic sphere, have become quite contentious. Moreover, the United States is formally allied with the Philippines and Thailand, and has a large military infrastructure in the former.

Most of the ASEAN countries have recognized China within the past 12 years and are still in the early stages of establishing broad relations with that country. There are many sources of discomfort, some arising simply from that fact that China is a very large country nearby. There is concern in ASEAN about the stability of China's political leadership and its ultimate intentions toward the region. China is also viewed as an economic competitor. Indonesia and China suspended diplomatic relations in 1967 and, although groping toward increased trade ties, have yet to normalize their relationship.

Although the ASEAN governments do not share the same concern about a Soviet threat as the countries of Northeast Asia, none can be described as having warm relations with the Soviet Union. The Soviet connection with Vietnam, the growth of Soviet military forces in Southeast Asia, and the lack of significant cultural and economic ties are factors. The challenge in this relationship is to assure Soviet respect for the interests and integrity of the ASEAN states. Once the ASEAN nations are satisified on this score, perhaps other facets of a broader relationship can be developed.

ASEAN IN THE ASIA–PACIFIC REGION

In the early years of ASEAN, the countries in the association were absorbed in the tasks of strengthening their internal solidarity, of dealing with new problems of regional order arising from the ending of the Vietnam War, and of bargaining with the advanced countries of the region for increased support. These important general tasks remain, although some of the specific issues and circumstances have been altered. In addition, however, ASEAN is being increasingly called upon to make a broader contribution to the larger Asia–Pacific region. In particular, Australia, Japan, and the United States have been urging ASEAN to join in a broader effort of Pacific regional economic cooperation.

There have been advocates of Pacific cooperation within the ASEAN countries, as well as many who have feared that the more advanced Pacific partners would overwhelm ASEAN and that Pacific cooperation would dilute the unity of ASEAN. The internal debate on Pacific economic cooperation has evolved towards a consensus favoring unofficial dialogue and practical cooperation under the aegis of the the ASEAN Foreign Ministers' meetings with their advanced-country dialogue partners. It can be anticipated, however, that there will be continuing incentives for expanding the scope of cooperation, both because the range of Pacific issues has expanded with increased regional interdependence and because the current arrangements do not encompass all of the relevant or potentially relevant economies in the region.

Aside from economic cooperation, ASEAN has found that it has an increasing stake in political and diplomatic issues in the broader Asia–Pacific region. Stability in the Korean peninsula, the evolving nature of Sino–Soviet or Sino–American relations, and the strategic equation in the South Pacific, for example, are important to ASEAN. How ASEAN might more effectively convey its interests and views on Asia–Pacific regional political and strategic issues is a question for the member countries to consider.

ASEAN's role in the broader Asia–Pacific region is closely bound with the social, economic, and political development of the member countries and with the future of the regional association. ASEAN is looking forward to its 20th anniversary in 1987, and plans have been mooted for a third summit. Yet there is concern that the association could become stale and lose political support in the member countries. Some believe that the younger generation of ASEAN citizens take for granted the association's past achievements and argue that ASEAN regional cooperation must be changed or intensified to make it relevant and exciting to them. For these reasons, ASEAN is engaged in a process of reassessment, and a third summit may prove to be the driving force that will crystallize into concrete measures some of today's tentative ideas for institutional development, a stronger economic community, or greater foreign policy cooperation.

A stronger ASEAN can only be welcomed by the other countries of the Asia–Pacific region. The history of ASEAN so far has demonstrated that increased confidence by the member countries in their ability to shape their destiny has made them more active members of the broader Asia–Pacific community. The East–West Center recognizes that ASEAN's development is and will be a product of ASEAN's own deliberations, but we hope conferences such as the meeting of parliamentarians and scholars upon which this book is based will strengthen consultation and encourage mutually beneficial exchange with other parts of the Asia–Pacific region. In addressing the social, economic, and political challenges ahead, ASEAN's almost 300 million people will inevitably play a greater role in shaping the future of the Pacific Basin.

LIST OF CONTRIBUTORS

Dr. Zakaria Haji AHMAD, *Fellow, Resource Systems Institute, East–West Center, Honolulu, Hawaii (Associate Professor, Strategic Studies Programme, Faculty of Social Sciences and Humanities, Universiti Kebangsaan Malaysia, Bangi, Malaysia).*

Dr. Narongchai AKRASANEE, *Senior Vice President, The Industrial Finance Corporation of Thailand, Bangkok, Thailand.*

Mr. Motofumi ASAI, *Director, Regional Policy Division, Asian Affairs Bureau, Ministry of Foreign Affairs, Government of Japan, Tokyo, Japan.*

Dr. Peng Lim CHEE, *Transnational Corporations Officer, Economic and Social Commission for Asia and the Pacific, Bangkok, Thailand.*

Mr. Bifan CHENG, *Associate Professor and Head, Asian and Pacific Area Studies Division, Institute of World Economy and Politics, Chinese Academy of Social Science, Beijing, China.*

Dr. Paul P.L. CHEUNG, *Lecturer, Department of Social Work, National University of Singapore, Singapore.*

Dr. Lee-Jay CHO, *Director, Population Institute, and Chairman of Directors, East–West Center, Honolulu, Hawaii.*

Dr. John A. DIXON, *Research Associate, Environment and Policy Institute, East–West Center, Honolulu, Hawaii.*

Mr. Timothy DOLAN, *Research Assistant, East–West Population Institute, and Graduate Student, Department of Political Science, University of Hawaii, Honolulu, Hawaii.*

Changes in title or affiliation that have occurred since the October 1985 conference are indicated in parentheses. For simplicity, the list is alphabetized by family names, which are capitalized and listed last, although methods of alphabetization and forms of address differ by country.

Dr. Carolina G. HERNANDEZ, *Professor and Chairman, Department of Political Science, University of the Philippines, Diliman, Quezon City, Philippines.*

The Right Honorable Dato Musa HITAM, *Deputy Prime Minister of Malaysia (Member of Parliament, Deputy President of the United Malays National Organization).*

Dr. Victor Hao LI, *President, East–West Center, Honolulu, Hawaii.*

Dr. Linda G. MARTIN, *Research Associate, Population Institute, East–West Center, and Associate Professor of Economics, University of Hawaii, Honolulu, Hawaii.*

Dr. Seiji NAYA, *Director, Resource Systems Institute, East–West Center, and Professor of Economics, University of Hawaii, Honolulu, Hawaii.*

Dr. Gerardo P. SICAT, *Chief, Public Economics Division, Development Research Department, The World Bank, Washington, D.C.*

Dr. Peter C. SMITH, *Research Associate, Population Institute, East–West Center, Honolulu, Hawaii.*

His Excellency General Prem TINSULANONDA, *Prime Minister of Thailand.*

The Honorable Robert G. TORRICELLI, *U.S. Congressman, Democrat of New Jersey, and member of the Subcommittee on Asian and Pacific Affairs of the U.S. House of Representatives, Washington, D.C.*

Dr. Vinyu VICHIT-VADAKAN, *Director, The South-East Asian Central Banks Research and Training Centre, Petaling Jaya, Malaysia.*

Dr. Sarasin VIRAPHOL, *Minister–Counsellor and Deputy Chief of Mission, Royal Thai Embassy, Tokyo, Japan.*

Mr. Jusuf WANANDI, *Executive Director, Centre for Strategic and International Studies, Jakarta, Indonesia.*

Dr. Gungwu WANG, *Professor and Head, Department of Far Eastern History, Research School of Pacific Studies, Australian National University, Canberra, Australia (Vice-Chancellor, University of Hong Kong, Hong Kong).*

The Honorable Aline K. WONG, *Member of Parliament, and Associate Professor, Department of Sociology, National University of Singapore, Singapore.*

LIST OF OTHER PARTICIPANTS

East–West Center
25th Anniversary Conference
on ASEAN and the
Pacific Basin

AUSTRALIA

Dr. Frank Frost
Director, Foreign Affairs Group
Legislative Research Service
Parliament

BRUNEI

Mr. Zainal Hj. Momin
Acting Commissioner of Labour
Ministry of Home Affairs

INDONESIA

Mr. Mardhani S. Dipo
Expert Staff
National Family Planning
  Coordinating Board (BKKBN)

Hon. Panangian Siregar
Member of Parliament

Hon. Hudjah Masjhur Harahap
Member of Parliament

Hon. Soegiyono
Member of Parliament

Dr. R. Henry Pardoko
Expert Staff
National Family Planning
  Coordinating Board (BKKBN)

JAPAN

Hon. Ichiji Ishii
Senator
House of Councillors

Hon. Eimatsu Takakuwa
Senator
House of Councillors

Dr. Toshio Kuroda
Director Emeritus
Population Research Institute
Nihon University

MALAYSIA

Hon. Omar Abdullah
Member of Parliament

Hon. A. Fadzil Che Wan
Senator

Dr. Hamid Arshat
Director General
National Population and Family
　Development Board

Hon. Dato Mohamed Rahmat
Member of Parliament

Hon. Idris Basri
Member of Parliament

Hon. Daud Taha
Deputy Minister of Public
　Enterprises

PHILIPPINES

Dr. Mercedes B. Concepcion
Professor of Demography
University of the Philippines

Hon. Antonio M. Diaz
Deputy Minister of Tourism

Hon. Edilberto A. Del Valle
Member of Parliament

Hon. Concordio C. Diel
Deputy Minister of Local
　Government

Hon. Omar Dianalan
Member of Parliament

Hon. Carmencita Reyes
Deputy Minister of Social
　Services and Development

SINGAPORE

Hon. Chin Hock Ow
Member of Parliament

Hon. Zulkifli Mohammed
Member of Parliament

THAILAND

Hon. Pinich Chandrasurin
Member of Parliament

Hon. Vira Ramyarupa
Senator

Hon. Tridhosyuth Devakul
Senator

Hon. Prasop Ratanakorn
Senator and Chairman
Senate Committee on Aging
　and Social Development

Mr. Kosit Panpiemras
Assistant Director General
National Economic and Social
　Development Board

Hon. Direk Sakunathawong
Member of Parliament

UNITED STATES

Dr. Mary G. F. Bitterman
Director
Institute of Culture
  and Communication
East–West Center

Dr. Wimal Dissanayake
Assistant Director
Institute of Culture
  and Communication
East–West Center

Dr. William E. James
Research Associate
Resource Systems Institute
East–West Center

Dr. Charles E. Morrison
Research Fellow
Resource Systems Institute
East–West Center

FACTS AND FIGURES ABOUT THE ASEAN COUNTRIES

PREPARED BY TIMOTHY DOLAN

Appendix Table A.1

Demographic Indicators

	Brunei	Indonesia	Malaysia	Philippines	Singapore	Thailand
Area (km^2)	5,776	1,906,240	332,456	300,440	618	514,820
Total population (thousands)						
1960	90	96,194	8,205	27,904	1,634	26,867
1970	133	120,280	10,863	37,540	2,075	36,370
1980	228	150,958	13,870	48,317	2,415	46,455
2000	386	204,486	20,615	74,810	2,976	66,115
Density (population per km^2)						
1960	16	51	25	93	2,812	52
1970	23	63	33	125	3,571	71
1980	39	79	42	161	4,156	90
2000	67	107	63	249	5,122	129
Average annual population growth rate (percent)						
1950–60	6.71	1.90	2.71	3.06	4.69	2.79
1960–70	3.91	2.23	2.81	2.97	2.39	3.03
1970–80	5.39	2.28	2.44	2.52	1.52	2.45
1980–2000	2.63	1.52	1.98	2.19	1.04	1.76
Expectation of life at birth (years)						
1960–65	N.A.	42.5	55.7	54.5	65.8	53.9
1970–75	N.A.	47.5	63.0	60.4	69.5	59.6
1980–85	N.A.	52.5	66.9	64.5	72.2	62.7
2000–05	N.A.	62.1	71.6	71.4	74.9	68.0

(continued)

Appendix Table A.1 (continued)

Demographic Indicators

	Brunei	Indonesia	Malaysia	Philippines	Singapore	Thailand
Infant mortality rate (infant deaths per 1,000 live births)						
1960–65	N.A.	145	63	97	30	95
1970–75	N.A.	112	40	68	19	65
1980–85	N.A.	87	29	50	11	51
2000–05	N.A.	49	18	24	8	24
Total fertility rate (children per woman)						
1960–65	N.A.	5.42	6.69	6.57	4.87	6.42
1970–75	N.A.	5.53	4.87	5.02	2.60	5.01
1980–85	N.A.	3.89	3.69	4.20	1.74	3.59
2000–05	N.A.	2.25	2.25	2.46	1.74	2.44
Percentage of population under 15						
1960	N.A.	40.2	44.9	46.9	43.2	45.6
1970	N.A.	42.3	45.1	45.5	38.8	44.9
1980	N.A.	41.0	39.1	40.6	27.1	40.2
2000	N.A.	29.8	30.8	32.9	21.4	29.4
Percentage of population 65 and over						
1960	N.A.	3.3	4.2	3.6	2.1	3.3
1970	N.A.	3.1	3.2	2.7	3.3	2.9
1980	N.A.	3.3	3.7	2.9	4.7	3.1
2000	N.A.	4.6	4.5	4.1	7.0	4.5

Marital status ages 50–54 (percent)	Male	Female	Male	Female	Male[a]	Female[a]	Male	Female	Male	Female	Male	Female
1960 Married	83.3	71.8	N.A.	N.A.	84.8	59.9	89.7	72.2	85.3	55.1	87.9	67.7
Single[b]	3.7	6.4	N.A.	N.A.	6.6	1.7	3.0	7.7	7.3	5.9	2.0	2.3
Widowed	9.5	19.7	N.A.	N.A.	6.6	33.1	6.8	19.1	6.8	38.5	6.2	24.6
Divorced/Separated	3.6	2.1	N.A.	N.A.	2.0	5.2	0.5	0.9	0.4	0.3	2.4	5.1
1970 Married	90.5	74.1	91.4	53.6	90.0	70.0	90.8	75.2	90.1	70.9	90.5	72.7
Single	5.1	4.6	1.8	1.0	3.1	1.7	3.2	7.3	5.5	4.1	3.1	2.5
Widowed[c]	4.3	21.2	5.5	41.1	5.1	25.8	5.1	16.1	3.6	24.0	4.4	20.4
Divorced/Separated	1.5	2.4	1.3	4.2	1.8	2.6	0.6	1.1	0.8	1.1	1.8	4.3
1980 Married	90.6	76.7	94.1	63.6	92.1	73.5	90.1	79.5	90.6	75.3	90.5	73.5
Single[b]	4.9	5.0	1.0	1.3	3.4	2.2	4.9	6.0	5.4	2.9	3.2	3.4
Widowed	3.0	15.9	3.5	28.6	3.3	20.4	4.4	13.5	2.6	19.4	4.3	18.5
Divorced/Separated	1.5	2.4	1.4	6.5	1.2	3.9	0.5	1.0	1.4	2.5	1.7	4.1
Percentage of population urban												
1960	N.A.		14.6		25.2		30.3		77.6		12.5	
1970	N.A.		17.1		27.0		33.0		75.3		13.2	
1980	N.A.		22.2		29.4		37.4		74.1		14.4	
2000	N.A.		36.5		41.6		49.0		78.5		23.2	

Sources: For this and subsequent tables see pp. 241–246.

N.A. Not available.

[a] For Malaysia 1960, figures are a composite of the censuses of Peninsular Malaysia in 1957, Sarawak in 1960, and North Borneo in 1960.

[b] For Thailand 1960 and 1980, priests were categorized separately. They are combined with single here. Also "unknown ever-married" and "unknown" categories are excluded, thus figures do not sum up to 100%.

[c] 1970 figures for Brunei combine widowed with divorced.

Appendix Table A.2

Health Indicators

	Brunei	Indonesia	Malaysia	Philippines	Singapore	Thailand
Population per physician						
1960	N.A.	46,780	7,020	6,940[a]	2,360[b]	7,950[b]
1970	N.A.	26,510	4,310	9,100[a]	1,520[b]	8,450
1980	N.A.	11,530[c]	7,910[d]	7,970[a]	1,150	7,180[c]
Calorie supply per capita (percentage of requirement)						
1961–65	N.A.	86.5	107.2	98.5	112.2	99.0
1970	N.A.	93.9	108.9	99.0	126.3	100.7
1980	N.A.	109.7	120.5	116.2	134.5	104.5
Protein supply per capita (grams per day)						
1961–65	N.A.	38.2	49.2	45.8	64.5	44.7
1970	N.A.	42.4	49.2	48.4	77.0	48.7
1980	N.A.	48.7	60.3	52.7	80.4	47.3
Percentage of national budget spent on health						
1973	N.A.	1.3	7.1[e]	2.9	7.8	4.0[f]
1980	N.A.	2.5	5.1	3.9	6.9	4.1

[a] Personnel in government services only.
[b] Registered (not all practicing in country).
[c] 1979.
[d] 1977.
[e] 1972.
[f] 1974.

Appendix Table A.3

Education Indicators

	Brunei	Indonesia	Malaysia	Philippines	Singapore	Thailand
Adult literacy rate (percent)						
1960	N.A.	39.0[a]	52.8[b]	71.9	N.A.	67.7
1970	N.A.	56.6[c]	58.5[d]	82.6	68.9	78.6
1980	N.A.	62.0[e]	60.0	75.0[f]	83.0	86.0
Daily general interest newspaper readership (per thousand population)						
1960	N.A.	11.0	60.2	17.7	142.6	10.6
1970	N.A.	N.A.	72.1	13.6	N.A.	20.5
1979	N.A.	17.7[g]	132.6	20.7	246.8	42.3
Percentage of national budget spent on education						
1965	10.1	N.A.	18.5	N.A.	N.A.	20.1
1970	13.9	N.A.	17.7	24.4	11.7	17.3
1980	11.3	8.9	16.4	10.3	7.3	20.6
Primary school enrollment ratio (gross)						
1960	N.A.	71	96	95	111	83
1970	N.A.	77	87	108	106	83
1980	N.A.	112	92	110	107	96

(continued)

Appendix Table A.3 (continued)

Education Indicators

	Brunei	Indonesia	Malaysia	Philippines	Singapore	Thailand
Secondary school enrollment ratio (gross)						
1960	N.A.	6	19	26	32	13
1970	N.A.	15	34	46	46	17
1980	N.A.	28	51	63	59	29
Post-secondary school enrollment (gross)						
1960	N.A.	0.7	1.2	12.7	6.4	1.9
1970	N.A.	2.8	1.6	19.8	6.8	1.7
1980	N.A.	3.9h	4.1	26.1	8.1	13.5

a 1961.
b 1962.
c 1971.
d Peninsular Malaysia only (includes semi-literate persons).
e 1978.
f 1979.
g 1976.
h 1981.

Appendix Table A.4

Labor Indicators

	Brunei	Indonesia	Malaysia	Philippines	Singapore	Thailand
Total labor force participation rate (percent)						
1960	N.A.	36.7	34.1	39.8	33.8	51.3
1970	N.A.	35.4	33.8	36.6	35.0	46.6
1980	N.A.	35.9	35.0	35.5	39.6	47.8
Male labor force participation rate (percent)						
1960	N.A.	54.2	48.8	52.1	51.2	52.7
1970	N.A.	49.5	45.7	48.6	50.6	49.3
1980	N.A.	51.0	47.6	47.6	57.1	51.3
Female labor force participation rate (percent)						
1960	N.A.	20.0	18.9	27.4	14.5	49.8
1970	N.A.	21.6	21.5	24.4	18.7	43.9
1980	N.A.	20.9	22.1	23.2	21.5	44.2

Appendix Table A.5

General Economic Indicators

	Brunei	Indonesia	Malaysia	Philippines	Singapore	Thailand
GDP in constant 1980 national currency (billions)						
1960	N.A.	14,568	N.A.	N.A.	4.19	164.05
1970	N.A.	21,085	24.02	146.20	10.14	351.04
1980	N.A.	45,446	51.84	266.01	24.29	684.93
GDP in millions U.S.$						
1980	N.A.	72,483	23,814	35,414	11,344	33,450
Average annual GDP growth rate (percent)						
1960–70	N.A.	3.7	N.A.	N.A.	10.3	7.6
1970–80	N.A.	7.7	7.7	6.0	8.7	6.7
GDP per capita in constant 1980 national currency						
1960	N.A.	151,444	N.A.	3,092	2,564	6,106
1970	N.A.	175,299	2,211	3,814	4,885	9,652
1980	N.A.	301,051	3,738	5,486	10,056	14,744
GDP per capita in U.S.$						
1980	N.A.	480	1,717	730	4,697	720
Percentage of income received by lowest 20 percent of households						
1960	N.A.	N.A.	3.2	4.2[a]	N.A.	6.2[b]
1970	N.A.	N.A.	3.3	5.2	N.A.	6.1[c]
1980	N.A.	6.6[d]	N.A.	N.A.	N.A.	5.6[d]

234

Gross national savings as a percentage of GDP						
1960	N.A.	N.A.	23.1	14.8	-0.8	14.1
1970	9.1	N.A.	22.1	19.2	19.3	21.5
1980	24.8	N.A.	27.2	24.6	32.0	20.0
Gross domestic investment as a percentage of GDP						
1960	N.A.[e]	N.A.	14.1	16.0	11.4	15.7
1970	13.6	N.A.	20.7	21.2	38.7	26.2
1980	20.9	N.A.	28.4	30.5	45.4	27.2
Food production index (1974–76 = 100)						
1971	87.8	N.A.	79.1	79.7	147.7	83.2
1980	124.7	N.A.	132.4	119.8	155.0	118.3
Per capita energy consumption (kilograms of coal equivalent)						
1960	129	N.A.	616	159	2,110	63
1970	143	N.A.	770	333	4,303	216
1980	266	N.A.	881	380	8,544	370

[a] 1961.
[b] 1962.
[c] 1968.
[d] 1976.
[e] An estimate is shown in Table 3.17.

Appendix Table A.6

Foreign Trade Indicators

	Brunei	Indonesia	Malaysia	Philippines	Singapore	Thailand
Total value of exports (millions U.S. $)						
1960	88.0	840.0	956.0	560.0	1,136.0	408.0
1970	92.2	1,009.3	1,686.4	1,061.7	1,553.7	710.2
1980	3,756.9	21,908.0	12,958.0	5,741.1	19,378.0	6,505.0
Main trading partners (exports)						
1960	Sarawak / Singapore / Hong Kong	Singapore / United States / Fed. of Malaya	Singapore / United Kingdom / Japan	United States / Japan / Netherlands	Fed. of Malaya / United Kingdom / United States	Japan / Fed. of Malaya / United States
1970	Malaysia[a] / Singapore / United Kingdom	Singapore / United States / Germany (FRG)	Singapore / Japan / United States	United States / Japan / Korea (ROK)	Malaysia / United States / Japan	Japan / United States / Netherlands
1980	Japan / United States / Thailand	Japan / United States / Singapore	Japan / Singapore / United States	United States / Japan / Netherlands	Malaysia / United States / Japan	Japan / Netherlands / United States
Total value of imports (millions U.S. $)						
1960	22.0	574.0	703.0	604.0	1,332.0	453.0
1970	87.7	893.4	1,412.7	1,210.2	2,461.3	1,293.4
1980	641.7	10,834.0	10,820.0	8,295.3	24,007.0	9,214.0
Main trading partners (imports)						
1960	United Kingdom / Singapore / United States	Japan / United States / China	United Kingdom / Indonesia / Thailand	United States / Japan / Germany (FRG)	Indonesia / Fed. of Malaya / United Kingdom	Japan / United States / United Kingdom

1970	Singapore Australia Japan	Japan United States Singapore	Japan United Kingdom United States	Japan United States Germany (FRG)	Japan Malaysia United States	Japan United States Germany (FRG)
1980	Singapore Japan United States	Japan United States Saudi Arabia	Japan United States Singapore	United States Japan Saudi Arabia	Japan United States Malaysia	Japan United States Saudi Arabia
Official development assistance: Total bilateral flows from Dev. Asst. Committee (OECD) member countries (net, millions U.S.$)						
1970	N.A.	449.0	22.9	41.3	26.8	69.4
1980	—	844.2	106.2	205.4	9.4	304.9
Direct foreign investment (millions U.S.$)						
1970	N.A.	83.0	94.0	−25.0	93.0	43.0
1980	N.A.	183.5	875.9	260.3	1,668.6	186.1
Terms of trade index (1975 = 100)						
1960	N.A.	36.5	169.3	166.6	N.A.[b]	110.0
1970	N.A.	48.2	134.3	135.3	98.2	113.9
1980	N.A.	149.2	149.1	78.1	99.4	86.4
International reserves (millions U.S.$)						
1960	N.A.	352.0	356.0	127.0	115.0	371.0
1970	N.A.	160.0	664.0	251.0	1,012.0	906.0
1980	N.A.	5,498.3	4,490.7	2,932.2	6,566.8	1,670.8

[a] 1969.
[b] 1972.

Political Indicators

	Brunei	Indonesia	Malaysia	Philippines	Singapore	Thailand
Title and name of head of government	Sultan Hassanal Bolkiah	President Soeharto	Prime Minister Mahathir bin Mohamad	President Ferdinand E. Marcos	Prime Minister Lee Kuan Yew	Prime Minister Prem Tinsulanonda
Age (as of 31 October 1985)	39	64	59	68	62	65
Years head of government (as of 31 October 1985)	18	18	4	19	26	5
Year of last election	1965	1982	1982 (Pen. Malaysia) 1985 (Sabah) 1979 (Sarawak)	1984	1984	1983
Major political parties and voting strength after last election (percent or number of legislative seats)	None	GOLKAR (64%) Unity Development (28%) Indonesia Democracy (8%)	(Pen. Malaysia) National Front (132) Democratic Action Party (9) Islamic Party (5) Independents (8) (Sabah) Parti Bersatu Sabah (25) USNO (16)	New Society Party (117) UNIDO (59) Independents (7) Appointed (17)	People's Action Party (73) Worker's Party (1) Singapore Democratic Party (1)	Social Action Party (101) Chart Thai (108) Democratic Party (57) Prachakorn Thai (36) National Democratic Party (15)

	Berjaya Party (6) (Sarawak) National Front (45 of 48)			Progress Party (3) Social Democratic Party (2) Prachaseri (1) Thai People's Party (1)[a]
	1	1	3	2	0	7

Number of changes of government head since 1960

[a] Final allocation of seats.

Appendix Table A.8

Defense Indicators

	Brunei	Indonesia	Malaysia	Philippines	Singapore	Thailand
Military expenditure (millions current U.S.$)						
1963	N.A.	143	50	80	N.A.	78
1970	N.A.	263	132	121	105	200
1980	N.A.	1,594	1,110	612	571	1,000
1983	N.A.	2,649[a]	1,432[a]	771[a]	995[a]	1,539
Military expenditure per capita (current U.S.$)						
1963	N.A.	1	6	3	N.A.	3
1970	N.A.	2	12	3	50	5
1980	N.A.	11	79	16	258	21
1983[b]	N.A.	15	91	13	366	29
Percentage of national budget spent on defense						
1960	0.3[c]	41.8	8.5	10.4	2.7	20.5
1970	20.4	N.A.	15.0	10.0	28.3	18.5
1980	34.6[d]	12.7	16.1	13.5	14.0[e]	18.0
1983	N.A.	13.7	11.8	15.1	17.1	19.9
Armed forces personnel (thousands)						
1963	N.A.	375	14[f]	45	N.A.	85
1970	N.A.	358	58	59	14	175
1980	N.A.	250	82	156	57	224
1983	N.A.	280	105	157	60	250

[a] Estimate based on partial or uncertain data.
[b] In constant 1982 dollars.
[c] 1961.
[d] 1979.
[e] Includes justice and police.
[f] Parliamentary forces not included.

SOURCES TO APPENDIX TABLES

Demographic Indicators (Appendix Table A.1.)

Area — United States Central Intelligence Agency, *The World Factbook* (Washington, D.C.: Central Intelligence Agency, 1983), pp. 29, 103, 139, 179, 198, 219.

Total pop. — United Nations, *World Population Prospects: Estimates and Projections as Assessed in 1982* (New York: United Nations, 1985), table A-2 (medium variant), pp. 48–49.

Density — Ibid., pp. 396–97, 420–21, 430–31, 436–37, 442–43. Brunei calculated from area and population figures above.

Average annual pop. growth rate — Calculated from total population figures.

Expectation of life at birth — United Nations, op. cit., Table A-15, pp. 122–23.

Infant mort. rate — Ibid., Table A-16, pp. 134–35.

Total fert. rate — Ibid., pp. 396–97, 420–21, 430–31, 436–37, 442–43.

% of pop. under 15 — Ibid.

% of pop. 65 and over — Ibid.

Marital status ages 50–54 (%) — For Brunei 1971: *Report on the Census of Population 1971,* table 12(a), p. 106.

For Malaysia 1960: United Nations, *Demographic Yearbook 1962* (New York: United Nations, 1963), pp. 436, 442, 444. (Data based on the results of the 1957 Census of Peninsular Malaysia and combined with the results of the 1960 Census of Sarawak and the 1960 Census of North Borneo).

For Malaysia 1970: *1970 General Report: Population Census of Malaysia* Vol. 2, table 2.16, p. 86.

For Malaysia 1980: *General Report of the Population Census* Vol. 2, table M31, p. 46.

For Thailand 1980: *1980 Population and Housing Census: Whole Kingdom,* table 6, pp. 25–26.

All others 1960: United Nations, *Demographic Yearbook 1968* (New York: United Nations, 1969), table 7, pp. 235, 245, 247.

All others 1970: United Nations, *Demographic Yearbook 1976* (New York: United Nations, 1977), table 41, pp. 803, 807, 813, 815, 817.

All others 1980: United Nations, *Demographic Yearbook 1982* (New York: United Nations, 1984), table 40, pp. 861, 865, 873.

Figures are percentages of total male and female population ages 50–54. Totals do not necessarily add to 100% due to exclusion of those categorized as unknown and due to rounding error. For Thailand 1980, priests are classified as single.

% of pop. urban   United Nations, *World Population Prospects: Estimates and Projections as Assessed in 1982* (New York: United Nations, 1985), pp. 396–97, 420–21, 430–31, 436–37, 442–43.

Health Indicators (Appendix Table A.2)

Pop. per physician   World Bank, *World Tables Vol. II (Social Data)* (Washington, D.C.: World Bank, 1983), pp. 43, 58, 75, 80, 89.

Calorie supply per capita   Ibid.

Protein supply per capita   Ibid.

% of national budget spent on health   Calculated from data in International Monetary Fund, *Government Finance Statistics Yearbook* (Washington, D.C.: International Monetary Fund, 1984), pp. 401, 514, 650, 694, 774 (table B).

Education Indicators (Appendix Table A.3)

Adult literacy rate   World Bank, *World Tables Vol. II (Social Data)* (Washington, D.C.: World Bank, 1983), pp. 43, 58, 75, 80, 89.

Daily general interest newspaper readership   Ibid.

% of national budget spent on education   For 1960: UNESCO, *UNESCO Statistical Yearbook 1978–79* (Paris: UNESCO, 1980), pp. 638–42.
For 1970–80: UNESCO, *UNESCO Statistical Yearbook 1984* (Paris: UNESCO, 1984), pp. IV-12, IV-15.

Primary school enrollment ratio   For 1960: Op. cit., pp. 172, 178, 180, 181, 183.
For 1970–80: Op. cit., pp. III-49, III-52, III-54, III-55, III-56.

Secondary school enrollment ratio   Ibid.

Post-secondary school enrollment ratio   Ibid.

Labor Indicators (Appendix Table A.4)

Total labor force participation rate	World Bank, *World Tables Vol. II (Social Data)* (Washington, D.C.: World Bank, 1983), pp. 43, 58, 75, 80, 89.
Male labor force participation rate	Ibid.
Female labor force participation rate	Ibid.

General Economic Indicators (Appendix Table A.5)

GDP	For the Philippines 1970, 1980: Figures were calculated from data in Asia Development Bank, *Key Indicators of Developing Member Countries of ADB* Vol. XV (Manila: ADB, 1984), pp. 256, 263.
	All others: International Monetary Fund, *International Financial Statistics Yearbook* (Washington, D.C.: IMF, 1984), pp. 332–33, 406–07, 498–99, 522–23, 570–71.
	Figures in the first three rows are in billions of constant 1980 national currency. The fourth row is reported in 1980 U.S. dollars calculated from data above and using the 1980 exchange rate found on pp. 331, 405, 483, 521, 565 of above. Exchange rate used is the end of period average (IMF category code rf).
GDP growth rate	Calculated from the above.
GDP per capita	Derived from dividing GDP by total population as reported above. Format follows that of the GDP table with the first three rows of data reported in constant 1980 national currency and the fourth row reported in 1980 U.S. dollars.
% income received by lowest 20% of households	World Bank, *World Tables Vol. II (Social Data)* (Washington, D.C.: 1983), pp. 43, 58, 75, 89.
Gross national savings as % GDP	Calculated from data in World Bank, *World Tables Vol. I (Economic Data)* (Washington, D.C.: World Bank, 1983), pp. 86–87, 112–13, 146–47, 158–59, 176–77. Figures derived from dividing gross national savings (excluding net current transfers from abroad) by GDP.
Gross domestic investment as % GDP	Ibid. Figures derived from dividing gross domestic investment by GDP.
Food production index	Food and Agriculture Organization, *1982 FAO Production Yearbook*. Vol. 36 (Rome: FAO, 1983), p. 76 (table 4).

| Per cap. energy consumption | World Bank, *World Tables Vol. II (Social Data)* (Washington, D.C.: 1983), pp. 43, 58, 75, 80, 89. |

Foreign Trade Indicators (Appendix Table A.6)

Total value of exports	For 1960: International Monetary Fund, *Direction of Trade Annual 1960–1964* (Washington, D.C.: IMF, 1965), pp. 148, 232, 273, 315, 338, 359. (Hereinafter referred to as *1965 IMF Trade Annual*.) For 1970: International Monetary Fund, *Direction of Trade Annual 1968–1972* (Washington, D.C.: IMF, 1973), pp. 246, 259, 264, 268, 271, 273. (Hereinafter referred to as *1973 IMF Trade Annual*.) For 1980: International Monetary Fund, *Direction of Trade Statistics Yearbook 1982* (Washington, D.C.: IMF, 1982), pp. 98, 205, 250, 308, 334, 361. (Hereinafter referred to as *1982 IMF Trade Yearbook*.)
Main trading partners (exports)	For 1960: *1965 IMF Trade Annual,* pp. 148, 232–33, 273–74, 315–16, 338–39, 359–60. For 1970: *1973 IMF Trade Annual,* pp. 246, 259, 264, 268, 271, 273. For 1980: *1982 IMF Trade Yearbook,* pp. 98, 205–06, 250–51, 308–09, 334–35, 361–62.
Total value of imports	For 1960: *1965 IMF Trade Annual,* pp. 148, 232–33, 273–74, 315–16, 338–39, 359–60. For 1970: *1973 IMF Trade Annual,* pp. 246, 259, 264, 268, 271, 273. For 1980: *1982 IMF Trade Yearbook,* pp. 98, 205–06, 250–51, 308–09, 334–35, 361–62.
Main trading partners (imports)	For 1960: *1965 IMF Trade Annual,* pp. 232–33, 273–74, 315–16, 338–39, 359–60. For 1970: *1973 IMF Trade Annual,* pp. 246, 259, 264, 268, 271. For 1980: *1982 IMF Trade Yearbook,* pp. 98, 205–06, 250–51, 308–09, 334–35, 361–62.
Official development assistance	United Nations Conference on Trade and Development, *Handbook of International Trade and Development Statistics 1983* (New York: UNCTAD, 1983), p. 380.
Direct foreign investment	Ibid., pp. 311, 313, 315.
Terms of trade index	International Monetary Fund, *International Financial Statistics: Supplement on Trade Statistics* Supplement Series, No. 4 (Washington, D.C.: IMF, 1982), pp. 158–59. (1975 = 100.)
International reserves	For 1960, 1970: United Nations Conference on Trade and Development, *Handbook of International Trade and Development Statistics 1979* (New York: UNCTAD, 1979), p. 386.

For 1980: United Nations Conference on Trade and Development, *Handbook of International Trade and Development Statistics 1983* (New York: UNCTAD, 1983), p. 348.

Political Indicators (Appendix Table A.7)

Title and name of gov't head	United States Central Intelligence Agency, *The World Factbook* (Washington, D.C.: Central Intelligence Agency, 1983), pp. 29, 103, 140, 179, 199, 219.
Age	For Prem Tinsulanonda: Newspaper Enterprise Association Inc., *The World Almanac and Book of Facts 1985* (New York: Newspaper Enterprise Association, 1984), p. 585. All others: Europa Publications Ltd., *The International Who's Who 1979–80* (London: Europa Publications Ltd., 1979), pp. 135, 715, 786, 801, 1213.
Years head of gov't	Europa Publications Ltd., *The Far East and Australasia 1984–85* (London: Europa Publications Ltd., 1984), pp. 234, 405, 572, 779, 809, 867.
Year of last election	United States Central Intelligence Agency, *The World Factbook* (Washington, D.C.: Central Intelligence Agency, 1983), pp. 29, 103, 140, 179, 199, 219.
Major political parties and voting strength after last election	Ibid. For Thailand: Europa Publications Ltd., *The Far East and Australasia 1984–85* (London: Europa Publications Ltd., 1984), p. 882. For Sabah: Suhaini Aznam, "Sabah on a Tightrope," *Far Eastern Economic Review* (6 June 1985), pp. 14–15. For Philippines: Furnished through the Philippine Consulate, Honolulu, Hawaii.
Number of changes of gov't head since 1960	Europa Publications Ltd., *The Far East and Australasia 1984–85* (London: Europa Publications Ltd., 1984), pp. 234, 405–07, 571–72, 779–80, 809–11, 865–68. For Malaysia: Ibid. and Far Eastern Economic Review, *Asia Yearbook* (Hong Kong: Far Eastern Economic Review, 1983), p. 212.

Defense Indicators (Appendix Table A.8)

Military expenditures	For 1963, 1970: United States Arms Control and Disarmament Agency, *World Military Expenditures and Arms Trade 1963–1973* (Washington, D.C.: United States Government Printing Office, 1975), pp. 37, 45, 51, 54, 59. For 1980 (except the Philippines and Singapore): United States Arms Control and Disarmament Agency, *World Military Expenditures and Arms Transfers 1971–1980* (Washington, D.C.: United States Government Printing Office, 1983), pp. 52, 58, 63, 66, 69.

For 1983 (and the Philippines and Singapore 1980): United States Arms Control and Disarmament Agency, *World Military Expenditures and Arms Transfers 1985* (Washington, D.C.: United States Government Printing Office, 1985), pp. 66, 72, 77, 80, 83.

Military expenditures per capita

Calculated from population and defense expenditure data above.

For 1983: United States Arms Control and Disarmament Agency, *World Military Expenditures and Arms Transfers 1985* (Washington, D.C.: United States Government Printing Office, 1985), pp. 66, 72, 77, 80, 83.

% of national budget spent on defense

For 1960, 1970: Calculated from United Nations Economic Commission for Asia and the Far East, *Statistical Yearbook for Asia and the Far East 1971* (Bangkok: United Nations Economic Commission for Asia and the Far East, 1972), pp. 55, 145, 253, 341, 355, 372.

For 1980 (except Indonesia and the Philippines): Calculated from United Nations Economic Commission for Asia and the Far East, *Statistical Yearbook for Asia and the Far East 1981* (Bangkok: United Nations Economic Commission for Asia and the Far East, 1982), pp. 110, 338, 453, 485–86, 528.

For 1983 (and Indonesia and the Philippines 1980): United States Arms Control and Disarmament Agency, *World Military Expenditures and Arms Transfers 1985* (Washington, D.C.: United States Government Printing Office, 1985), pp. 66, 72, 77, 80, 83.

Armed forces personnel

For 1963, 1970: United States Arms Control and Disarmament Agency, *World Military Expenditures and Arms Trade 1963–1973* (Washington, D.C.: United States Government Printing Office, 1975), pp. 37, 45, 51, 54, 59.

For 1980 (except Thailand): United States Arms Control and Disarmament Agency, *World Military Expenditures and Arms Transfers 1971–1980* (Washington, D.C.: United States Government Printing Office, 1983), pp. 52, 58, 63, 66, 69.

For 1983 (and Thailand 1980): United States Arms Control and Disarmament Agency, *World Military Expenditures and Arms Transfers 1985* (Washington, D.C.: United States Government Printing Office, 1985), pp. 66, 72, 77, 80, 83.

INDEX